NOBODY
EVER
ASKED ME
ABOUT THE
GIRLS

NOBODY EVER ASKED ME ABOUT THE GIRLS

Women, Music, and Fame

LISA ROBINSON

HE YORK

Henry Holt and Company

Publishers since 1866
120 Broadway
New York, New York 10271
www.henryholt.com

Henry Holt® and 🅗® are registered trademarks of Macmillan
Publishing Group, LLC.

Library of Congress Cataloging-in-Publication Data

Names: Robinson, Lisa (Music journalist) author.
Title: Nobody ever asked me about the girls : women, music, and
    fame / Lisa Robinson.
Description: First edition. | New York : Henry Holt and Company,
    2020. | Includes bibliographical references and index.
Identifiers: LCCN 2019052296 (print) | LCCN 2019052297 (ebook) |
    ISBN 9781627794909 (hardcover) | ISBN 9781627794916 (ebook)
Subjects: LCSH: Women musicians. | Women singers. | Women in the
    music trade. | Fame.
Classification: LCC ML82 .R633 2020 (print) | LCC ML82 (ebook) |
    DDC 781.64082—dc23
LC record available at https://lccn.loc.gov/2019052296
LC ebook record available at https://lccn.loc.gov/2019052297

Our books may be purchased in bulk for promotional,
educational, or business use. Please contact your local bookseller
or the Macmillan Corporate and Premium Sales Department
at (800) 221-7945, extension 5442, or by e-mail at
MacmillanSpecialMarkets@macmillan.com.

First Edition 2020

Designed by Meryl Sussman Levavi

Printed in the United States of America

1 2 3 4 5 6 7 8 9 10

For Deane Zimmerman

CONTENTS

PROLOGUE | 1

HOPES, DREAMS & AMBITIONS | 3

HAIR & MAKEUP | 19

FAME | 42

ABUSE | 60

LOVE & MARRIAGE | 79

MOTHERHOOD | 97

SEX | 111

DRUGS | 122

FAMILY | 143

BUSINESS | 158

STAGE FRIGHT & BAD REVIEWS | 183

MUSIC & INFLUENCES | 192

AGE | 209

EPILOGUE | 230

ACKNOWLEDGMENTS | 233

INDEX | 235

Prologue

Nobody ever asked me about the girls.

Until now.

Over my four-decade career interviewing and writing about musicians, I was most often asked what Mick Jagger or Michael Jackson or David Bowie or Jay-Z were really like.

For the most part, women were dismissed.

Women didn't really count in this world.

But with the recent domination of female stars—which seems to happen once a decade—this, to some degree, has changed.

In the more than one thousand interviews I've done with women, I've heard all their stories. The paths they took were different. The level of talent was different. Their luck was different. The effects of success or failure on their lives was different. But their goals and struggles were often similar. To be heard. To be seen. To be loved. To be famous. To be rich was probably part of it, but no one really owns up to it. Not at first. If ever. These women had obsessions that were often limitless, hopes that were unrealistic and ambitions that might have been unachievable. Like all women, life has not been easy for the women in music.

HOPES, DREAMS & AMBITIONS

"Can I tell you how many lives *Life* magazine ruined?" Bette Midler said to me in 2018 about the weekly picture magazine that was always in her house—and in millions of others'—when she was a girl growing up in the 1950s in Hawaii. "It was such a strong magazine. People who were out in the hinterlands were so caught up in it. It exposed you to a lot of things you did not know existed. Even if you went to the movies, you knew it was a movie—they were actors. In *Life* magazine, those were real people in wonderful clothes and wonderful cars, living fabulous lives and you thought, 'Wow, what am I doing in this backwater?'"

Bette Midler was sitting in her fabulous New York apartment with spectacular views of Central Park. We were sipping champagne. She had just come back from some fabulous vacation somewhere in Europe, and she was preparing to do forty-two more shows on Broadway in *Hello, Dolly!*, following her starring, sellout, Tony

Award winning performance the year before. Bette and I have known each other since the 1970s, when she first got major attention singing in the gay baths in New York City's Ansonia Hotel basement. Without question, considering the longevity of her career, her continued popularity and success, and everything she's been through—underground theater on the Lower East Side, cabaret, a Broadway chorus, the music business, the movie business, back to Broadway—she's handled fame and success better than anyone I've interviewed in over four decades. "It never went to my head," she said. "If it had gone to my head, I would have been either a drug addict or dead by now. Or something terrible would have happened. I said to myself, 'This is how it is, I know I'm well known,' it's in the back of my mind and I tamp it down because I think it's unhealthy. I never let it go to my head, never."

As Bette and I continued our talk that summer day, I remarked that she isn't at all showy: she doesn't flaunt houses, cars, jewelry. None of the material trappings of success that so many female stars—or just rich people in general—parade all over Instagram. "Why would I?" she said. "Why make people feel bad or angry or jealous that they don't have what you have? It's like *Life* magazine. And now, it's like *Life* magazine times 150,000." Bette told me she wanted to get out of her childhood hometown in Hawaii, because she knew she had a talent, and she was poor, and she didn't want to be poor. She didn't want to be famous, she said, she didn't even want to be rich—she just didn't want to be poor. "I was poor for a long time," she said. "For nineteen years. I shoplifted, I filched money from my mother, I walked two and a half miles to school and two and a half miles back because we didn't have fifteen cents for the bus. I would watch *The Ed Sullivan Show* or other TV variety shows and I would think, 'I can do that.' And they all looked like they were having so much fun. That's what they were selling. Who knew?"

"But," she continued, "real life is real. And when you get caught up in the fantasy of it, it takes years—years and years—to realize that you've been had. And that's big. To realize that you fell for something that's incorrect, that's a lie. It took me fifty years to realize it."

✦

At 9 years old, Joni Mitchell had polio, and because of the effects of the disease on her hands, she eventually had to figure out her own weird guitar tunings. She had a baby, gave it up for adoption, and sang in coffeehouses in her native Canada and in New York City, until she was "discovered" in a Greenwich Village folk club by Byrds guitarist (and later Crosby, Stills and Nash's) David Crosby.

Donna Summer sang in her Boston church and performed in school musicals. She left Boston for New York City, joined a rock band, then got a job in the German production of the rock musical *Hair*. She sang background vocals for producer Giorgio Moroder in Munich until he convinced her, as a joke, to sing the orgasmic vocals of "Love to Love You Baby."

As a teenager, Sheryl Crow was an athlete, a majorette, a member of the Pep Club and a winner of the Paperdoll Queen beauty contest. She was a music teacher before she got into her car by herself to drive from her native Missouri to Los Angeles, where she started a career that began by singing background vocals for Michael Jackson.

Courtney Love was expelled from school, put in foster care, and was legally emancipated at 16. She was a topless dancer in Portland, a stripper in Los Angeles, and a founding member of several bands in the Pacific Northwest before forming Hole in 1989.

Raised in Kansas, Janelle Monáe worked as a maid in order to get to New York City to learn how to act, how to perform. "It was in my DNA," she said. "This is why I'm here. I developed myself behind closed doors before anybody knew me."

Growing up in Queens, New York, Cyndi Lauper said she'd do anything to get noticed. She said she always felt like an outcast, but it was what made her feel like an artist.

Years before she was discovered singing in a California coffeehouse, Jewel sang as a child at open mic nights in Alaska with her father, lived in a van with her mother, washed her hair in Kmart sinks and lived on food stamps.

Cher had so little money as a child of divorced parents that she tied rubber bands around her shoes to hold them together. After she acted, directed and choreographed school plays when she was 9 years old, she knew she wanted to be famous, and ultimately went to Los Angeles' Sunset Strip to introduce herself to anyone and everyone she thought could give her a break.

Debbie Harry was born in Miami, moved to Hawthorne, New Jersey, with her adoptive parents, then moved to New York City. She worked as a go-go dancer, a waitress at Max's Kansas City and a Playboy bunny before joining several bands, and then, with her partner Chris Stein, formed Blondie—which they thought of as a "pop art project."

Janet Jackson initially wanted to be a racehorse jockey or an entertainment lawyer, but she didn't have a chance in the family that spawned the Jackson 5, and was eventually pushed into showbiz by her father, Joseph Jackson.

◆

In July 2005, Beyoncé sat in the living room of her cousin/assistant Angie Beyincé's apartment overlooking the Hudson River on Manhattan's Upper West Side. This was several years before she moved in with, and then married, Jay-Z in his Tribeca penthouse. She talked about her Houston, Texas, childhood, her family and her "obsession" with music. "I wasn't doing this to support my family or get out of a bad situation," she said. "This just was what I dreamed of. I was so determined; this is what I wanted to do so bad."

Her mother, Tina Knowles—still known to everyone in showbiz as Miss Tina—put Beyoncé and her sister Solange in dance classes, and when Beyoncé was 6, her teacher, Miss Darlette, had her perform in front of everybody in a talent show. She sang John Lennon's "Imagine," and, because she was shy and quiet around other kids, she said she was "terrified. I didn't want to go out there, but Miss Darlette said, 'You can do it, you do it all the time.' She always would say, 'This little girl is different, this little girl is special.' She would always have me sing for everyone in class—I was like her little baby. My parents—who had never seen me perform before, were shocked; it was like 'Is that my child?'"

The young Beyoncé entered talent shows like the Texas Sweetheart pageant, but eventually her mother said no more of those, and Beyoncé started performing at a bunch of local award shows. She was asked to join a girls' group, and, she said, "That's when I fell in love with being in a group." There were around fifty girls; some could dance, some could sing, and it was, according to her, "a big mess. So I got Kelly [Rowland] and my father started helping us get a record deal. I did *Star Search* when I was nine and we did everything—we rapped, we danced, we sang. It's embarrassing, but it was cute. I hear those demos now and it's like, oh my god, it's like hearing another person." When that first incarnation of Destiny's Child lost *Star Search*, "We were devastated," she said. "We were kids—we were crying, sobbing . . . but our mothers were there and they were like, 'Get over it, we're going to Disney World.' Still, we thought the group was over, we had a producer who quit, I was so sad. But then my dad started trying to find producers for us and shopping us a deal."

When Beyoncé was thirteen, the then four-member Destiny's Child did a showcase for Columbia Records, signed to Elektra Records, got dropped by Elektra, signed to Columbia and moved to Atlanta to work with a producer. They lived with one member's mother in one room in a basement. "It sounds crazy," Beyoncé said, "but it was nice. We had a couch, a bed and a cot, and we had the best time. We'd get up and go to the studio, then go back home. Each time there was a showcase we would think it was the most important thing in our lives, our big break, everything we had been working for." She took singing lessons. Her father media-trained them and taped mock interviews. None of it felt like a chore. By the time they were sixteen, the girls knew how they wanted to sound, how they wanted to look. They were "developed" before they had their record deal. "The other girls were not as obsessed as I was," Beyoncé said. "I was always focused. Different things excited me. Going out did not excite me. Boys did not excite me. I had a boyfriend, I went to his prom, but I preferred to be at home in front of a stereo making songs. All I wanted to do was watch videos and write songs and perform."

✦

Joan Jett, who always wanted to play electric guitar at a time when girls didn't play electric guitar, told me in 1983, "I just never thought that women shouldn't be allowed to do certain things. It never occurred to me that there was some sort of protocol. There's so much hypocrisy about what a man can do and get away with and what a woman can do. When we were in The Runaways, we took a lot of shit because we were all girls who picked up a guitar or a drumstick. We were considered a novelty act. But I have to credit my parents for always telling me I could grow up and do whatever I wanted to do."

In 1986, Chrissie Hynde said, "I got into a band because I didn't want a career. I still associated a rock and roll band with an anti-establishment, renegade sort of thing. Everybody wanted to be the Beatles or the Rolling Stones because they just had the coolest clothes and they made brilliant songs. For my twenty-first birthday, my mother wanted to give me a watch or some kind of traditional thing. And I said, 'Well, if you're going to give me something, there's this Gibson Melody guitar advertised in the paper for sixty dollars. Do you think I could have that?' I had a very colorless background in Ohio, and when I left and went to England to get into a band, nobody knew who I was and I had a real freedom to experiment and experience things."

At age 4, in Arizona, Stevie Nicks sang country duets with her grandfather. Recently, Stevie told me that when she was in sixth grade, she was in a play called *The Alamo*, playing the child of the only adult woman in the Alamo. "I went home and told my mother I was so bad; don't ever sign me up for any acting again. I'm a singer."

Annie Clark, who records and performs as St. Vincent, said, "In high school, I would read the *New York Times* Arts section and I knew I needed to see the world outside of Oklahoma and Texas—I had to be where it was happening." Instead of going out on a Friday or Saturday night, Annie said she would stay in her room, light candles, listen to John Coltrane, write and wait for magic to happen.

Brandy, who was singing at the age of 2, appeared on several TV shows as a child, and, with the help of what used to be called a "stage mother" manager, was a TV star at 16. "I've always been very serious about it," she told me in 1995. "It was something that was a dream for me."

In 1977, Céline Dion said, "Ever since I was a baby, I wanted to be a singer. I remember watching TV when I was 8 or 9 years old in Canada, seeing all the big American stars, and I wanted to be part of it, I wanted to be onstage with them. That was a dream for me." Her first big break came when her demo tape reached René Angélil—who mortgaged his house to finance Céline's first album, married her thirteen years later and remained her husband, manager and father of her children until his death in 2016.

According to Diana Ross, "Even when I was a kid with pneumonia, they were wheeling me into the hospital room while I sang 'Open the Door, Richard.' The music has always been in me, the music is my life." She hung around her neighborhood Motown recording studios until Berry Gordy let her sing background vocals for other Motown acts, then built The Supremes around her, mentored her, became her lover and the father of one of her children.

Fiona Apple's debut album made her a star at 19. She told me that for a long time, she didn't tell anyone she wanted to be a songwriter.

"It was very precious, very sacred to me," she said, "and I didn't want anybody else's incorrect judgment to influence me. I was very vulnerable to being discouraged. I didn't want people to think it was some kind of hobby. I didn't even really admit to myself that I wanted to do it because it was such a long shot, and if it didn't work out and people knew I had been trying it, I would have been embarrassed. I wanted to do it on my own and have complete control of the situation."

Björk, who was on the radio and famous in her native Iceland while she was still in school, said in 1995 that she hated the celebrity aspect of stardom, so she became a drummer in a punk band. "What I was obsessed with," she said, "was writing the best song ever written. I know that sounds big-headed, and I haven't done it, but that's what turned me on."

◆

"I'm happier now than I've ever been in my life," Tina Turner told me in the mid-1980s. I was in her dressing room at the Ritz in New York City when her album *Private Dancer* was in the Top 20 on the Billboard charts. Her single "What's Love Got to Do With It" would eventually go to Number One. After her show that night, David Bowie, Keith Richards and Patti Hansen, John McEnroe and I celebrated her success. It had been a long, hard time coming for the woman who told me her voice had always sounded like "screaming dirt."

Before the show, she talked to me about how, as Anna Mae Bullock from Nutbush, Tennesee, she lived through segregation in the 1940s and 1950s. She knew she had to call white people *sir* and *ma'am*. She was exposed to Holy Rollers and speaking in tongues by the Pentecostals—which she found more fun than her own Baptist church, where, when she sang in the church choir, her repertoire included "Onward, Christian Soldiers" and "Amazing Grace." When she got older and moved to St. Louis, she was intrigued by the juke joints that she said "evoked sex"—even though at 10 years old, she didn't exactly know what that was. She had dreams of wearing her hair differently—not in braids—and dreams of Hollywood glamour, even though she wasn't sure of what that was either. At 16, when she saw Ike Turner and his Kings of Rhythm onstage at a local club, all she wanted to do was get up and sing with them. Night after night she waited, until she finally got hold of the microphone and sang. Ike paid attention, took her under his wing and, for years afterward, taught her how to perform onstage. Offstage, he beat her, cheated on her and made her consider, on multiple occasions, ending her life.

After everything Tina had gone through with her ex–musical partner and by now ex-husband Ike—the years on the road in the clubs on the chitlin' circuit, the other women, the abuse, the breakup, her attempts at a solo career—she finally had a solo hit. She said, "I'm talented. I can sing. It's not a pretty voice but it's a voice that can bring out emotion. But you can't put me with Diana Ross or Olivia Newton-John. Tina doesn't sound pretty. She makes a statement. After Ike, no one found me and made me a star. In fact, people didn't want to touch me—because they thought the duo broke up and what would I do on my own? But I had a dream. It always was to sing. At first it was to be an actress, then my dream was to be the first black rock and roll singer to pack the places that the Stones or David Bowie or Rod Stewart did. And the competition I had to move out of the way to get up there. . . . Look how long I've been going. And I still don't have the fans that the Rolling Stones or Michael Jackson does."

"I had years of playing the small clubs on my own for no money, just to pay my rent," Tina said. "Even if it was Las Vegas or the Fairmont Hotel, I did it until I realized this is not what I want to do. I don't want to put those sequin dresses on anymore. At first, it was exciting to go to Bob Mackie and get those gowns, until I realized—I want to get into those rock halls. Janis Joplin had the credibility, the ability and the power to sing very black, and to scream. No white girls sang like her. I think if I was a white woman I would have gotten here much faster. We still have not broken that thing where man is the ruler and white people are the ruling race. I've said why did God make me a woman so someone could beat me up? That's not fair. And yes, I did doubt, but I didn't doubt that solo success would happen. It was just like—how long do I have to wait? It's almost shameful. It's still a slavery thing." And, she added—and remember, this was in the 1980s—"We're still niggers. I don't care how much a woman has a claim to fame, she's still a nigger."

✦

Alanis Morissette was a teenage star in her native Canada, where her first album went platinum and her second one went gold. But, she said, "In Canada, I was wearing high heels and low cut dresses and I wasn't writing what I really wanted to write. I didn't think it was what people wanted to hear and I wasn't prepared to fight for what I thought was right. When I left Canada and came to LA, I started from scratch. The record companies had no idea who the hell I was and that gave me the opportunity to be myself."

The British singer PJ Harvey said, "I got into this because of my love of performing. It had nothing to do with making money or wanting to be in the limelight."

Jennifer Lopez told me that she was so obsessed with being a great dancer that she slept in the Broadway dance studio where she took lessons. "Obsessed. I was obsessed with being a great dancer—thinking that I wanted to do Broadway. I wanted to be down at that dance studio twenty-four hours a day. When I was little, I danced in front of the mirror constantly; I idolized Michael Jackson, Janet Jackson, Tina Turner, Madonna."

Alabama Shakes lead singer Brittany Howard endured working in the post office in her small Alabama town while she pursued her dreams of being in a rock and roll band.

In the 1980s, the beautiful and mysterious British/Nigerian singer Sade, who had hits with silky songs like "Smooth Operator," told me, "I never had any dreams or aspirations of being a singer. But

I always sang. I auditioned for a band that turned me down, but then they came back to me. So, I just sort of fell into it."

The musician/singer/songwriter and producer King Princess grew up around her father's Brooklyn recording studio where she learned how to play several instruments, how to write songs, how to produce records and how to navigate her way around the misogynistic music industry.

✦

With unparalleled hopes, dreams and ambition, Madonna fled Detroit to come to New York, to Be Somebody. "I thought of being everything," she told me in 1984. "At first I thought about being an actress. Then I wanted to be a singer. Then I got more into dancing; I just felt that I needed a skill to go to New York. I loved to dance, I was really good at it, so I thought in New York, I could start with that and take it from there. I had to arm myself with something." When Alvin Ailey didn't work out, she joined a band and started a singing career, and with what would mark her ever-continuing confidence, she said, "I always knew this would happen. I thought once the public knew who I was, I wouldn't have any problems because I feel that I know what the public would like."

The shy Romy Madley Croft would sing quietly in her London home so her father wouldn't hear her. Later, she sent music back and forth to friends online, and they formed what initially was considered an "underground" British group, the xx.

Rihanna was a tomboy who played outside with her brothers in her hometown of Bridgetown, Barbados. When inside, she said, she was "obsessed" with music. "I would just dream and watch TV from when I was 5 or 6 years old—getting into Mariah Carey, Celine Dion, Whitney Houston. I always wanted to do this. I'm a dreamer. I dream very big."

✦

Katy Perry was sitting yoga-style on a sofa across from me in a suite at the Ritz Carlton Hotel across the street from Staples Center in downtown Los Angeles. It was Grammy week, February 2011, and although Katy was nominated for four awards, she would win none. She was, at that time, still married to the British comedian and actor Russell Brand, who was barely around that week. She'd already had a monster debut hit, "I Kissed a Girl," and was now performing in her full-on pastel pink, polka-dotted, cupcake-adorned, girly stage shows strengthened by massive hits such as "Teenage Dream" and "Firework." For several hours, we ate room-service food and she talked about how, as Katheryn Hudson, the daughter of Pentecostal preachers who moved around from city to city, she lived in a household where if her mother read to her, it was only Scripture. She attended church services where people spoke in tongues. She wasn't allowed to listen to secular music. She wasn't even allowed to say "deviled eggs." She had to sneak out of her house to listen to rock and roll or watch MTV. When she was a teenager and her family settled in Santa Barbara, she started making demos at a studio in what she described as "a Christian place that does a lot of outreach for homeless people and charity work." With a repertoire that included "Oh Happy Day" and "His Eye Is on the Sparrow," she went back and forth with her mother from Santa Barbara to Nashville to record Christian music. "I didn't know anything else," she said. "But I was excited. When I was 13, my church bought me a blue guitar I saw in a shop window and I was learning how to write songs. When you're young, you feel invincible; when you're a kid, you get bruises and cuts but you don't care. I just thought—always—that I had something to offer that no one else had brought to the marketplace."

At 17, with her parents' blessing, she moved to Los Angeles to make secular music—pop songs—and to work with producer Glen Ballard. She got by, she said, by selling her clothes to vintage clothing stores and singing background vocals for the likes of Miley Cyrus. She was signed to several labels and was dropped, but now, she said, "Rejection is God's protection. I was never in a rush. I don't have a time bomb ticking about where I want to be. Growing up, I always had cool friends who would sneak me CDs in towels. I'd listen to girls like Shirley Manson, Gwen Stefani and Alanis Morissette. I'd go to my friends' houses and turn on MTV, and they'd say 'Let's do something else.' But to me, that was the something else."

◆

The 13 year-old Lauryn Hill came from South Orange, New Jersey, to Harlem and the Apollo Theater's Amateur Night, where she was booed by an unforgiving audience when she sang a Smokey Robinson song ("Who's Lovin' You"). She eventually won the crowd over, but afterward, she cried backstage.

Describing herself as a "painfully shy, library person," Lorde—who had global success at age 16 with her hit song "Royals"—considered herself a writer. "It makes no sense that I'm doing this," she told me in 2016. "I always knew I'd do something, but I never thought it would be music."

Adele knew at age 4 that she could carry a tune. She would get on a "weird little platform" in her mother's boyfriend's house and sing "Dreams," by a British singer she loved named Gabrielle, as well as songs by the Spice Girls and Destiny's Child. Her goal was to get out of where she grew up—upstairs from a convenience store in Brixton. "I didn't care how I was getting out," she told me in 2017. "I didn't care where I'd be living. But I knew from 7 years old that I wasn't living there."

When Gwen Stefani was 17, her brother Eric got her to join his ska band No Doubt and while she just sort of fell into it, she quickly became the visual focus and lead singer of the group.

Marianne Faithfull wanted to be—and was—an actress, but as Mick Jagger's girlfriend in the 1960s, she had a Number One hit with a song ("As Tears Go By") that Mick co-wrote with Keith Richards for her, which began her music career and a life of wildly careening highs and lows.

Mariah Carey knew from the age of 4 that she wanted to be a singer. "I always loved music," she told me in the 1990s, at the height of her early fame. "My mother was an opera singer and a vocal coach, and she would always tell me to sing for people. When I was 13, I was in studios, listening and learning about my voice. I hung out with friends and went to parties, but I kept my music to myself because I wanted it to be sacred and special."

In 1978, Linda Ronstadt told me, "When I was in first grade, and I had trouble with arithmetic, I said to myself that I didn't have to learn arithmetic because I could sing, and that's what I was going to do for a living."

Mary J. Blige had to overcome abuse and drug problems in her rough Bronx neighborhood, but she always sang in church and listened to the R&B songs her mother played in their house. In the 1990s, when hip-hop embraced a female who could really sing, Mary was discovered and mentored by record executives Andre Harrell and Sean "Puffy" Combs, who brought her into the mainstream.

Lady Gaga's hopes, dreams and ambitions have been well documented. She grew up in New York City, always wanted to be a star, took singing lessons and piano lessons, and was a self-described "theater girl" in her private high school before moving into an East Village walk-up. It was there that she took drugs, wrote songs, performed as a go-go dancer in clubs, formed a band, got signed by a record label and got dropped by that record label. Then came the catchy hits and the outrageous costumes that turned her into a worldwide phenomenon.

✦

In my apartment on November 8, 1974, Patti Smith told me, "I remember the exact moment I met rock and roll. I was 6 years old and I was in front of my clubhouse. I was a creepy, homely kid, I had an eyepatch, I weighed about ten pounds. This boy had a little RCA Victrola and we had an extension cord running into the clubhouse. He said, 'Wait until you hear this,' and he put a record on. It was 'The Girl Can't Help It' by Little Richard and the only thing I can compare it to is when I saw the Stones on *Ed Sullivan*. It was instant recognition. I didn't know what it was, but it got me at 6 years old, and it never stopped."

Over hundreds of hours of the interviews I did with Patti in the 1970s, she talked about what she has since written about in her memoirs: moving from New Jersey to New York City, meeting Robert Mapplethorpe, wanting to do great work, mainly because of Robert— who wanted so badly to be famous. He was shy, she was not, so she championed and hustled for them both. She's written and talked a lot about her love of poetry and writing and books. But, by 1973, when she formed The Patti Smith Group, in the numerous times she was in front of my tape recorder, or we talked on the phone, or backstage at CBGB or other concert venues, or in a van on tour in the early days of her band, we talked about music and her childhood dreams. "I wanted to be a total relentless artist poet," she said, "but I really didn't know what I wanted to do. I knew I wanted to do something and I knew I had these rhythms in me, but I didn't know what to do with them."

"Even when I was 5 years old, I was very impatient," she said, "because I was just trying to get bigger, to get all this stuff out. As a kid, I had the sense that it was waiting. And then I got bigger and felt it coming, but I was frustrated, I didn't have any skills. I wasn't ready. And I didn't know exactly what it was, but I knew something was coming out." Early on, when she was starting to merge poetry with rock and roll and she performed at Max's Kansas City, "It was like a bird flew out of my mouth," she said. "And halfway through the show, I was really singing. To suddenly sing is fantastic, but it's also frightening. Because if you thought it was never going to happen to you, it's such a monstrous responsibility, it's such an honor, it's a little scary, but right now, I'm watching myself unfold." Patti's rock and roll heroes were all men—Bob Dylan, Jim Morrison and Keith Richards—and, she said, "I never thought about doing anything new. I just wanted to be the best version of what was. And now I feel myself becoming something I don't know about. It's the singing and the sense of freedom."

✦

In 2014, Florence Welch, of Florence and the Machine, told me, "I had no idea what would happen with my first record. I was just happy to have made it. Then I won a Brit Award before I had even finished the album. It was terrifying. I was unable to cope. I was completely unprepared for what came next."

HAIR & MAKEUP

MTV changed everything.

In 1980, when MTV took the mystery out of the music, videos with storyboards and concepts often specified what the song was supposed to be about. Prior to that, there were a few TV shows with popular musicians lip-synching to their records: *Shindig!* (with girls go-go dancing in cages), *Don Kirshner's Rock Concert, Soul Train* and the one that started it all—*American Bandstand*. You could see The Ronettes with their hair piled up high and cat-eye black eyeliner, or the white, British soul singer Dusty Springfield with her blonde bob and shift dresses. There was the occasional full length movie— the *T.A.M.I. Show*, which featured the Rolling Stones, James Brown, and girls go-go dancing in cages. But most American rock bands, and the singers who fronted them—especially women—were seen only in concert, on their album covers or in the few magazines that catered to the rock and roll fan. In the late 1960s, The Mamas & the Papas had huge hits and the model-gorgeous looks of Michelle

Phillips—in contrast to the overweight Mama Cass, who had the much better voice. Except for Janis Joplin and Grace Slick, who were lead singers in hippie, "psychedelic" rock bands during the Summer of Love—which seemed to last six years—most young, white, female singers were considered folk singers. Joan Baez, Judy Collins and Joni Mitchell played guitar, wore flowered dresses and sang what were considered suitable, sweet, non-threatening songs to those who weren't listening to the lyrics. Joni Mitchell especially—with her long, straight blonde hair, great cheekbones and unusual guitar tunings—was an extraordinary writer who considered herself akin to a jazz musician, like John Coltrane. By the 1970s, Fleetwood Mac had giant hits and the benefit of Stevie Nicks' amazing voice— but they also had Stevie's adorable blonde looks combined with her "witch-like" image: the flowing long, black dresses, fringed shawls, and platform boots. (Stevie always told me that she couldn't sing unless she wore those boots; they made her "feel tall.")

Janis Joplin was the first real female rock and roll star without any sort of conventional female beauty. In fact, she was once called "the world's ugliest man" and was compared to a dog. But there was no way you could deny her deeply emotional, gutsy voice—it came at you like Bessie Smith or Big Mama Thornton or Little Richard or all of the great blues belters of yesteryear. Janis Joplin was a misfit in her native Port Arthur, Texas, who fled as soon as she could to San Francisco. She was sweaty, she howled, and she commanded a stage like no other white woman had before and, quite possibly, since. In addition to an extraordinary stage presence, she also had great style— before there were stylists—without the benefit of any special hair or makeup assistance. Her voice went along with the look: the feather boa on top of her head, the bell-bottoms, the big sheepskin hat, the round tinted glasses, and all that tie-dyed, crushed velvet of the late 1960s.

◆

In the 1960s and 1970s, before MTV, record labels promoted their acts with 35 millimeter color slides, or black and white promotional photos sent to journalists with press kits that included a bio and reproductions of good reviews. In the handful of rock magazines that existed at the time—*Crawdaddy, Rolling Stone, Creem, Hit Parader* and, later, *Rock Scene*—there were "candid" shots from photographers Annie Leibovitz, Bob Gruen, Jim Marshall, Henry Diltz, Ethan Russell, Mike Putland, Leee Black Childers, Baron Wolman, Mick Rock, Lynn Goldsmith, Roberta Bayley, Neal Preston, Andy Kent and Richard Creamer. These magazines featured Janis Joplin, Joni Mitchell and Linda Ronstadt—but not nearly as much as they did the Beatles, the Rolling Stones, The Who or Led Zeppelin. Janis Joplin existed primarily on record, in concert, rarely on radio, so visually, she lived in those few rock magazines or the photos on her album covers. She and Grace Slick and Linda Ronstadt and Stevie Nicks were all flying blind; there were no female Beatles or Rolling Stones for them to emulate. They were just themselves. When the 1960s ended, sometime around 1973, more rebellious, hard-edged female stars emerged. Patti Smith and Chrissie Hynde projected androgynous images at the exact moment when girls were "allowed"—as were Suzi Quatro and Joan Jett—to pick up guitars and play in the boys' club. None of the "looks"—Janis' feather boa or Stevie's fringed shawls, Suzi's or Joan's black leather pants, Patti's ripped Haile Selassie t-shirt or Chrissie's motorcycle jacket—were accidental. The difference was that these girls didn't have marketing teams telling them how to dress or helping them create an "image." Rihanna once told me that when she was starting out, she won an award on Canadian TV, and, she said, "I'll never forget it. I got an awful text about the color lipstick I wore. I was told it was too dark of a pink. I was like, 'Are you serious? Thank you for congratulating me on the first award I ever won in my career—and you're talking to me about lipstick?'" But even back during the reign of MTV, no one discussed their "brand." No one designed sneakers or sold their own fragrance. That all changed thirty years later—when file sharing ruined the business model of what had been the record business, and people had to start getting their music heard in other ways—mostly in advertisements, or campaigns for whatever else they were hawking—because no one was selling millions of physical albums (CDs) anymore. Except Adele.

✦

So, when the "I Want My MTV" campaign bludgeoned its way across the country in 1980 and cable television was forced to broadcast the channel, we got Madonna. She was considered a "rebel" and a "chameleon" by some of the squarest people on the planet. She was determined to be considered stylish and sexy and free and strong. In 1984 she told me, "I think I have an original sense of style and I know for a fact that there are people who are copying my style. But I don't always 'dress up'—and if I want to walk on the street and not have people annoy me, I don't wear my jewelry or any makeup. It's the videos that get me recognized—my 'Boy Toy' belt, that's my symbol." That was what she said. That was the myth. The reality is that Madonna's style was copied from the girls on 8th Street in Greenwich Village, and from Cyndi Lauper and the designer Maripol, who made the rubber bracelets Madonna wore in her videos. And most definitely Debbie Harry—whose neighbor Stephen Sprouse made clothes for her years earlier in the 1970s. (Debbie once told me that she knew she was considered the original "Marilyn of rock," adding, "My cheekbones were the secret to my success. They seat six." She also told me that yes, she did think Madonna copied her: "I wore the wedding dress first, goddammit!" She then quickly—and tactfully—added, "I suppose it was a compliment.") Surely Madonna was aware too, of Tish and Snooky—who had the "punk" boutique Manic Panic on St. Mark's Place. And Patricia Field, who had a shop on West 8th Street that catered to drag queens, downtown trendsetters and the uptown "vogueing" ballroom crowd. (Pat Field would finally get her due, and a payday, dressing the women for the unfortunately popular *Sex and the City* that gave a tourist's view of what New York City was like.)

Madonna was well versed in the so-called downtown scene of the 1980s—which, like everything else, has achieved legendary status in hindsight. She also had a team at her record label before people actually started referring to it as a "team." A creative director. A stylist. A famous photographer. They shot an expensive video in Venice, Italy, in a gondola, with Madonna in that wedding dress, singing the laughable "Like A Virgin" lyrics. It was a hit, inspiring little girls everywhere to look like her, dress like her. Ruining the culture. Her voice, such as it was, didn't really matter. She was aggressively sexual, but not sexy. Styled, but not stylish. Successful in spite of her tinny little voice. Successful because of her drive and her image. She came along at the right moment, when MTV needed her and she needed MTV. This was not a concert where you actually had to leave the house or pay money to see your favorite star. This was "free" on pay cable TV, in your living room. Or your bedroom. Countless girls growing up could sing and dance along while looking in the mirror. When the novelty of MTV wore off and everyone became accustomed to this twenty-four hour a day visual radio, it was nowhere near as exciting as seeing Janis Joplin on a stage. Still, when something is seen in context, and it's the first—as in Madonna, Michael Jackson and Prince, who were all considered the stars of the 1980s—they're remembered for just being there. People who weren't there believe that they all mattered. The music of Michael Jackson and Prince mattered. Madonna spawned girls who wanted to be famous like her, have hits like she did. But what really came in her wake? The adorable young pop star Britney Spears and others who either had a good run, couldn't take the pressure and had nervous breakdowns, or knew better than to hang around for forty years.

✦

In the 1970s, Sony came out with a portable videotape recorder called the Portapak, and there were a few of us who understood that this would change everything. My husband Richard directed the first Blondie video, shot in black and white against a white back-drop. It featured close-ups of Debbie Harry and her cheekbones—but it had little, if any, exposure. There was nowhere for this to be shown, except on one or two local cable channels that broadcast homemade porn. (It's hilarious to think that now, almost fifty years later, everyone can, and does, make their own homemade videos and posts them on Instagram for everyone to see on their phones. Back to the future.) Even at the end of the 1970s, when we told record company publicists that they should start videotaping their acts, we were told that those 35 millimeter color slides were enough. When MTV became the main music promotional tool, hundreds of thousands of dollars were spent by the then very flush record companies on acts that were considered priorities. It was not unlike the movie studio system in the 1930s and 1940s, when stars were groomed to look a certain way. Just like talkies killed the silent movie stars who didn't have good speaking voices, that Buggles song wasn't a joke: video killed the radio star. This is ancient history now, but when it happened, fashion photographers, hairdressers, makeup artists, stylists and models slid right into music and took over. These images were often the very antithesis of musicians who, on their own, had actual style. The result: today's "glam squads" and elaborate videos that only get seen on YouTube, on computers or phones—often the size of a postage stamp. But someone like Brittany Howard, who has a voice that comes the closest to Janis Joplin we've heard in fifty years, initially couldn't get into fashion magazines because she's heavy. Or Adele—who, despite that voice and that beautiful face, was at first told she was too fat for the cover of a glossy mainstream magazine. (When Adele lost something like one hundred pounds last year, it was "breaking news" all over the Internet.) Things have changed somewhat: the very large Lizzo has had no problem getting on award shows and magazine covers wearing both skintight gowns and something akin to one of those Ice Capades outfits.

One woman who has long been forgotten but who defied the category of what women were expected to look like in rock and roll was a Scottish singer named Maggie Bell. Before she went out on her own, Maggie was the lead singer in a band called Stone the Crows. The band's lead guitarist, Maggie's boyfriend Leslie Harvey, was electrocuted and died onstage in May 1972. Maggie was a big girl with long, curly reddish hair—not especially pretty in any sort of conventional way. But she had an amazing voice. One that could be compared to a blues belter like Janis Joplin then, or Brittany Howard today. And of course, at that time, there weren't many photos of Maggie Bell in rock magazines—except for the ones I put in *Hit Parader* or *Rock Scene* when I edited those magazines. Maggie was managed by Peter Grant, who also managed Led Zeppelin and Bad Company, so she opened for those bands on their U.S. tours. But she didn't have the cute blonde looks of Debbie Harry, or the androgynous swagger of Patti Smith and Chrissie Hynde, or the hippie aura of Stevie Nicks, or the ethereal good looks of Joni Mitchell. And she didn't have hits or a marketable image, so she eventually faded from the U.S. music scene. She's sung with British blues bands and her voice is as strong and tough as ever. But, among the thousands of women I've interviewed over the last four decades, there has yet to be one who has credited Maggie as any kind of inspiration. And there's only one who seriously mentioned Janis Joplin to me—and that's Brittany Howard.

◆

A word about weight: Even in the 1960s, when miniskirted skinny English models like Twiggy and Jean Shrimpton were in fashion, Janis Joplin managed to get famous with a normal figure. You could see her normal figure in a famous black and white photo taken of her in her prime by Bob Seidmann. No one used words like *anorexia* or *bulimia* in the 1960s—even though lots of us stayed skinny with the help of "diet pills" like Dexedrine or Eskatrol. Diana Ross was skinny, Mama Cass was huge, Grace Slick was just . . . normal. In the 1970s, cocaine replaced diet pills, and certainly all of the male rock stars—Mick Jagger, Jimmy Page, Keith Richards, David Bowie, Lou Reed—were rail thin. They babbled. The women were not immune to either cocaine or alcohol. Janis Joplin died. Judy Collins, Bonnie Raitt and Stevie Nicks have talked at length about addiction. Even the so-called punk rockers who rebelled against all the "bloated" dinosaur rock bands were big customers for cocaine and, eventually, heroin. It's certainly still around today. Visually, the late Amy Winehouse had a style influenced by The Ronettes—who came fifty years before her—but heroin undoubtedly kept her weight down. The gym and all those SoulCycle classes can only do so much. Lady Gaga told me she'd been bulimic but didn't want her fans to know. She smoked cigarettes but didn't want her fans to know. She told me she only ate one meal a day, but it's certain that when she's in "training" for a tour or a Super Bowl performance or an Oscar red carpet, that one meal a day isn't the pasta at her father's Upper West Side restaurant. (More about drugs later—but suffice to say, alcohol, cocaine and heroin are no beauty treatments.)

Weight wise, Mariah Carey has been up and down for years, but so has Bono. And supposedly, Mariah is selling her *voice*. But we all know women are judged differently, and women singers and musicians are no different than actresses or models—except many of the musicians have actual talent. As delusional as Mariah or Madonna may be about their age-inappropriate dressing, they beg to be "treated like a human being" (Mariah) or go into a snit when criticized (Madonna). A very young and cute Mariah told me in the 1990s that she knew she would succeed faster than some hideous slob who had a great voice. But, she said, "I want to be taken seriously. I don't want it to be, 'Oh, Mariah Carey, doesn't her body look great in this shot?' I want it to be, 'Did you listen to this song? Doesn't her voice sound good?'" And in 1994, Jewel told me, "I think that it's sad that a lot of women in music still find their worth in their ability to sexually attract men. And I have a really hard time in interviews. . . . I notice my male friends get interviewed in a whole different way than I do. I can't even read fashion magazines because everyone is so emaciated and beautiful and perfect. I grew up on a frigging homestead with dirt underneath my nails, driving tractors. You never get over that. You have days where you're just like, 'I can't be on television today, because I ate a whole pint of Ben and Jerry's last night and I can't face the world.' But I've never been one of those girls who can starve herself."

◆

Some women are incredibly disciplined. In 2010, Jennifer Lopez told me that when she was starting out, she wanted to be a dancer and an actress, and didn't think about her image. "It's not until you're faced with people talking about you and looking at you and discussing your image that you really start looking at yourself. I mean, just like any other person, you get dressed and you want to look nice, but I never— ever—really thought about 'image' until probably after my first album." She certainly thought about her image in 2000, when she appeared on the Grammys wearing that green print Versace dress with the neckline plunged down to her navel. She wore a similar version after she turned 50, at both a 2019 fashion show and on *Saturday Night Live*. This street-smart girl from the Bronx was never naïve. (Still, several years ago at a video shoot, another singer who was there told me that Jennifer—who was at that time in her late forties—ran around asking everyone on the set if her famous posterior still looked good.)

Once, at a party, Beyoncé cut a small brownie into four tiny little squares in front of me and ate only *one* of the squares. Another time, when I was interviewing her, Beyoncé ordered a pizza and had *only one slice*. "My personality is all or nothing," she told me. "I either give all I have or I'm not going to do it. With food, I had to tell myself that this is my *job*. I treat it like it's my job, and when I say that to myself, I really believe that I can do anything." And who can forget those famous cayenne pepper, honey and vinegar "cleanses" that

Beyoncé went on to prepare for a movie role, or an album release, or an appearance at the Super Bowl? Still, I've seen her after she's been in the studio—once when she stopped by her husband's private suite in the 40/40 Club wearing cutoff denim shorts, espadrilles and a tank top, with no makeup whatsoever and her hair pulled back, and she looked adorable. And now, having had three children, she seems to have come to terms with a fuller, curvier body.

After awhile, it just becomes too much of a drag to maintain one's "performance" weight. In 2015, over a meal of gnocchi, ravioli and spaghetti, Rihanna told me, "I have been in the gym every day because of this. I'm not willing to give up my food, but I will sacrifice an hour for the gym." These days, with social media and all that butt-baring and body shaming going on, it's a miracle that any female has the guts to make a record, put herself out there or get on a stage. Some mainstream stars don't care: Kelly Clarkson's weight changes on a regular basis. Pink is a big, strong girl who refuses to adapt to any stereotyped demand. Alessia Cara claimed that you're beautiful just the way you are. There is a whole crop of younger girls in indie rock bands who say they couldn't care less. But even Romy Madley Croft of the xx got smaller as the band got bigger.

These days, Beyoncé and Rihanna and Nicki Minaj and Katy Perry and Lady Gaga have all taken charge of their own careers and image in a way that Janis Joplin and Tina Turner and Stevie Nicks and Diana Ross never did. Along with the auto-tuning of the voice comes the photoshopping of the Instagram pictures—to say nothing of the actual "real" fashion shoots. Ed Sheeran and Post Malone are stars who clearly are no beauties. Just imagine if they were girls. If a female star leaves the house without makeup, she winds up in one of those "Stars Without Makeup" pictorial spreads in a tabloid magazine. And everyone's idea of glamour depends on what you saw or where you were from: Dolly Parton, who left the hills of Tennessee for a country music career in Nashville, said her idea of glamour was the town tramp—makeup, high heels, big hair, sequins, glitz, sparkle, fancy cars, sunglasses, fur coats. And while many female rock stars got their visual inspiration from men (Patti Smith/Bob Dylan, Patti Smith/ Keith Richards, Madonna/David Bowie), or the choreography of Michael Jackson (Beyoncé), every female musician's "look" can probably be traced back to someone who came before.

✦

"I watched videos of Diana Ross and the Supremes over and over," Beyoncé told me in 2005. "Diana was so elegant and so poised. Her hair, those dresses, I wanted to look like that, to do that." She was set to star in the 2006 movie *Dreamgirls*, which was previously a Broadway show loosely based on The Supremes. I asked her which role she was going to play. She looked at me with surprise. "The lead singer of the group," she said, as if there would be no other role she would consider. I stupidly blurted out, "Oh, then you don't get to sing *that* song"—referring to the barnburner "I Am Telling You I'm Not Going." For one second, Beyoncé looked slightly stricken; she realized that it was that song that would be remembered from the movie. And in fact, it was that song—as well as her intense performance—that eventually won the *American Idol* runner-up Jennifer Hudson the Oscar that Beyoncé wants to win one day.

Rihanna told me that when she was seventeen, she wore white jeans, white boots and a turquoise tube top from Forever 21 to her first audition for Jay-Z and Def Jam Records, and, she said, "My hair was wavy, parted to the side, and I'd had my first weave." Years later, she was above the fold on the front page of the *New York Times*, photographed at the 2015 Met Ball wearing a yellow satin Guo Pci–designed extravaganza that flowed all the way down the museum steps. And, she also told me that she was "thrilled" to be the first black woman to be the star of an advertising campaign for Dior.

Gwen Stefani was a normal sized teenager from Southern California when she joined her brother's ska punk band that would eventually become No Doubt. She loved Debbie Harry's cute blonde looks. Then, through the visual transformations that inevitably accompany success and fame, Gwen became the skinny, adorable blonde star with colorful, slightly madcap outfits, and the clear visual focus of No Doubt. Cyndi Lauper told me, "I colored my hair because it made me feel good, and I wore a lot of jewelry because it made me feel good. Then, when everything got out of hand in 1984 and I became well known, I had to hide all of that in order to walk on the street."

Lady Gaga was a normal sized brunette from a New York City family and emulated the style of the British socialite Daphne Guinness. Before she was famous, before she had money, she had a glue gun and studded her jeans with sequins. After she became *Lady Gaga,* she wore an Alexander McQueen red lace gown that went all the way up to cover her face—as well as her hands and her shoes. She wore a dress made out of raw meat. She wore backless eight inch platform boots. She referred to Alexander McQueen and Donatella Versace as her close friends. In 2011, she made her Grammy red carpet entrance lying inside a transparent egg carried by shirtless men. When I first met her in 2010, she walked into a bungalow at the Beverly Hills Hotel completely encased in a black lace catsuit and wearing black leather fingerless gloves, eight inch black leather backless boots and a black lace veil—which I finally got her to lift so we could sip wine and talk. I have previously written about how she told me that people always asked her who the *real* person was behind all that drag. And she said that even with the wig on her head, the Chanel outfits and the eight inch backless boots, that *was* the real her; Lady Gaga was the real person.

Björk has an unbelievably beautiful voice with a great range, and an eclectic body of work, and she is *still* remembered for wearing that swan dress to the 2001 Oscars. Erykah Badu once told me that even though it's the music business and some people have gimmicks and costumes, "before I was signed [to a record label], I still dressed like this. I throw a head wrap on and that takes two minutes. What I wear—long African print dresses and a plethora of beaded necklaces—is not that extraordinary; it's how you feel when you have it on. In the subculture of hip-hop, I feel I am adorning myself with my culture." But not everyone felt that way. Once, at a *Vanity Fair* photo shoot, Mary J. Blige asked photographer Marc Baptiste if he could photograph her in such a way that her tattoos weren't visible. Or, could we airbrush them out later—because she couldn't get advertising endorsements if she looked too "hip-hop." Translation: thuggish. And this was fifteen years ago, when tattoos were still considered "rebellious" as opposed to just another fashion accessory. From the '60s right up to today, the way women look—their clothes, their hair, their makeup—has been analyzed, dissected, praised and criticized. Often, it fueled their success. None of it would have mattered if the music wasn't good, or catchy, or both. But the image is part of the currency. It's an old story: no one—*no one*—is judged on their looks the way women are. Look at poor Madonna—with what appears to be all that extreme plastic surgery. And Cher—beloved as she is, well—it's still hard to remember what she used to look like. In an attempt to fight the inevitable, they don't look younger, they just look like they've had work done. In 2012, Lady Gaga told me she was "too chicken shit" to do anything to her face, but surely she's been in Hollywood long enough to have been pressured into having had something done. Even Gwen Stefani and Jennifer Lopez—who've sworn to me they've done nothing to their face—look like they're no strangers to Botox or fillers, or nose jobs or eye lifts, or more. In 2004, Jennifer Lopez told me she had absolutely nothing at all done to her face: "Want to look close?" she said, pulling her hair back behind her ears. Fifteen years later, when she celebrated her 50th birthday for what seemed like a month-long series of parties, she still looks like herself as opposed to some freak; but she looks like she's been freshened up a bit. This is the burden that is now placed on every single woman who steps on a stage to sing, play a guitar or to make music. Unless you just don't care, and who does not?

✦

The photo shoots of the 1960s and 1970s captured rock and roll stars in dressing rooms, backstage, onstage, at an occasional studio or, if there was a large enough budget, at an exotic location. These shoots were nothing like the elaborate ones that came in the 1980s—when pictures had to keep up with the videos on MTV. Today, photos have gone back to the candid shots of before—except that they're selfies, taken, controlled and photoshopped by the stars themselves in order to reinforce their image. Still, there are the occasional elaborate shoots done for magazines that still exist and have a budget (albeit a dwindling one), such as *Vogue*, *Vanity Fair*, *Elle* and the like. If someone is powerful enough—like Beyoncé—she gets photo approval. These days, Cardi B is demanding photo approval. And now that nearly every female star (except Adele) is hawking a perfume, or a clothing line, or sneakers, or all of the above, there are the ad campaigns. Or someone is the face of something, and this all seems normal now.

But in the olden days, it was much funkier. The first woman I recall seeing in a dressing room before a show was Patti Smith in 1974 in the so-called backstage at CBGB. The backstage at CBGB consisted of a couple of rooms with lumpy, broken-down sofas. I'm not even sure if there was a mirror in there. Patti's preshow routine may have included applying some kohl eyeliner, but mostly it was rumpling her hair and some vague sexual foreplay with one of her boyfriends at the time. Over thirty years later, in 2011, I sat in Katy Perry's dressing room prior to the Grammy Awards and, for what seemed like an interminable amount of time, watched her get "done." It was at least a two to three hour mind-numbing process that involved the application of false eyelashes, fake nails, hair extensions and a complete facial transformation. There were five people involved in this production, all crammed into what was a fairly small space. This dressing room was actually half a dressing room, curtained off from the other half where Rihanna was getting "done." There were discussions about whether or not Katy had too much foundation on, and what lipstick color looked best with which outfit and whatnot. Katy went from being a cute girl to a made up doll—"camera ready"—for television. She had to go through three costume changes: one for the red carpet, one for her live singing performance and yet another to sit in the audience where she would smile and applaud the Grammy winner in her category when she lost. I understand that it's show business, but I always wonder (a) how much of these masks cover up deep rooted insecurities and (b) how much confidence does this really give these women? And does that confidence disappear when the makeup comes off at the end of the night? Katy Perry had done an infomercial for the skin-care line Proactiv—and when I asked her why she did it, she said she had terrible acne, this was the only thing that actually worked and she never went anywhere without it. As I've previously recounted, Lady Gaga told me that in high school, she would put her makeup on at night before she went to bed: "So I would be ready for school in the morning and feel like a star."

Very few women are like Bette Midler, who told me that when she started out in show business, she didn't really know what she looked like, because growing up, "We had no mirrors in the house." Obviously, not everyone is as naturally beautiful as Alicia Keys—who decided to go completely natural and wear no makeup whatsoever. (It must save a fortune as well as alleviate the soul-crushing routine of it all.) And Christina Aguilera never looked better than when she appeared on the cover of *Paper* magazine in 2018 without a trace of makeup on her face. It didn't last—she reportedly hated it and went back to the red lipstick and full-on glam look shortly thereafter. But even a singer as breathtakingly talented and naturally beautiful as Adele feels she needs all that "drag," as she laughingly refers to it, as well as Spanx, before she can go onstage. "I don't wear makeup except when I'm working," Adele told me in 2016, backstage at Staples Center in 2016. "You see how much fuckin' makeup I have to wear? It's like a whole fuckin' tub of powder, I swear, it takes two hours. So I meditate."

And . . . I keep going back to Janis Joplin . . . who actually was considered ugly and never would have been on any *Vogue* cover (although the savvy editor Diana Vreeland had Richard Avedon shoot her in 1968 for a famous inside portrait). She didn't need two hours of makeup, or a makeup artist hovering about. She just looked like . . . Janis.

✦

I always thought it was hilarious that they were called makeup "artists." Granted, the late, famed Way Bandy actually *painted* a face on the face he was working on, way before the so-called first celebrity makeup artist Kevyn Aucoin left his native Louisiana for New York City and the bigtime. Still, the first time I observed a makeup artist on a tour was on the 1975 Rolling Stones tour of the Americas. Pierre La Roche was a flamboyant and temperamental Frenchman who had done makeup for Bianca Jagger and was hired to do Mick Jagger's makeup for every show. I never could understand why Mick felt he needed that makeup every night; the shows were in massive stadiums before the existence of those Jumbotron screens that showed the singer's face. To most of the crowd, Mick looked the size of an ant. Obviously, David Bowie wore makeup before that, as did Marc Bolan and Gary Glitter and Alice Cooper and Bryan Ferry and the entire glam rock crowd. But this was the first time I saw it done as an actual job by someone who received a salary, was part of the traveling entourage and whose function was to pile on foundation and do Mick's eye makeup for every show. Eventually, it became routine. Now even Bono has his own makeup artist on tour.

✦

But when it comes to women, tours and photo shoots are operatic. I spent quite a lot of time on photography sets in the 1980s, when I was friends with the fashion photographer Steven Meisel. I've been witness to more than twenty years of shoots for *Vanity Fair* and I've seen a lot of tedium and drama. Janelle Monáe once took four hours to get ready for a photo that wound up looking like every other photo she's ever taken. At another photo shoot, in the middle of getting her makeup done, Solange burst into tears and ran out of the building. I never found out why—we were told that it was a "personal matter." I don't think it was the makeup, but you never know. And at a major Ariana Grande cover shoot, the 27 year-old star, who is treated like a child by her team, allegedly kept bursting into tears and refusing to come out of her trailer because she didn't like the way she looked. For one Lady Gaga shoot, Annie Leibovitz had Gaga get into five different looks: nude in Tony Bennett's art studio (where he was painting a portrait of her), in a gold lamé gown "eating" a hot dog on Fifth Avenue near the Plaza, in another ensemble on the Staten Island Ferry, another costume in an East Village laundromat, then a red gown and hat for the cover picture. (Drama ensued when one of the pictures was printed with a visible piece of tape pulling back the Gaga temples.) Nothing like this was ever done in rock and roll in the 1960s or 1970s. The first time the influence of fashion with music hit home for me was in 1983, when Steven Meisel rented a room at the St. Regis Hotel for Madonna to lie on a bed wearing a bustier for the cover shoot of her *Like A Virgin* album. When Annie Leibovitz shot Linda Ronstadt for the cover of *Rolling Stone* sometime in the 1970s, she managed to convince Linda to lie on a bed in lacy lingerie. Linda protested that she didn't want to do it; she was worried that it would wind up on the cover. Annie said oh no, it was just for them, and of course, it wound up on the cover. And some forty years later, Linda told me that in hindsight, she didn't regret it—because she looked so good.

Back in the 1970s, I was backstage with Linda Ronstadt before one of her concerts in her hometown of Tucson, Arizona. She told me then, "When I was a little girl I looked in movie magazines and I saw pictures of Brigitte Bardot and I wanted to look like her. I don't look like her, I never did grow that kind of figure, or that kind of face. But when you grow up in this culture, it was fun to try and too hard to resist. But I don't know what it has to do with my work. It's just the package that the voice comes in."

✦

As the editor of *Hit Parader* and *Rock Scene* in the 1970s, I had to pick photographs to run with the stories. All of the *Rock Scene* pictures were black and white photos that were either taken candidly at parties, backstage or on tours. I used to drag the young Bob Gruen around by the nape of the neck at parties and set up posed shots. When it came to such *Rock Scene* staples as Patti Smith or Debbie Harry, I always picked flattering shots. But those girls were young, they embodied the spirit of the so-called punk scene, they didn't have to spend hours trying to look like that. They just looked like that. Years later, fashion magazines would do all sorts of tributes to that time, and I can only imagine certain fashion photographers poring over the pages of vintage copies of *Rock Scene* and people doing hair and makeup for hours so that the models looked like what people just looked like naturally in the 1970s. Or the 1960s. Remember grunge? Same thing. For *Hit Parader*, I mostly covered male groups like Led Zeppelin or The Who or the Stones, and I would "commission" photographers like Bob Gruen or Neal Preston or Andy Kent to shoot the band in concert or set up the rare staged photo shoot. (Such a shot was the one hastily arranged by me when Bob Gruen shot Led Zeppelin standing by the wing of their private plane at Teterboro Airport on the way to a concert in Pittsburgh. Now it's a postcard.) An example of a staged shoot was one with the New York Dolls outside of Fredrick's of Hollywood on Hollywood Boulevard for *Creem* magazine. Or Debbie Harry on the streets of New York lying across the hood of a convertible. Or the Ramones on the subway. Or Talking Heads in a supermarket. Or Patti Smith onstage at Gerde's Folk City the night Bob Dylan showed up to watch her perform. But all this stuff usually just happened—with a minimum of effort and/or fuss.

✦

Hence, when MTV changed everything in the 1980s, color slides and candid black and white photos were no longer sufficient to publicize a band. Elaborate videos for the likes of Michael Jackson or Madonna were the norm for a priority act, which meant someone for whom there were great commercial expectations. As it went on, it got more and more theatrical: think of the Destiny's Child "Survivor" video with those three girls crawling on a beach. Or Whitney Houston on the stage of some opera house singing a song that Dolly Parton wrote ("And I Will Always Love You")—while no one thought to ask Dolly to make a video of her own song. The images of the 1980s and 1990s were Prince, Michael Jackson, Guns N' Roses and Nirvana. Women? Madonna and Cyndi Lauper and Gwen Stefani. When hip-hop came in, there was the talented and beautiful Lauryn Hill, and the talented Missy Elliott—whose video director Hype Williams and stylist June Ambrose put her in an inflatable fat suit in one of the most clever videos of the 1990s—and that was about it. The male hip-hop, hair band and even Duran Duran videos featured bikini-clad women writhing around on yachts. And still, the strongest MTV female-centric video, the one that visually resonates years later, the one that shows the influence of the fashion business on music, was the David Fincher–directed clip with the five supermodels—Christy Turlington, Naomi Campbell, Cindy Crawford, Tatjana Patitz and Linda Evangelista—all lip-synching to George Michael's "Freedom." Or Robert Palmer's "Addicted to Love" clip, with a row of models—all dressed alike with their hair pulled back and red lipstick—standing behind Robert Palmer and pretending to play the guitar.

✦

By the early 1980s, I was firmly established as a rock columnist at the *New York Post*, had a syndicated column in one hundred newspapers via the New York Times Syndicate, was editing *Hit Parader*, *Rock Scene* and *Rock & Soul* magazines, was the American editor of the British music weekly the *New Musical Express* and a contributor to *Creem* and *Interview* magazines. In addition to a syndicated radio show, I was the host of one cable TV show (*Radio 1990*) and a featured interviewer on another (*Night Flight*). In many parts of the country where there still was no MTV, these were the only shows that featured rock and roll musicians on a regular basis. I started to be concerned—in a way I never had before—about hair and makeup. Not so coincidentally, this occurred at the same time I was friends with Steven Meisel and his coterie of makeup artists and hairdressers. In addition to the already famous makeup star Way Bandy, there was the hairdresser Oribe and makeup artists Kevyn Aucoin and François Nars—all three were beginners with careers kick-started by Meisel. They helped me. They did my hair and makeup for free for my TV tapings. Steven himself cut my hair into bangs and created a style for me that now, looking back, resembled a middle-aged Elizabeth Taylor going to a Prince concert, trying to look "punk." (Steven also told me to tweeze my eyebrows—he said they'd grow back. They didn't.) So, as I sat in the makeup chair getting "done" for TV, in addition to the usual and continuous gossip, there were always these little hints about my need for a touch of Botox here, maybe an eyelift there, a teeth whitening . . . and this was over thirty-five years ago. I wasn't very young, but I didn't look that bad. But this cadre of makeup and hair people also worked with celebrities—Whitney Houston, Cher and Madonna—as well as models, and plastic surgery was their religion. And even the models, beautiful as they were, were insecure. They had to compete for editorial pages in magazines, high paying advertising jobs, magazine covers and younger girls coming up behind them. Female musicians had the same insecurities about

their looks and different but similar concerns: whose song was higher on the Billboard charts, who sold more records, whose tours sold out faster, who could perform in a bigger venue, whose video was in heavy rotation on MTV and younger girls coming up behind them.

I cringe when I think of what I might look like today had I followed any of that nudging toward plastic surgery. I'm terrified of the dentist. My dermatologist once had to spray liquid nitrogen on one of my fingers to remove something, and I screamed so loud that nurses came rushing in from neighboring rooms. So when it came to all this hair and makeup and plastic surgery hubbub for my TV job, I just gave up. Or stood up for myself—depending on your point of view. I decided I did not want to live like that. And so I quit—and did not pursue—a career in TV. While the entire "aging gracefully" thing is anything but graceful, no one was hiring me for my looks. It was for the way I conducted an interview, or what I had to say, or write. When I look back at photos of myself in the 1980s, I think I looked pretty good. I once asked my husband if, in the 1980s, I complained a lot about my hair or my weight, and he said, "Always." I apologized. Had I known I looked that good, I would have had a much happier decade.

◆

I've been on several Beyoncé photo shoots and she never allows anyone inside her makeup and hair area other than her team or her glam squad. Or, as it is now referred to, her "Glam." (There are probably young women that grew up calling it "Glam" who quite possibly may not know that it is shorthand for "glamour.") Now there are budgets for "Glam" (which always includes straws—because when the subject is drinking a beverage, she cannot mess up the lipstick). If there wasn't a separate room set aside for hair and makeup, a makeshift one was erected with screens inside the photographer's studio, and the entire boring process is shielded from view. Except for the stylist, who darts in and out to ask about clothes. Or the photographer, who occasionally advises on the makeup to

go along with his or her "vision." Or not. A typical glam squad for a major star and a big shoot (or even a big night out, like the Met Ball or an award show where a red carpet is involved) might have easily consisted of the following: the hairdresser, the hairdresser's assistant, the makeup artist, the makeup artist's assistant. A manicurist and the manicurist's assistant—and occasionally there was an additional pedicurist for the painting of the toes while the fingernail polish is applied by someone else. And this doesn't even include the massage therapist, the stylist, the security guards standing watch over the entrance to the makeup area or the additional security guards watching over the borrowed jewelry. Then there were racks and racks of clothes and shoes and sunglasses and different "looks" that have been "pulled" from various designers. The costumes have to be shlepped from whence they came to wherever the shoot was—so that involved labeled trunks that house all this stuff. For her U.S. concert tour, Adele wore the same Burberry beaded gown every night—but she had three of them, so that while she was wearing one onstage, the other two were being dry cleaned. Others, like Katy Perry or Lady Gaga, had racks and racks—*rooms* of clothes to choose from.

This is all a far cry from Patti Smith's artfully ripped Haile Selassie t-shirt, leather pants or black motorcycle jacket, but make no mistake, that was no less contrived. Patti—and Joan Jett and Chrissie Hynde and every single woman who stepped on a stage (even Alessia Cara, who now wears a simple black dress and sings about how beautiful everyone is just as they are)—has thought very carefully about what they're wearing, what their hair looks like, how much makeup they need and the message this all sends. And there are often convoluted explanations and rationalizations about how the image needs to look like what the music conveys . . . the whole thing is just an exhausting burden on the women of the music world. It may cost more money than Janis Joplin's feather boa and bell-bottoms, or Stevie Nicks' platform boots, but it is no less of a *thing*. It is a thing

because it's show business and women can sell more tickets these days by wearing less (except for Adele and Billie Eilish), but also, because there is still that thing about being attractive to men who want to sleep with them and women who want to be them.

◆

While only a few of the men I've interviewed over four decades seemed overtly concerned about their looks (Bryan Ferry, Nick Rhodes, Sam Smith, to name the few), *all* of the women I've interviewed cared about what they looked like. The young Patti Smith would quietly ask me if she looked okay when she was interested in some boy in the room. Three years ago, Iggy Azalea made me wait almost an hour while she put on full makeup for an interview that wasn't even being photographed or taped for TV, nor was I writing about what she looked like. For all of these women, I feel a tremendous empathy. For the older ones who don't look good anymore but still sing great. For the older ones who never sang great but look like freaks because of the pressure put on them to try to look young. For the younger ones already getting work done because they're pressured to look perfect against all the others who look perfect. For the ones who look in magnifying mirrors and worry about when they need to start visiting a plastic surgeon. For those who get hysterical if they have a pimple or acne. For those who have had work done and lie about it. The whole thing is a mess.

FAME

"Growing up, I didn't want to be famous, but famous people were my hope," said Adele (real name Adele Laurie Blue Adkins). We were sitting on a sofa backstage in her spacious dressing room at Staples Center prior to one of her sold out concerts on her 2016 tour, and she told me that while she manages to be fiercely protective of her son and her private life, she recognized fame as fuel. "People dream to be famous, people cling on to what it must be like to be famous; to be adored, to be able to do nice things, to be creative. But when you get there, you can't say 'Being famous fucking sucks,' because even if it does, you can't publicly say that; people don't see the bad sides of it." What were the bad sides? "My family selling stories about me," she said. "And friends from when I was younger selling photographs from school. I appreciate when there's money [involved], but you *could* go get a job. That was the worst thing."

"I love being famous for my singing and my songs," she continued. "But I don't feel like me going to a grocery store, or going to a playground with my child is me being famous, because everybody does that. There's such a massive difference between what I do for my work and what I do for my real life. I don't think anybody should be famous for their fucking life." She added that it was really hard, because no one can see the downside of fame. "I have no disrespect for anybody who's famous because it's hard work," she said. "I think it's hard work for people who enjoy it as well. But it's persuasive and cruel and it can really ruin a person if you let it."

✦

Fame.

Lady Gaga (real name Stefani Germanotta) titled her second album *The Fame Monster*. David Bowie (real name David Jones) sang that fame "puts you there where things are hollow." Alanis Morissette (real name Alanis Morissette) said it's isolating. Every woman who's become successful and famous who sought it, when she got it, publicly or privately complained about it. The lack of privacy, being put on a pedestal, living in a bubble. Then they apologize for complaining. And all of them—all—say they wouldn't trade it. They wouldn't give it back. This was their *dream*. They worked so hard to get it that when they got it, even when it wasn't what they thought it would be, they put up with it. Also, no one was rushing to turn down the money or the perks that came along with it. Or they always longed for the glamour, the fame and the riches and the attention, and when they got there, it was exactly what they wished for. It was everything they thought it would be until it went away—and then they missed it. Or the struggle to keep it going, to churn out "product," becomes so exhausting and debilitating that the addictive nature of it turned them into monsters—or they checked out altogether. Many of them wanted to be famous but won't admit it. Or they love being famous but won't admit it. Or, like Bette Midler (real name Bette Midler), they never really thought about being famous, they just felt that they had a talent and wanted to express it—singing, dancing, songwriting, performing—and had no idea what really came along with it. "I can do that" was the refrain from so many of the women I've talked to over the years. Or "I want to do that." Or someone told them they were special and they could do that. Then, when they get up there, or out there, or now, with the Internet, on there, there is a very mixed result.

✦

Taylor Swift (real name Taylor Alison Swift) was without question, the single most overtly ambitious musician I ever met outside of Madonna (who swears her real name is Madonna Louise Ciccone) and Patti Smith (real name Patricia Lee Smith). When I was introduced to Taylor at a Clive Davis pre-Grammy party at the Beverly Hilton, she was a fledgling country music singer with buck teeth, long curly hair, and a long, red lace hillbilly dress. The second she heard I was from *Vanity Fair* magazine, she grabbed my hand with such force that I thought she might break it, and her eyes lasered in on me like something out of *The Exorcist.* She had convinced her entire family to shlep from Reading, Pennsylvania, and move with her to Nashville to pursue her musical dreams and ambitions. Years later and millions of dollars richer, she briefly moved to New York City and made a fool of herself with an inane song called "Welcome to New York," which was adopted by the city for a minute as an anthem for tourists. She did not step out onto a street—at least according to paparazzi photos—without full hair and makeup and a "cute" outfit. Even going, supposedly, to and from the gym.

And no, I have never interviewed her. And no, I never wanted to. And yes, she is doing just fine without my approval—but so what. She's relentless. Like something buzzing around you that you want out of your range of vision. The idea that she, or anyone, thought she could play the Joni Mitchell role in the still-unmade "Ladies of the Canyon" movie is laughable. (Joni told me she put a stop to that.) But the idea that anyone would mention Taylor in the same sentence as Joni, as if they were even the same species, or on the same planet—is laughable. It would be like a 10 year-old girl who never picked up a tennis racket except in her bedroom, swinging it in front of a mirror, stepping on the court with Serena Williams. Still, Taylor keeps going. Included in the deluxe package of her 2019 album was a booklet of journal entries that she supposedly wrote as a teenager; this way, she could milk her fans for extra product. And then those entries were actually analyzed by besotted male rock critics from the *New York Times*—not unlike those guys who write books analyzing the lyrics of Bob Dylan. And still, she keeps going.

After a slew of stalkers were discovered both outside and inside Taylor's various houses, she became more private—cossetted by security guards and private jets. But she's still out there—on tour, with a newly revealed political correctness as a champion of the LGBT community—even though she claims she'd been there for them all along (it must have been privately)—and support for Democrats. She claims she's living her life in a fishbowl, but of course she wouldn't trade it and she keeps going. She is a willing prisoner of her lifelong dream of fame. As Joni Mitchell (real name Roberta Joan Anderson) once wrote in a song, Taylor is captive on the carousel.

✦

"You're supposed to be happy all the time because you have so much," Mariah Carey (real name Mariah Carey) told me in the late 1990s. "Not that I would trade it for anything, because this is all I dreamed about my entire life, but just because this success happened doesn't mean that you have to pretend that everything is happy and rosy and beautiful. I'm not regretting anything, I'm grateful for everything that I have. But you have the same problems no matter what it is that you do. People come out of the woodwork with all the crazy things that nobody on the outside knows about or realizes goes on in my life, and now, because I'm famous, they're public." At that time, she was referring not only to problems with her first marriage, to the then CBS Records chief Tommy Mottola, but also to scandals involving her sister, a nephew with problems, her own insecurities and so forth.

Years later, during her up and down career, she had an alleged meltdown in a Tribeca hotel—complete with plate throwing and whatnot. There was a bizarre appearance on an MTV show where she slurred her words, a messed up live televised 2016 New Year's Eve performance in Times Square and a very public broken engagement to a billionaire—followed by an ill-advised, ill-fated reality TV show, lawsuits with former assistants and a manager, all punctuated with a public admission on the cover of *People* magazine that she was bipolar. But in the 1990s, Mariah was still fresh, new, hopeful and pensive when she told me, "Sometimes I get upset because things are different now and the people who were around a lot when I first started out aren't around much anymore. I get lonely. I don't have that many friends. I like to go shopping, and when I didn't have money to buy anything, I couldn't go. Now that I have money, I still can't go—because I don't want to try clothes on and have people whisper that I'm in the store trying on clothes. And I can't grocery shop [more about *that* later]; my housekeeper shops for my food."

◆

In 2005, Beyoncé (real name Beyoncé Giselle Knowles) told me, "Nobody can prepare you for fame. The attitude is, you should be so happy—and you are—but if it was a normal world, you'd be able to just cut it off and go home." Then, she added quickly, "But I wouldn't trade it."

Sometime in the last decade or so, Beyoncé got labeled Queen B. She didn't start it, but she hasn't stopped it either. If you know her, you would not accuse Beyoncé of being grand, or having attitude. In person, she's still shy, albeit driven and ambitious. Even though Adele and possibly Taylor Swift have sold more records, and Adele has won more of the bigger Grammy categories, and Cardi B (real name Belcalis Marlenis Almánzar) had higher digital streaming numbers (until Ariana Grande—real name Ariana Grande-Butera—surpassed her), Beyoncé, since she left Destiny's Child and went solo in 2003, has been considered the biggest pop star on the planet. Whether she would have ascended to that position without pairing up with her husband Jay-Z and acquiring some of his street credibility to form the sum-is-greater-than-the-parts, royal coupleness of it all remains a question mark. She was groomed for this. She studied this. She may say—as she did in a self-directed mini-documentary she released on YouTube a few years ago, that she often wishes she could walk down the street and be anonymous. But her Instagram feed says otherwise. There are photos of matching mother/daughter outfits with her and her adorable 8 year-old daughter Blue Ivy. The 2017 photo that announced the birth of her twins, Rumi and Sir, with Beyoncé surrounded by flowers, evoked Our Lady of Guadalupe. The video for "Apeshit," of her and Jay in the Louvre (and there is now a "Carters tour" in the Louvre showing the artwork they included in that video)—all of that would lead one to believe that she is keeping her Beyhive fans happy. And keeping that fame machine rolling.

◆

There's an entire category of female stars who claim they never ever even *thought* about being famous. It was always just about the work. Sade (real name Helen Folasade Adu) had jazzy, soulful hits in the 1980s. Then she disappeared from the music world three separate times in the past thirty years to take extended "hiatuses," raise a son, move to the Caribbean, come back and release more music. She rarely ever does interviews, but in 1985 we talked and she was adamant: "I'm not impressed by stars, I'm not taken in by fame. There are as many entertaining taxi drivers in New York as there are people in the entertainment industry. It's very easy for some people to become stars—and I wouldn't give them the time of day." She was equally emphatic about her hatred of industry events: "Why should I stand next to Simon Le Bon and make faces? Why should I do that in my limited free time? It's a waste of time. I'd rather stay at home and write or see my friends."

It's a familiar refrain. Like Sade, or Adele, who told me she would do anything to avoid a red carpet, in 2017, Lorde (real name Ella Marija Lani Yelich-O'Connor) told me that she knows what she's good at, and one thing she is not good at is "looking nice on a red carpet." She said that her success was "crazy, but because it happened when I was so young, it normalized quickly. It just felt like a weird symptom of my life. But I try my hardest to live my life in a way that makes me feel normal. I don't think it helps the work to feel like a big deal. It's a terrible thing to feel like a weird giant. I'm not a monster; I'm a writer."

The Irish singer/songwriter and performer PJ Harvey (real name Polly Jean Harvey) was famous in the alternative rock world of the 1990s. In 1995 she told me that her love of performing had nothing to do with wanting to be in the limelight or wanting to be seen as some sort of popstar. "That's actually what I *didn't* want," Polly said. "I suppose with me, it's just a very big need for self-expression, it's a compulsion, really. But I wasn't prepared for success. When the first few interviews started happening, I was really taken aback and found it very odd that people would suddenly be very interested in you and your private life because of the artwork that you make. I find it very invasive, very upsetting."

✦

One woman who handled sudden, massive fame with astonishing low-key grace was Norah Jones (real name Geethal Norah Jones Shankar). In 2002, she released her debut album, *Come Away with Me*, with its hit single, "Don't Know Why." I remember at the time, pulling her CD out of a stack of CDs, seeing the photo of a beautiful woman on the cover, and being impressed with her jazzy, soulful voice. It was one of those voices that immediately sounded like no one else. I remember too, telling her producer, Arif Mardin, that Norah was going to win all the Grammys that year. And when, in 2003, she was nominated for eight Grammys and won five—including Best Album, Best New Artist and Best Record—I laughed with her and Arif at her after party that she had, in fact, won almost *all* the Grammys.

The woman who was the daughter of the late Indian musician Ravi Shankar and American Sue Jones (Norah eventually legally changed her name to just Norah Jones), reacted to her almost overwhelming and unexpected fame with a quiet dignity. She has sold fifty million albums, collaborated with Willie Nelson, Ray Charles, Outkast, Q-Tip, Dolly Parton, Mavis Staples, Keith Richards and numerous others, and manages to maintain her privacy. She is elegant and unassuming—living quietly in Brooklyn with her two children and husband, keyboardist Pete Remm—and she still records and tours all over the world. Hits may come and go, but great voices—and Norah has one of them—last.

✦

The dancer, singer and performance artist FKA twigs (real name Tahliah Debrett Barnett) was mobbed by paparazzi while engaged to heartthrob Robert Pattinson. She rarely talked about him, and they're no longer together, but when they were, in 2016, she told me, "I really keep my life very simple. I've lived in the same place in London for the last seven years, I go and do my shopping, I get on buses, and all the rest is outside of who I am. It's like another dimension, really, that I don't associate myself with. In the beginning [when she and Rob were mobbed], it was a bit of a shock—mind-boggling, really. But my mum told me when I was very young that you can't reason with the unreasonable, and that phrase has got me through so many things. I just try to keep my dignity and carry on with my day."

In the 1990s, Gwen Stefani (real name Gwen Stefani) had eye-catching MTV videos as the front woman with No Doubt. In 2017, recalling those early days, she said, "I always felt like a star in my own small pond. When we started No Doubt [in 1986] we played shows, people were there, we were good, and there was a lot of confidence in that." She said she would walk into Tower Records, she'd see their albums on the racks (when there were albums, racks and record stores), people would recognize her, and it was all fine. Then, a few years ago, she went on the NBC TV competition show *The Voice* and everything changed. Her marriage to rock singer Gavin Rossdale broke up and her eventual romance with her co-judge on *The Voice*, country star Blake Shelton—who was going through his own divorce with the country singer Miranda Lambert—initiated nonstop tabloid headlines. "I never saw myself in that category," she told me. "I never did anything controversial. All I did was write songs about heartache and dress up in clothes. I didn't have a lot of boyfriends, that's not who I am—I'm not that cool. So when *this* all happened, I think a lot of it had to do with being on a network TV show, and being with someone who also has a high profile career. It kind of puts you on another level."

No one would ever accuse the mainstream pop star Katy Perry (real name Katheryn Elizabeth Hudson) of being shy or avoiding the spotlight. But when I spent time with her in 2011, she talked about how she spent so many years trying to Make It, that when she finally did, she didn't have a day off. "I wouldn't be working at this pace if I didn't know that fame is fleeting," she said. "Everyone thinks the famous have fabulous, charmed lives of dressing up and going on red carpets," she told me, "flying hither and yon, to and fro—and they have no idea of the actual work involved. And if you complain, they just think you're being a spoiled brat diva. Sure, you have the big house, but you can't *leave* the big house."

◆

But before fame flees, stars have big houses. And way back, when *MTV Cribs* started showing stars showing off their mansions, their swimming pools, their media rooms—all of that became fodder for envy on the part of ordinary people. The definition of *covet*, which is warned against in the Tenth Commandment, is "*to yearn to possess or have something.*" And the dictionary definition of *obsess* is "*to pre-occupy or fill the mind continuously and intrusively and to a troubling extent.*" In this tabloid and Internet age, when the enormously rich are often aimless, we see these words used, as in: *I'm obsessed with that color lipstick*, or *What purse do you covet this season?* Everyone who follows famous people's Instagrams is obsessed with something, or covets something that they want and don't have. People look at TMZ or *People* magazine or *Us* magazine or Beyoncé's Instagram or Gwyneth Paltrow's Goop, or the myriad of websites hawking something or other and are "obsessed." Or they look at the pictures of a star on a yacht in Amalfi, or stepping off a private plane, and they get jealous. Of the clothes, the vacations, the houses, the jewelry—they want all that—none of which they can afford. I am convinced that women have had *children* because they see pictures of Gwyneth Paltrow or Jennifer Lopez with their children (without realizing that all those people have nannies to take care of said children), and so they want some of *those*. The ordinary person has absolutely nothing to do with these famous people or their lives—other than being a fan of their work. But more often than not, they are fans of their life. Their possessions. Their fame. The members of the audience don't have the talent. They haven't put in the work. Or they never had the opportunity, or the luck. They still want . . . that. They wish they were on that boat cruising around Italy with Beyoncé. Forget sea-sickness or being trapped on a boat with the same people for days. It just all looks so shiny and luxurious and fun. Like Bette Midler said, that's what they're selling; they're selling their *life* as much as they're selling their record albums or their digital streams or their makeup line or their sneaker line or their lingerie line or concert tickets. The un-famous cannot imagine that the life of the famous is anything but a fabulous life. What on earth do these people ever have to complain about? They're rich, they're successful, they're *famous*. What could be better? (Being thin is also good.) And if they get robbed or dumped or divorced or stalked—no one has a shred of sympathy for them because they're *famous*. They asked for this life. They sought it. They *chased* it. They won the lottery. Stop whining.

✦

In 1993, the indie rock singer/songwriter Liz Phair (real name Elizabeth Clark Phair) had a big success with her debut album, *Exile in Guyville*—which was intended as a concept album with "answers" to all of the Rolling Stones' songs on *Exile On Main Street*. After *Guyville*'s critical acclaim, commercial success and the rejection she got from her indie music scene in Chicago, Liz told me, "The fame stuff doesn't make you feel better about yourself. It only makes you scrutinize your-self so much that nothing is ever good enough. You go in there and find something that's wrong, before somebody else tells you it's wrong. If I'm alone in my house, I don't take any of it seriously. I fit right back into life as I left it. But nothing's thrilling anymore—because you see behind the scenes. What would have been glamorous for you, or what would have been exciting in your life or what you might have looked forward to as a magic moment—it's all been unveiled. Everything is sort of programmed and planned. Crazy nights don't look so crazy anymore."

With the exception of a true artist like Joni Mitchell—who has an understandably confident sense of self-worth—the woman I've talked to who may be the most anti-fame was Linda Ronstadt (real name Linda Maria Ronstadt). In the 1970s, Linda was an adorable country-rock star and for her, it was always—always—about the music. We've talked several times over the past four decades, but early on, she told me, "The work always came first, and I didn't have a choice about the work that I do. It never was about the stardom. People think you're aiming for fame and visibility, but those things just come along with the package. I think they're a drag, and they destroy people, because celebrity just causes you to become more and more isolated. And the more isolated you become, the harder it becomes for you to do your work. And if you don't do your work, then you're nothing except a celebrity." She added, "When I'm not being paid to perform, it's nobody's business what I do. I feel I have no obligation to the public whatsoever. What Humphrey Bogart said is the greatest: 'You don't owe the public anything but a good show.' Also, when you're a celebrity, everyone flatters you. I don't like it. Flattery never does you any favors."

◆

Then there's Rihanna (real name Robyn Rihanna Fenty), whose reputation is that of a wild and crazy, sex-mad party girl. In real life, Rihanna is lovely, elegant and down to earth. In 2016, we talked in a private room of a Los Angeles restaurant while paparazzi were outside screaming her name. This happens to her all the time; she appeared totally oblivious to it—and it reminded me of sitting in a glass-walled restaurant with Mick Jagger somewhere in America during the Stones 1975 summer tour. A girl was right outside, screaming his name—shrieking and sobbing—before she was carted away by security guards. As Mick sat there quietly, sipping white wine, I asked him how he dealt with it. What else could he do, he said. The implication: he'd been famous for twenty years and such was the level of his fame at that time that he couldn't possibly greet every person who screamed his name.

One aspect of my hours-long talk with Rihanna that struck me as hilarious was that she said she tells her friends all the time that she wishes she could go and buy her own groceries. "I literally sit there and dream about buying my own groceries," she said. "Swear to god. Because it's something that is real, and normal. And you need to have something in your life that isn't so comfortable. I like to feel free. I have security but I like to sneak out, get into a cab, nobody's paying attention, and I just go. I did that in Japan—and it was the best experience ever. No one bothered me."

As I've previously reported, Rihanna told me that fame has protected her. She said she's had to be so conscious of her surroundings, what people say, why people want to be with her, why people want to sleep with her. "It makes me very guarded and very protective," she said. "People expect the day we become famous, we become perfect, and that doesn't make any fucking sense to me—because famous is the furthest thing from perfect." We discussed how certain stars are so inaccessible and on such a pedestal, and she said, "I'm very—very—afraid of being on that pedestal. It looks fucking beautiful and very glittery and blinged out, but it is way too scary, way too unrealistic. There's just this long way to fall when you pretend that you're so far away from the earth, and far away from reality. You're floating in this space or this bubble that's protected by fame or success. It's the thing I fear the most; to be swallowed up by that bubble. I never want to be that person. It's like a fungus. It can be poison to you, fame."

◆

A note here about shopping for groceries: You would be extremely surprised at the number of famous women who have bemoaned the fact that they can't go grocery shopping anymore. As if this was some sort of *treat*. A *pleasure* that's denied to them. Of course, most of them have the money to hire assistants or housekeepers who can purchase food to nourish these stars and keep them from starvation. Obviously, it's more than just a metaphor for the tradeoff—the lack of privacy, the people bothering them for a selfie or an autograph in a supermarket aisle. They don't want to have to put on makeup or do their hair just to be able to go out to buy milk. But if they don't, they're all over the Internet photographed looking like a slob. Not a one of them would trade their fame to be able to go and buy lettuce, but Shopping While Famous is something that often comes up in a sort of wistful manner. Rihanna longs to be able to buy her own groceries. FKA twigs proudly claims she does her own shopping. When we first met in 2010, Lady Gaga defiantly told me she went to the market to purchase a melon. Adele puts on a baseball cap and sunglasses and goes to the Beverly Hills Bristol Farms to buy special cheese. Iggy Azalea (real name Amethyst Amelia Kelly) told me she likes to shop for things in the supermarket like cake mix—even though she has zero plans to bake a cake; she just likes the way the box looks in her cupboard and she remembers the days when she didn't have money to buy either cake mixes or a cupboard. Pat Benatar (real name Patricia Mae Andrzejewski) told me she likes to "blend in" in the grocery store. But for someone such as myself, who actually *has* to go to the grocery store and is *constantly* food shopping, it is a mind-numbing chore, and I think, who are they kidding? These girls can't seriously long for such an outing . . . can they?

◆

The Icelandic singer/songwriter Björk (real name Björk Guð-mundsdóttir) first became famous in the late 1980s with her band The Sugarcubes before embarking on a successful solo career. In 1995 she told me, "I know you're not going to believe this, but I never wanted to be famous. That was never a target of mine. Long before I even wanted any attention, people asked me to do things, and so I guess I'm spoiled rotten that way. I was eleven, just singing in my school, and they wanted me on the radio. At first I refused, and then I said okay. Then they asked me to do a record and I said no way, but my mother said, 'Well, maybe you can do it your way with friends on it.' So I said okay. Then they put me on the front pages of the newspapers in Iceland and I hated it—so I became a drummer in a punk band. Then they wanted to put me on the front pages because it was so unusual that a girl was a drummer in a punk band."

"But in Iceland you could never really become a star because you meet the people anyway, just walking down the street all the time. I think it would be completely different to being an 11 year-old in the U.S.—it's like black and white. I think I was really very lucky, because when that notoriety happened to me, and the kids in my school all wanted to hang out with me because they thought I was cool, I instinctively knew that when a person came to me, I knew what they were after. Do they want the creativity, do they think I'm funny, do they want the glamour, are they jealous? My instincts about all that are good." Summing up the absurdity of fame, she told me, "I had to go to the gynecologist for a checkup, and he was putting these sticks in me to do tests. He's Malaysian, and we just got to chatting; he asked me what I was doing next, and I said I was going on tour—to Asia and Malaysia. He said, 'Really?' And he started recommending four-star hotels, and went to his drawer and pulled out a booklet about hotels in Malaysia and asked me what kind of swimming pools I liked. There I was with my legs spread and sticks sticking out of me and this Malaysian doctor is discussing hotels with me. And I thought, whose job is stranger—his or mine?"

◆

In the 1980s, there was Madonna, who never pretended that her goals were anything other than worldwide fame. Now that she considers herself a great artiste, the emphasis is on her art and her family—including four adopted African children. When she first came to New York City, she shamelessly embraced fame. Yes, Madonna wanted to "express" herself, but not in the PJ Harvey sort of way—although she absolutely believed her talent matched her unbridled ambition. She actually said to many people, on many occasions, "I want to rule the world."

But two other women who came to fame in the 1980s had very different—and way more down to earth—stories. The rock singer

Pat Benatar had an enormous hit with "Hit Me With Your Best Shot." Cyndi Lauper (real name Cynthia Ann Stephanie Lauper) had hits that included the bouncy yet subtly feminist anthem "Girls Just Wanna Have Fun" and the gorgeous ballad "Time After Time." In 1986, Pat Benatar told me, "I thought it would feel good to be the center of attention. I thought it would be exciting and wonderful to be fussed over. And then you get there, and you can't even blow your nose without someone picking the tissue off the floor. It's ludicrous. And you either go for it or you don't. It's like having a baby. You read everything you can about it and you talk to anyone it happened to, but until it actually happens to you, you're never really prepared. I was pretty freaked out. It takes a long time to realize that somebody thinks it's important to talk to you, or you can't just sit in a restaurant and have dinner anymore, or people are trying to break into your hotel room."

"I have a pretty low profile," Pat added at that time. "I don't want to make a big fuss, I don't drive a flashy car, and I don't live in a flashy house, and I don't dress flashy when I go out. I'm kind of private. You can't escape the feeling that you're a star, but I don't feel very much different than I always felt. It's just odd that children run up to me in the street—that's a little strange to me sometimes. The trappings of being a rock and roll star are silly. I mean, it's a great thing, it's a fantasy—it certainly was mine—and there's nothing greater than standing in front of twenty thousand people and singing songs you wrote and music you want to play. But being a *star*—that gets in the way of being a person."

Cyndi Lauper had a variety of hair colors, a thick Long Island accent, and a "kooky" style featured on popular MTV videos in the mid-1980s. Talking to me at that time about how fame affected her life, Cyndi said, "Now all the people in the old neighborhood come up to my mother and say, 'Hi, how *are* you?' And she says, 'Fine—same as I was before when you didn't care.' There were a lot of people there that snubbed us, and now they come out of the woodwork. For me, it's been kind of great, because you're famous somewhere else, and then you come home, and you're home. I don't want to be in the ivory tower; it's not pretty there."

◆

When a man becomes successful and famous, he gets more of everything. When a woman gets successful and famous, she loses something. In her 2018 documentary, Lady Gaga said that when she sold ten million albums, "I lost Matt," her then stylist/boyfriend. When she sold thirty million albums, she said she lost Luc—her on-again, off-again Lower East Side bartender/drummer boyfriend. When she landed the leading role in the Bradley Cooper remake of *A Star Is Born*, she broke off her engagement to the actor Taylor Kinney, and when she was nominated for an Oscar, she had to end things with her agent/boyfriend Christian Carino.

I have previously written about how I asked Gaga in 2010 when she knew she was *really* famous. She told me it was after a concert somewhere on tour in Australia. She didn't remember the city, but she remembered leaving the arena and there were, she recalled, about five thousand people standing on stairs leading to a train station just screaming. The roar was like nothing she had ever heard before. So she made her security guy stop the car she was in, got out, went to the fence where the fans were, and signed as many autographs as she could without the fans pulling her through. She said it was *insane,* and, she thought, how could she possibly be better for them? She wanted to make sure, she told me, that she made even one melody that really saved someone's spirit. It wasn't pressure, she said, it was an "obligation."

Courtney Love (real name Courtney Michelle Harrison) was in a foster home as a young girl. In 2018 she told me, "I wanted to be famous at the age of 4—because I thought then, life will be fair." As a teenager, she hung around bands in the Pacific Northwest, then went to London and hung around with British bands—like Echo and the Bunnymen. She came back to the U.S., worked in strip clubs, formed bands and eventually started a really good rock band—Hole. She also met and married Kurt Cobain and became really famous. And then, as she summed it up to me, "I got famous. And I found out that life still wasn't fair."

ABUSE

Beyoncé may sing that girls run the world, but that's just wishful—or delusional—thinking. In fact, there probably isn't a girl over the age of 12 who hasn't, at some point in her life, been the object of unwanted sexual attention, harassment, innuendo, inappropriate touching, inappropriate remarks, discrimination or actual physical violence from the men who really run the world. The music business is show business. Why would the record industry be any different than the movie industry or the fashion industry or politics or, for that matter, any business?

✦

Before she ever was a professional musician, Fiona Apple was raped at the age of 12 in the hallway of her New York City apartment building; she wrote a song ("Sullen Girl") about the experience.

Tori Amos was raped at knifepoint by a guy to whom she gave a ride after one of her shows at a club. She wrote a song ("Me and a Gun") about it.

Lady Gaga admitted that she was raped by a producer many years her senior when she was 19; she sang "Til It Happens To You" at the 2016 Oscars with a chorus of fifty sex abuse victims. (The song, from a 2015 documentary about campus rape was, ironically, distributed by Harvey Weinstein's company.)

Madonna said she was dragged up to a roof and raped when she first came from Detroit to live in New York City.

As a young girl, Donna Summer was a devout Christian who was allegedly molested by her priest. She told me that for years she suffered from depression.

Tina Turner was routinely beaten and bloodied by her musical mentor and husband Ike until she managed to escape.

Carole King was beaten by her third husband.

Ronnie Spector was kept captive in the mansion she shared with her then husband Phil Spector until she managed to escape.

Mariah Carey married the much older boss—the then head of Columbia Records Tommy Mottola—in a lavish 1993 ceremony wearing a bridal gown modeled after Princess Diana's. The couple lived in a huge Westchester mansion, and, in 1997, toward the end of that marriage, Mariah called me in the middle of the night to vent about how she was being kept in the house by the jealous, controlling Mottola. (Years later, Tommy told his side of the story, which included some of Mariah's erratic behavior and public meltdowns.)

And in 2015, in a well publicized incident following a Grammy party, Rihanna was beaten by her boyfriend Chris Brown.

✦

Then, there are all the other, more subtle forms of abuse: the "locker room talk," the "bad behavior," the "sex addiction," the "mistakes," the "boys will be boys." The verbal abuse in a recording studio when the male record producer undermines a female singer's confidence. Tina Knowles told me of incidents when her teenage daughter Beyoncé was recording vocals and the producer was dismissive, paying no attention in the control room, chatting away on his cell phone. (However, you can be certain he was paying attention when the royalty checks were due.) That climate, those situations, undoubtedly put Beyoncé on the eventual trajectory to produce her own music, to control her own career. In 2005, in a rare moment of candor, Beyoncé told me that she knew the "record business was a dirty business, but I don't have dirty people around me." She said this prior to firing her father/manager Mathew Knowles—whose rumored inappropriate behavior ranged from allegedly sleeping with Beyoncé's dancers to ultimately fathering an illegitimate child. Her parents' divorce and her husband Jay-Z's self-admitted infidelity are just two of the difficult private things Beyoncé has had to deal with on her relentless and determined climb to her current megastar status.

◆

Stevie Nicks was allegedly abused by her controlling, possessive boyfriend and Fleetwood Mac bandmate Lindsey Buckingham. For years, she also was in a relationship with guitarist Joe Walsh, who would do whatever he liked on the road—but she, of course, could not.

Taylor Swift brought charges against a radio disc jockey who grabbed her ass at a photo op during a meet and greet before one of her concerts.

Kesha was involved in well-publicized, years long lawsuits with her producer Dr. Luke, who she claimed forcibly and sexually harassed her. Her claims were eventually dismissed, but his suit against her for defamation and breach of contract is still pending. (The recording may be over, but the melody lingers on.)

And, after many years together, Bette Midler fired her early boyfriend and longtime manager Aaron Russo because he hit her. Twice. (More about that later.)

The Australian rapper Iggy Azalea had a former boyfriend who, she described to me, was a "convicted criminal" with arrests for fraud, auto theft and domestic battery. "He basically forged a contract with my name on it," she said, "that stated he had the rights to my music." When her 2014 hit single "Fancy" made her famous, he tried to sell a sex tape he claimed they had made which, she said, they hadn't. "The thing I find so disgusting about that," she said, "is if you did make a sex tape, it would be a private, intimate thing. Not something to be made public; that's sexual harassment." Two years later, Iggy was publicly humiliated when her then boyfriend, the then Los Angeles Laker basketball player Nick Young (who ridiculously nicknamed himself "Swaggy P") bragged about how he cheated on her. That brag was taped in the Lakers locker room by his then teammate (D'Angelo Russell), put online, and went viral. (Clearly, Iggy doesn't have the best taste in men.)

✦

If cheating and lying about it constitutes abuse, there are very few—if any—female stars who have not dealt with that—especially from threatened, less successful boyfriends or husbands. A sad example is when Gwen Stefani discovered her husband, the fading rock singer Gavin Rossdale, cheating on her with the nanny. In 2014, Jennifer Lopez told me that when she was dating Sean "Puffy" Combs, she was totally paranoid that he was cheating on her ("He's that guy," she said). But no one would tell her the truth. Until someone finally did. When J.Lo was engaged to Ben Affleck, it was his gambling, visits to strip clubs and drugs that probably caused her to break off their engagement just days before the planned wedding. Mary J. Blige discovered that her longtime husband/manager was fooling around with one of her own protégés, a young woman signed to Mary's own record label.

✦

"I had a broken jaw once," Tina Turner told me. "Ike and I had a fight between shows in the dressing room, and when I tried to sing and hit the notes, there'd be blood gushing, and I had to try to swallow it. That was just one of the horrible experiences when I had to work afterwards. A black eye, a broken jaw, a busted lip." Tina and I were in her dressing room at the Ritz in 1984 in New York City. Ike Turner, the man who discovered her, took her out of Nutbush, Tennessee, put her in his band, married her and beat her for years, was still alive. She told me she would never write a book about what happened in her abusive marriage until he was dead. "You sure he's six feet under? How about cremating him?" She laughed, then added, "I'm not wishing death on him. But I'm waiting. And the life he's led—he can't be around that long." (She must have changed her mind; Tina co-wrote her autobiography with Kurt Loder in 1986, twenty-one years before Ike died in 2007.) After sixteen years together as Ike & Tina, with his terrible reputation for abusing Tina and his own drug use, Ike was down and out. No one wanted anything to do with him, but everyone was thrilled for Tina's success. "My triumph was in leaving Ike," she told me. "Anything else that might have bothered people or frustrated people in trying to have commercial success, I could deal with. It was like cake for me, because it was nothing compared to what I came from. I didn't even think or dream of a hit record. I was just happy I was working, because at the beginning, when I left him, a lot of promoters wouldn't touch me. They thought the team was broken and I was no good without Ike."

After she got away from him, he suggested an Ike & Tina reunion tour. She told him that if she brought him back into her life, everything she did to make a break would have gone down the drain. "I regret I had to take those beatings," she said, "but I learned so much. All that stuff he did onstage, all that control—he did it right but he handled it wrong. It was twisted. He felt threatened, so he handled it violently. I'm fortunate that I came out with very few scars; my mind and my body wasn't really damaged. I don't regret it—except for the woman part; his cheating was so horrible that the lady side of me . . . that was so very ugly. I don't forgive or forget that." She said that in the beginning, she loved him. They were friends. When she fell out of love, she still cared for him. Then there were children and their combined careers and the money they made: "I didn't want to throw all of that down the drain. I tried to fix it by just being partners, but he didn't want that. I stayed as long as I could because I tried to hold it together. There's something about us women—we're always trying to change men, to see things a different way. Always trying to be mother. I had to realize that there's nothing more important than me." She added that she didn't think Ike really remembered it: "When you're giving punishment, you don't remember it as much as the one receiving it remembers it."

✦

Things were different in the 1960s. Female liberation was a fight for mere recognition. For some it was for the still not passed Equal Rights Amendment. For others it was equal pay. For others, it was to move up from the secretarial pool. And women protested segregation, the Vietnam War, Nixon and so forth. But the lives of those of us who came of age in the 1960s held all sorts of secrets and in some cases, shame. The decade brought with it the birth control pill, which meant sexual liberation. You could sleep with anyone you wanted to and not get pregnant. I myself so did not want to ever get pregnant that for a long time, I simultaneously took both the pill *and* used a now archaic rubber diaphragm that was no picnic to insert. But this also meant that if you put yourself in a position where you wound up with a guy in a hotel room, or his apartment, or you invited him into your apartment, or you traveled with him on an overnight trip, you were just expected to "go all the way" with him. It was just taken for granted. And many of us just went through with it whether there was genuine passion there or not. We were expected to, we succumbed to it. I know I did. It wasn't really forcible sex, but it wasn't a trip to the moon either.

✦

As a young journalist breaking into the music industry in the 1970s, I witnessed such outrageous and disgusting behavior from male rock musicians toward groupies, and yet, I wrote nothing about it. I did nothing about it. Who would I have called? The police? I was an invited "guest" journalist on the private planes and the tours of the Rolling Stones, Led Zeppelin, The Who—and later, Van Halen and many others. By not writing about the private side of those tours, I was trusted to accompany them and get the stories that no other rock journalist would get and many of which I would never write. Looking back on it—and we're talking about more than forty years ago—was I complicit in some of this? Possibly. But it was "the way it was." And there was pressure on me: I had to make a choice. If I wrote about what really was going on, I wouldn't "get to go" on these tours or have this access. Probably in much the same way political reporters didn't write about the women President Kennedy allegedly snuck into the White House, or George Bush's rumored girlfriend, or how today's sports journalists don't write about well known athletes' "side pieces" (and think about that word—piece—used in 2020)—I kept quiet. I convinced myself that these guys had a right to their private lives. And "everyone" knew about it. "Everyone" did it. "Everyone" thought it was delightful—sex and drugs and rock and roll. Fun. Until it wasn't. Now in fact, I never personally witnessed any violence, pressure or predatory behavior against any of these groupies who, quite frankly, basically threw themselves at these guys. That is not to say that I didn't see grown men in their twenties take advantage of often underage girls who were thrilled to swan in backstage on the arm of someone like Jimmy Page, or actually wait in a line to get on a tour bus to give a blowjob to a roadie in the hope of then moving on up to another line to be able to service the band's drummer, or bass player—or if she was really hot, the guitarist or lead singer.

The Runaways now tell stories of how their manager Kim Fowley either raped them himself or set up situations where rape was involved. Among the most gross of musicians was Gene Simmons of Kiss—who kept numbered polaroids of the girls he bedded on his tours. (I once told him that these numbered pix reminded me of the numbers tattooed on the arms of his Holocaust survivor parents.) In Van Halen's case, a roadie would go into the audience and pull out girls who would get the chance to meet David Lee Roth and spend the night with him. This was all considered consensual sex. It was the "culture" of the time. In some circles it's *still* the "culture." In the case of Led Zeppelin, the band members usually had mistresses or road girlfriends who were by their sides during their U.S. tours while their actual wives were back at home in England with their children. Pamela Des Barres has written extensively about her experiences as a star groupie; she considered herself a 20th century courtesan. No one ever put me in any sort of compromising situation—other than just being considered "one of the boys." Or, more likely, they were mindful that I still was, after all, a journalist. I was the recipient of a lot of jokes; I got the nickname "Hot Pants" on the 1975 Stones tour as a sarcastic nod to my prudishness.

One night in Buffalo on that tour, in Keith Richards' hotel room, I hung out with Mick Jagger, Ronnie Wood and others until five in the morning, hoping to get a long-promised interview with Keith. They were all screaming at the TV, I was taping all this for some reason; I guess you had to be there to think that this inane, stoned babble would one day become historically important. But then, as the only woman in the room, I was, of course, the one enlisted to take the breakfast order, write it down and call room service. (I still have that written out order. I saved everything.) And, unlike the other three women on that tour, I probably was the only one who went back to my hotel room every night, alone. When a drunken Mick Jagger once called my room in the middle of the night to ask if I'd like to come down to his room to keep some other guy who was visiting him company, I hung up. Once in the 1980s, at the end of an interview I did with Mick in his suite at the Carlyle Hotel (interviews were routinely done in hotel suites), he stood right in front of my face and smiled at me in this sort of comically come-hitherish way. I laughed, he laughed, we both turned away and that was the end of that. I assure you, he doesn't remember it. But you have no idea how many people there are—both men and women—who have said to me over the years, "If I'd had the chance to sleep with Mick Jagger, I wouldn't have turned him down." Once, Lady Gaga told me that she would have been one of those girls in the audience who could have been pulled backstage to meet David Lee Roth—but I think she was kidding.

What was much more common, and what happened often, was that the CEO of Atlantic Records, Ahmet Ertegun, would just casually slip his hand under my blouse while we were on the plane—or even at a press party—with the Stones or Zeppelin. (I even saw him do it once to *Yoko Ono.*) I would laugh and brush his hand away. It's what we all did. I heard rumors about women who went into his office and saw him masturbating behind his desk, but luckily, I never saw anything that disgusting. There was always genuine discomfort, and there were the shared whispers: "*Don't get into an elevator with that guy,*" and "*Stay away from that guy at the office Christmas party.*" But there also was the knowledge that these were the men in power, they had the ability to help grant proximity to the bands and had the access I needed in order to make a name for myself in a world of the all boy rock journalists. And when I think back now to the things I heard men say, things that you would think would be impossible today with a woman in the room—it's archaic: "*She's a great fuck*" or "*She looks like she'd be a bad fuck.*" "*I'd fuck her.*" "*She's got great tits.*" "*She's got some body on her.*" Today, if a man is caught in a sexual harassment situation, or they're called out for making public sexist remarks, they all give a shout-out to their female family members: "*I've got daughters,*" they say, like they're wrapping themselves in the American flag. "*I have sisters, my grandmother was the strongest woman I know, I have nothing but the utmost respect for women, my mother raised me as a single mom with three jobs . . . blah blah blah.*" When men do bad things to women, we women are never surprised. We women are used to it. We women believe all of it. But keeping quiet about the male boss—which means nearly every boss—has been the rule. Because the alternative—losing your job, not getting another job, having your name smeared because maybe the way you were dressed meant you were "asking for it," or "what were you doing in his hotel room to begin with"—we've all lived with this. Maybe it's changing. But not fast enough, and maybe not until, as Beyoncé sings, girls run the world.

◆

Then there are the even more subtle forms of abuse. When I first met Joni Mitchell prior to a 2001 *Vanity Fair* music cover shoot, she was one of the only people in the group Annie Leibovitz would photograph for that three-panel cover that I had never met before. (The rest of the lineup was David Bowie, Beyoncé, Jewel, Beck, Stevie Wonder, Emmylou Harris, Gwen Stefani, Maxwell, Jay-Z, Missy Elliott and Chris Cornell.) Joni's makeup artist and our mutual friend (the since-deceased) Paul Starr arranged for us to have a drink the night before the shoot at the Carlyle Hotel—where Joni could still smoke in the lobby lounge. Within five minutes of our meeting, I casually mentioned that I felt Madonna had ruined the culture and from that moment on, we were kindred spirits. It always annoyed me that Joni—a brilliant songwriter and extraordinary musician—was never mentioned in the same paragraphs by male rock journalists as were Bob Dylan, Jimi Hendrix, Neil Young. And that Jann Wenner once had the balls to run a despicable *chart* in *Rolling Stone* magazine about all the men in the Laurel Canyon scene that Joni had supposedly slept with. First of all, it was none of his damn business. Second of all, how did he know? Would he have done that with Bob Dylan? With James Taylor? I think not. Once, during one of our conversations, Joni talked to me about that Laurel Canyon scene—where, granted, she was regarded as one of the most talented of the songwriters, where some of those guys knew they couldn't match her talent on the guitar—but where she was still, a girl.

She told me, "I remember one night specifically when a group of us were somewhere and they passed the guitar around, and Neil [Young] had a new song, and he'd sing, and there'd be raves all around. They never passed the guitar to me; I had to ask. I'm thinking of one specific night—when I said, 'I have a new song,' I played it, and the room was dead. No response. And I'll give you another example of what it was like to be a girl in a boys' club: when I made *Court and Spark*, it was a big breakthrough for me, because it was my sixth album and I'd finally found a band that could play my music. And one night, I think we were at David Geffen's and Bob Dylan was there, and they played Bob's new album first, and of course everyone raved. Then I put on *Court and Spark*—and they all just nodded at me. Even to the point where afterwards, one of the guy's girlfriends came over to me and said, 'I don't know why they're doing this to you.' I received a lot of that."

✦

In Ann Arbor, Michigan, in the late 1960s, the MC5 and The Stooges began their careers. It was a scene fueled by the political fervor of the self-named White Panthers and their leader, John Sinclair. He was sentenced to ten years in jail for one marijuana joint, until John Lennon and Yoko Ono gave a benefit concert for him that got him out. And it was there, in that hotbed of "power to the people," that the women were in the kitchen cooking while the men sat around a table plotting the upcoming revolution. John Sinclair was considered a "rock star." Iggy Stooge was a rock star. (Everyone still uses the words "rock star" to describe someone who apparently has the most charisma and is the best at what they do—whether it's Mick Jagger or Oprah Winfrey or Bill Clinton or J. K. Rowling or Barack Obama or LeBron James. And, as long as we glorify this . . . *thing* that has gone on now for almost sixty years that was initially, and is still largely male, it reaffirms the misogyny.) Before she was considered a rock star, Madonna had to play nice with Seymour Stein, who signed her to his Sire Records. He was gay, and there certainly was nothing sexual going on between them. But she was used to batting her eyes at men—always men: DJs, producers, actors—all of whom could advance her career. Then there's a famous photo of Patti Smith sitting on Clive Davis' lap. They are both smiling. Clive signed Patti to his Arista Records before she was considered a rock star, and before he admitted to his "bisexuality." (Eventually he dropped the "bi.") There was, of course, nothing sexual going on between them either. He was interested in signing a "punk," and Patti was the right one at the right time. But even Patti—with her androgynous swagger and supreme self-confidence—would play that game and flirt or become involved with anyone who could help get her to the next step. I saw her do it with Clive and with other musicians and boyfriends. Years later, when she opened a show for her idol, Bob Dylan, she was glowing so much she appeared incandescent. She, like every other woman, always knew where the power was. And the lines of acceptable behavior have, for years, been blurred.

◆

Actual rape, of course, is different.

"It changes you forever," the 19 year-old Fiona Apple told me in 1996 about being raped when she was 12 years old. "But it's a few minutes of my life, it wasn't my fault, and then it's over." She said it was hard for her to prosecute anyone, because you can't really search for someone: "I went to a lineup once, but you have to be really sure that the person is the right person." Fiona told me that around the time of the rape, her mother gave her a book of poems by Maya Angelou. "It was a time when I just felt weak and sore all over as a human being. I felt I wasn't a whole person because I was a victim. Maya Angelou had written about her experiences; she had been through the same thing I had been through. I used to go to sleep with her book under my pillow every night and I feel she really raised me up through that sad experience. Not just because of the rape, but because of not fitting in anywhere."

Fiona Apple had a voice that sounded like a sexy, seasoned jazz singer. She had a hit debut album (*Tidal*) in 1996, but she got a reputation for being nuts (she once walked off the stage mid-show at Roseland in New York City; she later said it was because she couldn't hear the sound mix in the monitors). She was extremely skinny, bordering on anorexic; she told me that for years she wanted to make herself look less desirable so she wouldn't be considered sexy. However, her debut video for the song "Criminal" was almost an exact replica of a controversial Steven Meisel grunge-era, semi-porn Calvin Klein ad—with teenagers in underwear at some sort of druggy party in what looked like a 1960s era "rec" room, wood paneled basement. As a 19 year-old newcomer to the music business, Fiona had a male manager and marketing executive who thought this video would be a good idea. She went along with it. But Fiona was damaged. "People always thought I was weird and said things behind my back," she said. "I felt like nobody liked me. There were times I thought the rape was a really big deal, then there were times I thought it wasn't. Maybe I was affected by it more than I thought I was."

✦

According to singer/songwriter Rita Coolidge she gave part of what became the hit song "Layla" for Eric Clapton's Derek and the Dominos to drummer Jim Gordon—and she didn't receive any writing credit on it. At that time, when she complained to the music mogul

Robert Stigwood—who managed Eric Clapton—he told Rita she should stick to background singing, not worry about credit and not attempt a solo career, because, he said, "You're just a girl."

In 2016, Gwen Stefani told me that she wrote No Doubt's hit song "Just A Girl" because, "As you get older, you realize that girls are not equal. You don't think about it when you're little, but when you hit puberty, and you walk down the street someone's going to whistle at you, and you realize that you have this power with your sexuality. Then you realize that it makes you less—because you're just an object, you're just a girl. I was living at my parents' house and I realized there were limits on me. My dad said I had to be home at a certain time, I couldn't have the keys to the car. . . . I didn't mean for the song to be any sort of feminist anthem; it was very cynical and sarcastic. Like, 'I'm just a girl and I can't do anything, right?'"

Rita Ora told me that she couldn't perform any of the songs she worked on with her ex-boyfriend, co-writer/producer Calvin Harris, after they broke up, because he served her with an injunction that prohibited her from doing the songs live.

Pat Benatar, Debbie Harry and Chrissie Hynde all told me during one decade or another that they couldn't get their songs on the radio because, they were told, "We're playing a girl already." Even Kacey Musgraves, the winner of the 2018 Album of the Year Grammy and countless Country Music Awards, told me that she ran into trouble with the all-important country music radio stations because she wasn't "nice" enough to a particular radio programmer. Patti Smith didn't have a hit at all until she rewrote the lyrics and recorded a song ("Because the Night") written by and then given to her by Bruce Springsteen.

And despite her successful career with Fleetwood Mac, it took Stevie Nicks recording a duet with Tom Petty ("Stop Draggin' My Heart Around") to have her first solo hit.

✦

In June 1991, I was at the Greene Street Studios in New York City with the producer Phil Spector. This was years before he was convicted of the murder of Lana Clarkson and sentenced to a life in prison. He was, at that time, a friend of mine. He was remastering all of the hits he produced from his "Wall of Sound" 1960s heyday for a boxed set. He played The Ronettes' "Be My Baby." He played Tina Turner singing "River Deep, Mountain High." He played the Righteous Brothers hit "You've Lost That Lovin' Feelin'"—the title of which, he told me, some disc jockey had initially told him was too negative. The only other person in the room was Phil's longtime engineer, Larry Levine. The lights were down low, the air conditioning was extremely high—it was dark and freezing and I thought nothing of it—recording studios were often like this. At the time I remember thinking that it was like watching Pablo Picasso re-paint his pictures. I'm not building up to some sort of Phil attack here—that's not what happened. In fact, that never happened to me, although I was in two dodgy situations with him: once when he violently screamed at a woman at our table in a jazz club and another time when, very drunk, he wouldn't let me leave his hotel suite until I listened to him play some new song on the piano many many times. (To be fair, he did send me dozens of pages of apologies by fax the following day.)

But what did happen that day in the studio was that a song came on that I'd never heard before. It was by The Crystals, it sounded sort of like a funeral dirge, and it was "He Hit Me (and It Felt Like a Kiss)." (The lyrics were *"He hit me / and I knew he loved me / if he didn't care for me / I could have never made him mad / But he hit me / and I was glad."*) Phil had never released it before, he said, but he decided to include it in the boxed set. Since then, it's been covered by Courtney Love and Lana Del Rey. Reportedly, Amy Winehouse loved the song, and various performances of it can be seen and heard all over YouTube. The song was written in 1962 by Gerry Goffin and Carole King—the then married Brill Building songwriters whose maid, Eva Boyd (who, as Little Eva, sang "The Loco-Motion"), had told them her story.

Her boyfriend routinely hit her, she said, and she knew that meant he really loved her. She was one of those typical victims of domestic abuse—although I feel that is way too mild a term; it is violence against women, plain and simple.

Carole King, who herself was brutally beaten by her drug-addicted third husband, has said that she regretted ever having written that song. When I heard the song that day in the studio, I was shocked. Phil, of course, was nonplussed. Today, it's almost macabre: thinking about Tina Turner, who had one of her biggest solo hits with the Phil-produced "River Deep, Mountain High," and that Crystals song, and Phil, who may never see the outside of a jail again.

◆

In 2009, following Clive Davis' pre-Grammy party at the Beverly Hilton Hotel in Los Angeles, Rihanna and her then boyfriend, the R&B singer/dancer Chris Brown, got into a fight in his—as she put it, rented—Lamborghini. He punched her in the face, he busted her lip, she spit blood in his face. She jumped out of his car, screamed for help and went to the police. He was arrested for felony assault. Someone sold the photos of her battered face to TMZ. They are still online today. I told her that this would follow her to her eventual obituary; the first line would mention this incident, and she said she knew that she was the poster child for domestic abuse. Every time there is high profile violence against famous women, Rihanna is dragged into the story, brought up as an example of another victim. "It's like the victim gets punished over and over," she said. "I don't want to say, 'get over it,' because it's a serious thing. A lot of women, a lot of young girls are going through it. A lot of young boys too. And it's not a subject to sweep under the rug. So I don't dismiss it or not take it seriously, but for me, and anybody who's been a victim of that abuse, you don't want to remember it."

At that time, she pressed charges, they went to court, she had a restraining order against him. Then they briefly got back together, only to break up again. "I was that girl," she said. "I was that girl who felt that as much pain as this relationship is, maybe some people are built stronger than others. Maybe I'm one of those people who are built to handle shit like this. Maybe I'm supposed to be the guardian angel who is there for that person because they're not strong enough—they're not understanding the world. I was very protective of him. I felt people didn't understand him."

She felt that way even after the beating. As I've previously recounted, she said, "After awhile you're their enemy. Because you remind them of their failures or even bad moments in their lives when you say you're willing to put up with something. They think less of you because they know you don't deserve what they're going to give. And if you put up with that, then maybe you are agreeing that you do deserve it, that you are to blame. That's when I had to say I was stupid thinking I was built for this. Sometimes you just have to walk away."

◆

The first time I interviewed Lady Gaga, in 2010, she told me that from the age of 16, she had dated men much older than she was— although, she said, she wasn't sure the proper word was "dated." She said she'd always been in abusive and often traumatic relationships, that while she didn't get beaten up, she felt that mental abuse led to sexual abuse and there were times she felt she was in danger. Years later, she publicly admitted that she'd been raped when she was 19 years old.

In her 1991 song "Me and a Gun," Tori Amos sings "*Yes, I wore a slinky red thing / does that mean I should spread for you, your friends?*" Tori Amos was raped when she was 21 by someone she gave a ride to after performing in a club. In 1994, she told me, "It fucks you up. You have to look at the parts you've numbed. For me, the part I numbed was the capacity for violence, which was able to help me heal from being violated. It's okay to feel all different things; when I allowed myself to feel like a scumbag, or inferior, that really helped me. Okay, you feel inferior to other women when you walk into a room. And you've been using feeling like a victim to make you feel better. You depend on feeling like a victim to make you feel worthy. But if people are afraid of that vulnerability—that doesn't make you any less of a strong woman, or less of a feminist." Tori became a spokesperson for the rape crisis organization RAINN (Rape, Abuse and Incest National Network). She recounted a heartbreaking story to me about a girl who fainted at one of her concerts, then came backstage and begged Tori to take her home with her—because, she said, if she went back to her own home, her stepfather would rape her, as he did every night.

✦

In 1984, Annie Lennox told me that she felt that the world was changing. "There are a lot of women in positions now that fifty years ago, or even ten years ago, never would have dreamt would be possible. Society is changing. I see heterosexual couples where the guy is not so dominant or macho, and the girl is not so submissive and sweet. There's a lot of good association going on between men and women."

She was optimistic, and some of that is absolutely true. Then there's the part where maybe she didn't get it. These stories of abuse are not specific to female musicians. They are the same rumors and whispers and stories told by, or more often kept secret by, many—many women. But I have seen the music world up close. And I know what it takes for these women to get to the point where they can overcome anything and everything and still get up on that stage and project confidence, project the aura of an invincible, larger than life persona. Despite the damage. Despite abuse. Many managed to do it and have become successful. And many—we may never know how many—have not.

In 2018, Sheryl Crow told me, "I was pretty outspoken on my first album about the sexual harassment when I sang background vocals on the Michael Jackson tour by his manager, Frank DiLeo. I named Clarence Thomas in that song too. I'm dismayed by how slowly we've come to even where we are now. I definitely lived through all that, and even being the boss of my own band was always tricky; not only with your own band members being male, but also being on the road with other bands. It was like 'who's going to get in there first?' It's always the code."

LOVE & MARRIAGE

"All the men in my life have not just pursued me, but have pursued me in such a voracious way that I think, oh my god, nobody has ever loved me like this," Jennifer Lopez said. "That's how hard they go." We were talking at her house in Calabasas, California. It was 2010 and she was still married to Marc Anthony, her third husband and the father of her twins. She described him to me that day as "the love of my life." But the other men in her life to whom she referred included her first husband, Ojani Noa, who managed a restaurant she owned; Sean "Puffy" Combs; then her second husband—her backup dancer Cris Judd; and her ex-fiancé, the actor Ben Affleck.

Jennifer recalled how, when she first met Puffy, on a video shoot, he came up to her and told her he was in love with her. She told him he didn't even know her. Even though she was married at the time, Puffy called her day and night. She kept him at a distance, but eventually, she told me, it was exciting. They shared a love of music, he mentored her in the world of hip-hop and he swept her off her feet. "You have to realize," she said, "I had had one boyfriend, one husband, and I was very naïve. My mother raised me to be a good girl— you're supposed to be a good girl. My mother was a good girl, and she was with one man for thirty-five years. They got divorced, but it was very much that kind of upbringing, and it was a family full of girls."

When we talked, Jennifer told me that Marc Anthony made her feel safe. She said that was the biggest compliment you can give to someone. "You want to feel safe; unsafe would be bad for me. I always felt if I ever needed to call somebody in the middle of the night, it was Marc. If I was in Siberia and I called him in the middle of the night and said something was wrong and I needed him to come there, he loved me and cared about me so much that the world would stop and he would come. It's always been that way."

Perhaps I should have known at that time that something wasn't quite right, because it had been nearly impossible to get Marc to participate in the interview. And when he finally did, he showed up to the house—seemingly reluctant, moody and uncomfortable—and the two of them gave me a tour, which concentrated on her rooms full of clothes and his recording studio, where he was allowed to smoke. Two weeks after that talk, Jennifer's publicist called to warn me that there would be an announcement soon that she and Marc Anthony, "the love of her life," were getting divorced.

✦

In talking to all the women I've talked to over the years, I was mindful that they were serious songwriters, or talented singers, or great performers. Some of them were even all three. But because they were women and I was a woman, sooner or later, we talked about love and men (or, in fewer instances, love and women). And so, after the first intense sexual attraction and infatuation, if the relationship progresses, most female stars are no different than women everywhere: they want one someone to have their back, to share their life, to call their own. Or, for many, to have a family. And no matter how tough, how focused, how successful, famous or rich they all became, every single one of these successful female musicians still had the same female longing about finding The One. Having it all. Happily ever after. The fact that this so rarely works out perfectly when a woman has a big career, is another matter.

✦

Years ago, Bonnie Raitt was married to the actor Michael O'Keefe, and she told me that it didn't work out because everyone treated him like he was "Mr. Bonnie Raitt."

According to Jewel, "People think because you're selling a lot of records that there must be a lot of men who want to date you. But that doesn't mean that you can connect with someone. It separates you. A lot of men don't want to be around a situation and have it be 'Jewel, Jewel, Jewel' all the time."

And in the 1980s Cher said, "It takes a certain kind of man to be able to be with me. It's really hard for a man to be called 'Mr. Cher.' The attention was really hard on Rob [her ex-boyfriend, baker Rob Camilletti], but nowhere near as hard as being called 'bagel boy' by the press. People are really mean spirited. But they also don't realize that it makes the relationship difficult. At some point, if you want any sort of privacy, whatever you're doing, you'd better be doing it in your own house—and not near any kind of open window."

In 2017, Rita Ora admitted that she had really bad luck with men (her bad taste included boyfriends Rob Kardashian and the DJ Calvin Harris), and she said, "Love is great, but it also can be the most dangerous thing on planet Earth. People do crazy things when it comes to jealousy and love."

Lady Gaga has told me that despite her best efforts and even though she would cherish and take care of any man she let into her life, she had never written a song that was almost completely about being happy and in love. She said, "I'm lonely when I'm not in a relationship, and I'm lonely when I'm in a relationship."

When she was dating Jay-Z, but before she became Mrs. Shawn Carter in 2008, Beyoncé told me, "At one point, I was worried I couldn't find someone. Because I didn't go out, and I didn't expose myself to a lot of people, But I asked for this career, and I got it." And Beyoncé, who was once criticized for a song of hers with lyrics about bringing your man his slippers and whatnot, said to me, "It's ok to cater to a man if he's a strong man and he does the same for you. You can still be a strong woman and do that."

◆

"It hurt my feelings, and then it made me mad," country legend Tammy Wynette told me in 1994 about the 1992 *60 Minutes* interview when Hillary Clinton said she "wasn't just some little woman standing by her man like Tammy Wynette." Tammy told me, "I'm watching TV, and this comes out of her mouth, and I thought how could she do that? She's defending him against Gennifer Flowers and if she wasn't standing by her man, then what *was* she doing? What a contradiction."

Eventually, Tammy said, with the intervention of their mutual friend, the actor Burt Reynolds, Hillary called her, but at first, Tammy didn't want to take the call. "After awhile," Tammy said, "I took her call, she apologized, and said they'd been firing questions at her so fast that she just said that before she thought. All is well now."

But, Tammy added, "All I meant in my song ("Stand By Your Man") was that if you love somebody, stand by them. I was born and raised in the Deep South, and what my daddy said was god. Everything was the man, the man. . . . Still, I am very independent. I am not a mousy little woman, I don't like mousy little women who are afraid of some man. I never lived like that. I came to Nashville with no job, no husband, three kids, with no support from their father and nothing on the horizon. I came because of my love for singing. Even though at first I kicked myself for not going back to the beauty shop, I knew I could make a living singing. I raised all my children on my own, and I taught my girls to never have to depend on a man."

✦

Linda Ronstadt, who was involved for years with the musician JD Souther, was rumored to have had romances with many other musicians. "Well, who are you going to date," she asked me in the late 1970s, "the dentist?" But she told me that if you were smart, you didn't get romantically involved with a member of your own band. "I said if you were smart," she laughed. "The only thing I pray for is to never fall in love before a tour. The only thing that works out is if you fall in love *on* a tour. But that can be very sticky. I call it 'roadmance.' It's boring to be on tour," she added, "and lonely. It's different for the guys, because they can go out and get drunk and pick people up. It's miserable and disorienting, and so, the whole world becomes the people on the tour. It can be a real trap to not develop substantial relationships. But even though it's a drag, and boring, and tedious as hell sometimes—not to mention exhausting and terrifying—when you get home, you can always use it as an excuse. Like, 'Hey, you're starting to get boring—I'm going off to Cleveland.'"

"I never met anybody I wanted to marry," Linda added. "And not being married makes a big difference. For one thing, they don't take half your money when you leave them. Or half your house. If you want to leave, you pick up your bags and you leave. It's easier than getting divorced."

✦

In 2015, Joni Mitchell, recalling the Laurel Canyon scene in the 1970s, said that she and David Crosby were never the couple that everyone thought they were. "David used to act like he sort of discovered me in Florida," she told me, "and he would trot me out to play for people. We spent a lot of time together in Florida and it was very enjoyable; I guess we had what you would call a brief summer romance in Florida; we rode bikes in the Grove, and went on his boat. He was off drugs then, but his appetite was for 15 year-old harem girls waiting on him—and more than one. And whatever his idea was about me, it was unrealistic, because I would not be a servant girl. I guess I had a childlike quality that made me attractive to him, and my talent made me attractive. But we were never an item."

As for her love affair with Graham Nash, she told me, "Graham and I fell in love. And he got sick, and I Florence Nightingaled him back to health. We were a good couple; we laughed a lot and we played a lot. It was a very enjoyable relationship. But once the band [Crosby, Stills & Nash] got together and hard drugs set in, if we were having any trouble, Graham went to David Crosby—of all people—for counsel, and Crosby would tell him, 'I wouldn't take that from her.' I don't even know what our troubles might have been, but you know, relationships sometimes hit a point. I remember ours as being very harmonious. Graham was very tender, and he had a way of handling me. I'd be flustering around—the world is this, the world is that—and he'd just sit there with his arms around me and he'd cool me out. It was a very warm and delightful relationship. Until he became involved with cocaine."

✦

In 1969, after the Buffalo Springfield broke up, Stephen Stills was the guitar player in Judy Collins' band. (Later, when he was in Crosby, Stills & Nash, he would write "Suite: Judy Blue Eyes" for her.) Judy, who wrote about their love affair in her memoir, told me in 2015, "We fell in love immediately. Four days after Robert Kennedy was assassinated. When I went out to LA, I had already been in therapy for five or six years, and I had a very integrated life in New York where I had friends—people who had nothing to do with my musical career. Artists, painters, every kind of personality. And when I went to California, everyone was in the music business, and how boring is that? Very soon, it became clear that Stephen and I weren't going to go off together into the sunset of Malibu. I take the responsibility for that; I was probably too drunk at the time to handle it. But he didn't like New York, he didn't like shrinks, he was not impressed. He actually was outraged by my lifestyle."

♦

In 1994, Stevie Nicks told me that she was single because, "That's really the way it has to be. I'm getting ready to go on the road and my life is so busy that it would be hard to fit a relationship into it. That doesn't mean if one comes along I couldn't handle it, but it hasn't happened. That whole 'Mr. Stevie Nicks' thing absolutely exists. I wish it didn't, but it does. Even if I'm with someone in the rock and roll business, or a big rock star, or someone out of the business—it doesn't matter. They cannot relate to my lifestyle. I went with [guitarist] Joe Walsh for two years and even *he* couldn't handle it. That's really hysterical, isn't it? He said to me he couldn't deal with my lifestyle and I said, compared to what? It's an absolute double standard. Then I start feeling guilty that I'm not giving enough to the relationship. But the phone's ringing off the hook for other things that I absolutely can't get out of doing. You're guilt-ridden all the time. If you're not disappointing *him*, then you're disappointing *them*."

In 2016, Stevie told me that it wouldn't have been possible to have another relationship or get pregnant and have a child during the second Fleetwood Mac record: "Lindsey [Buckingham] would have been furious that I was having a baby with someone else," she said. "He would have been furious that I was having a relationship with someone else. He was happy I was keeping my relationships to myself and didn't ever bring any boyfriends around him. It would have broken up the band."

✦

I don't care how much things have supposedly changed, women still like having—certainly saying—"my husband." When I was growing up, I saw how my mother would not exactly flirt with, say, the butcher, but she would act a certain way—smiling, conciliatory, girlish—oh, the hell with it, flirtatious—to get a better cut of meat. And if you think this still doesn't go on, just stand at the lox counter at Russ & Daughters on the Lower East Side of Manhattan, or Murray's Cheese on Bleecker Street, or the prepared food counters at any Whole Foods anywhere in America and watch the way women still "have to" talk to men. When I was first married, I remember actually thinking to myself—although I never would have said it out loud—I'm home free. I too, could now say to the butcher (there still was a butcher down the block from where I lived in New York City), "my husband likes this," or "my husband likes that." As a woman, you were treated with a different kind of respect when you *had* a husband, when it was known that a man wanted to marry you. And I don't care what anyone says, it's still a form of currency. I know how the doorman acted to me when I walked through the lobby with my husband or when I walk through the lobby alone. Men never really believe or get to see this, because they are the man walking through the lobby. I also know how salespeople, contractors, workmen, building supers, real estate agents, bosses, accountants and lawyers all act when a husband is present as opposed to when one is not. (And gay marriage is not that much of an exception; it too shows that someone loved or valued you enough to make that commitment.) But as a woman dealing with a man's world, having a husband puts you in a totally different category.

When I used to attend friends' weddings back in the late 1960s or '70s, if the girl's family had money, the events were over-the-top, elaborate affairs. And now, for some reason, this mating ritual among millennials and those even younger has returned with a vengeance. Bachelorette parties have become destination events, or "girls' trips" to Mexico or Las Vegas or god knows where. Bridesmaids or just friends have to cough up money for plane tickets, hotel rooms, and piña coladas. And, I have been made aware, the weddings have actually become a competition for who can have a better set of photos for their Instagram.

Music stars aren't immune to any of this either. Tweets or Instagram posts with pictures of large, vulgar diamond engagement rings and captions like "I said yessssss!!!!" are an almost weekly occurrence, whether it's in the rock or the rap world. Weddings are a much bigger deal too, whether it was Katy Perry's wedding to Russell Brand on a protected tiger reserve in India or Gwen Stefani's *two* wedding ceremonies to Gavin Rossdale—one in London, where he lived, and one at the then Interscope chief Jimmy Iovine's house in Holmby Hills, California. Mariah Carey has had two husbands, a fiancé, and perhaps a husband-in-training with a younger boyfriend.

So, as antiquated and possibly ridiculous as all this sounds, having a husband still makes it easier for a woman to get that respect—even though marriage isn't usually consistent with prolonged sex or fidelity. There is now, as much as there ever was, the desire for the legitimacy that comes with that ring. Beyoncé memorialized the "put a ring on it," and right or wrong, with that, it gave her a totally different respect as a *married* woman.

✦

The songwriter Lucinda Williams, who wrote one of the best songs ever about a breakup (check out "Change the Locks"), has had obsessive love affairs where she too, as I've witnessed with others, seemed to turn from a tough, strong woman into a mushy, needy, clingy girl. This sort of behavior is familiar to any woman who has had the unfortunate experience of unrequited love (as who has not?) and who doesn't have the willpower to stop calling, or texting, or chasing that object of their love. Or lust.

"I've really only had two boyfriends in my life," Gwen Stefani told me in 2016, a year after she filed for divorce from her husband of fourteen years—Bush lead singer Gavin Rossdale. "When I met Tony Kanal [the bassist in her band No Doubt], I was 17 and he was only 16, and I was instantly obsessed," she said. "I was after him, I chased him. He didn't really feel the same way about me. The whole relationship was about me being obsessed with him and him tolerating it until he couldn't anymore. So when that relationship was over, I was crazy. I was 25, I was still living in my parents' house, and even after we broke up, there was that obsession. That's when I met Gavin."

For the next seven years, Gwen and Gavin were together. But she told me they weren't really together because both of their bands were always on tour. "We would see each other for four days. The most time we ever spent together before we were married was, I think, three weeks at one time. I had never lived with a guy. . . . I literally only had those two experiences. The first one was always insecure because I knew it was one sided, and the second one was hard because I was in a band and had a responsibility to the band."

After she and Gavin were married, she tried to keep the marriage going, but between the band and three children and the marriage—well, she admitted, "It's hard to balance everything. Because of the way I was brought up, I wasn't going to let this marriage get messed up. But obviously I couldn't keep it going. And I would physically get ill from the guilt of wanting to please everyone."

✦

In 1974, Carly Simon was married to James Taylor, and they had their first child. She told me that both she and James were great procrastinators, and it took her a long time to get him to write a song with her. "It's hard to have a professional relationship with a spouse," she said, "because you can't really criticize them the way you would with someone else. I feel much more comfortable writing with Jacob Brackman. Also," she added, "the first year and a half that James and I were together, we lived in a very small apartment, and when we were both home, we were really on top of each other. We couldn't work at home." What she alluded to, but would never come right out and say it, is that when there are two songwriters, or two performers in the same business, and one climbs the charts higher than the other, it is a recipe for discord.

✦

On May 9, 1980, at a show at Trax nightclub on West 72nd Street in New York City, I introduced Chrissie Hynde to Ray Davies. Chrissie's band, the Pretenders, had a Number One hit with a Kinks song, "Stop Your Sobbing," which was—as all the Kinks' songs were—written by Ray, who was brilliant, sophisticated, wry and witty. He also could be difficult, moody, erratic, depressed and alternately charming and understandably bitter. In other words, he was like most musicians. I have previously written about how Chrissie wanted to meet Ray—who I knew and who had an apartment in New York up the block from Trax. I told her this would be a mistake, that he'd break her heart, but she insisted. Don't be silly, she said, I just want to thank him for the song. When Chrissie, who usually wore jeans or black leather pants and a motorcycle jacket, arrived at the club wearing a skirt, I knew there'd be trouble. That night, they left the club together, and three weeks later Chrissie called and said they were still together. I said I wanted no credit or blame. I ended up getting both.

From what little she chose to state on the record in our numerous interviews, theirs was a highly volatile relationship. In 1981, she said, "I have this reputation of being this loudmouth American, or ex-American, kind of a public figure. Ray's always been an enigma. People don't want to infringe on his privacy, and I felt bad that I put him in an embarrassing public situation. The guy is a handful, but he's an essay on life itself. All the highs and lows; he's like the English weather. I've definitely met my match." What she didn't ever say, but what I'm certain of, was that he was with her during a time when the Pretenders were on the rise and The Kinks were taken for granted. While Chrissie's songs—"My City Is Gone," "Brass in Pocket" and many others—will stand the test of time, it's pretty damn hard to compete with the songwriting legacy of Ray Davies. And this afore-mentioned competition, whether it's stated or not, between a couple both checking their chart positions in *Billboard*, is not the basis for a blissful relationship. Chrissie debated whether or not to give up her music career to be with Ray, but of course, no such thing happened. They broke up, she eventually married another musician—Jim Kerr of Simple Minds—then they broke up. Years later, she told me, "Let's face it, we do have this mating instinct. Just when you think it's safe to come out, there it is again. You're driving down the street and it's the last thing on your mind and all of a sudden it's like, 'Oh, he looks nice,' and you're up the lamp post." As for that competition between two people who are together and in the same business: "I know exactly what you're talking about," she said, "but you have to get away from those guys, you have to get away from that on a per-sonal dignity level."

◆

The first album Mariah Carey released after her divorce from Tommy Mottola was the not-at-all subtly titled *Butterfly*. Tommy had been called her Svengali, her starmaker, but of course, Mariah couldn't have become the star she did had she not had the voice she had. But when she stopped listening to Tommy's advice—what songs to record, what clothes to wear—things started to fall apart. In 1998, she called me from her Tribeca penthouse, and while at that time she didn't want to be quoted, she laughed and said that she felt free at last. In fairness, when Tommy signed her to Columbia, he put so much marketing money and effort into her career that she had Number One singles, Grammy nominations and wins, and the career that had always been her dream. And then . . . she was miserable. Finally, she was free to live the life she said she wanted to live on her own. She added that when she had married the boss, she took a lot of cheap shots. People resented her success. If they didn't like him, they hated her. But mostly, she said, "I think I always had a fear of marriage because my parents got divorced when I was 3 or 4 years old. I never had a vision of what an ideal married couple was. I just had other friends whose parents were divorced or families that fought every night. I never knew how to handle marriage."

✦

In 2017, Romy Madley Croft of the alternative British trio the xx told me, "Since I was 16, I've always had a love interest. I always craved a connection and I've always been a hopeless romantic; always daydreaming and obsessing. But in the past, I wouldn't have enough confidence to live out those things. I always wanted someone to be romantic about, someone to text to." But, she said, "I lost both my parents when I was younger, and pushed it down. My mum died when I was 11, and my dad when I was 20 and I was on tour. I must admit that I didn't deal with it. I just drank and partied and numbed myself. But now I have a girlfriend, I've been with her for about four or five years and I'm very happy. She really helped me. She never did any drugs or really drank, she's really stable, and she had more confidence. She's a bit older, has been really supportive and she gets it." (Romy is no longer with that girlfriend.)

A few years ago, Adele, who was married to someone older than her by about fourteen years, attributed the age difference to the stability and happiness she found in their relationship. "He's perfect," she told me in 2016 about her partner Simon Konecki, the father of her son. "My friends who date people our own age don't always understand this, but he's confident in who he is, he's already the man he's become. After my first album, all the other people I was with couldn't handle it, but he's not threatened by my success—and that's an amazing thing." Adele emphasized that nothing was more important to her than her relationships with Simon and their son, saying, "If my relationships with them started to flounder because of a tour, I would pull out of the tour. My life is more important to me than anything else I'm doing—because how the fuck am I supposed to write a record if I don't have a life? If I don't have a real life, then it's game over anyway." In 2019, she shocked the world by announcing that she and Simon—after apparently spending months of quietly and privately living apart—were getting a divorce.

◆

Patti Smith, who always had a lot of boyfriends, once told me—in one of our many interviews—"After I accepted the fact that I was a girl, between the ages of 12 and 15, it was really rough, but I got over it. I was so boy crazy that I realized the one great thing about being a girl was that you could get boys. So, if you can't be one, you can at least get one." And, in 1994, after the death of her husband, Fred Smith, she talked about her decision in 1979 to walk away from her career to move to Detroit, marry Fred and raise a family. "I was so in love with Fred, I was really unhappy when I wasn't with him, and he just said that he really thought we shouldn't be parted. So I made the decision we wouldn't be. It didn't take me months; I made the decision in one night and I never regretted it. I think what I did required more strength, more independence and more depth of character than not doing it."

Patti never thought she gave up anything to be with Fred. She was a true romantic, and to her, being with the man she loved, putting everything else aside, was more than an adventure, it was a *mission*. It was Art. She wrote some letters to me from Detroit, and the theme was always the same: she never stopped working, and Fred started to teach her how to play guitar. They wrote some songs together. After Fred died, I asked her if when she first went there, did she think she would live in Detroit for as long as she did. "When I went there I didn't think we were going to live as isolated as we did," she said, "but I didn't pre-suppose anything. I went there with the thought that all I wanted to do was to be with him. He was very loyal to Detroit, he was very territorial. He didn't feel that people should go somewhere else to 'make it.'" At first, they lived in the fading Cadillac Hotel in downtown Detroit in one room. It had no kitchen, no sink, it was one big room and a bathroom. They had room service. After a year, they got an apartment in the middle of Detroit, and then later, moved to what she described as a romantic old house on a canal, twenty minutes from downtown Detroit, on a dead-end street with no sidewalks. "What I wanted in my life at that point," she said, "was to be with Fred and to develop my work to a higher place. And I've never regretted it, never in the most difficult of times. He was a complex man, but he was warm, generous and extremely soulful and private. In fifteen years of marriage we were only parted two nights—both were when I was in the hospital having children and even then, he was there at the hospital. I'm not comparing myself to Arthur Rimbaud," she added, "but I always found it incredibly astonishing that Rimbaud left France and essentially became a gunrunner, and coffee grower and coffee trader in Ethiopia. I found it astonishing and incredibly brave to go to an unchartered land."

✦

The country music star Kacey Musgraves told me in 2018 that before meeting her husband, Ruston Kelly, "I used to justify terrible relationships I was in because I thought I would get good songs out of them. What kind of personal torture is that?" One night, when she was at home in Nashville, she said, "I had cleared my schedule, my hair looked good, an ex-boyfriend was playing at the Bluebird Cafe, so I thought I'd go. I went alone, which is very out of character for me. I'm a homebody; I just like to stay home, put on some sweats, but something made me decide to go. I was fresh out of a bad relationship, tired from being on the road, and it was a weird, confusing time for me. Ruston was playing and his back was to me for his entire set. I didn't even see his face. But his songs really got to me, and I was like, 'Who is this guy—I really like his brain.' I went up to him afterward, told him his songs were incredible, and we should write together sometime. We kept in touch, a few months went by and we had a writing date. It sounds so cliché, but that day we just had a natural synergy, and I laughed my ass off. We had an instant connection, and we've been inseparable ever since."

"I'd been in closed, walled-off spaces before I met my husband," Kacey added, "and then I was like fuck, I'm not going to be able to be creative now that I'm happy. But it's actually been the opposite, I've been inspired by it; I dove right in." As for being married to another musician, Kacey said, "I've never been with another songwriter or an artist. It's a challenge, but we'll make it work." (She couldn't make it work; in 2020 they broke up.)

The singer Pat Benatar, who had hits in the 1980s with a hard rock band led by her husband, the guitarist Neil Giraldo, told me that "Home comes first, because home will be there later. When I was 20, I was a maniac, and I thought I'd be single forever. Of course it depends on the partner, but also, you want a refuge. Something that nobody else sees, that's just yours. Someone who loves and needs you just for you."

"Neil and I have our problems like everybody else," she continued, "but it's great to be able to share every aspect of your life with the person you care about the most. We've been together a long time and we know how to get around the problems. We're so used to this now, we don't know any other way. Neil is very adamant about home to be home, and work to be work. He's Italian, and he's very old school that way. And we still get jealous—but I think it's good; it gets me pumped up."

◆

In 1980, I visited John Lennon and Yoko Ono at the Record Plant in New York City, only a month or so before John was murdered. They were finishing up what would be their final collaboration—the double album *Double Fantasy*. Yoko talked at length about her art, her work, her relationship with John and men in general. As I've previously written, she told me that she'd always been involved with herself, that she was never the type to build her life around a man—men always built their lives around her. But, she said, John was such a strong character that he wasn't going to let her take him for granted. She said he made her listen to his story, how he grew up and his pain. She admitted that she hadn't had deep communication with other men before John, and they both had to reach out to each other. She added that it was all a nice lesson for her to know that society could be just as painful for men as it was for women.

✦

According to Rihanna, the music industry creates stories that can make her very uncomfortable just being friends with someone. "It changes the dynamics of the friendship," she told me in 2015. "If I'm standing next to somebody, what? I'm not allowed to do that? The fame, the rumors, it all makes me want to back away from even wanting to attempt to date. I don't have time to be lonely," she said. "And I feel guilty expecting someone to be faithful and loyal to me when I can't even give one hundred percent of my attention. The thing is that a woman will find herself giving all of herself, and by the end of it, it's either the right thing or not. But we give more sometimes than men deserve. It's a gift and a curse."

✦

When I had a lengthy sitdown in 2011 with Katy Perry, she was married to Russell Brand. She told me that she fell in love with him quickly, that she went off to India with him before she even really knew him. I said that was a ballsy thing to do, and she said, "I'm a ballsy girl." She hired a skywriter to write "I love you" and planned out where they would be when it happened. They got married in India where no helicopters with paparazzi could find them and take pictures. She was adamant about their privacy, and didn't reveal much about their life together, but she did say, "I wasn't promiscuous, but I was always smart about things. I didn't have insurance, so I would go to Planned Parenthood and I learned about birth control. But I was always scared I was going to get bombed when I was there. To me, growing up, that was the abortion clinic. I didn't know that it was for women and their medical needs." As for keeping her marriage to Russell really private, she did say that one day the real story of their great love would be written. That story will never be written; they broke up ten months after that talk.

◆

Sadly, for many of these stars, if the career is in good shape, the relationship is not and vice versa. Many women have had to make that choice. All the success, all the applause, the accolades, the recognition, the money, the awards—it starts to feel empty when there's no one except your manager or someone on your staff or road crew to talk to after a show, or to go home to after a tour. Or to not have that one person to whom you make that first call in the morning, and the last one at night.

MOTHERHOOD

In a VIP suite at a stadium concert three summers ago, a major music talent agent said to me—*apropos* of nothing—"You know there isn't a female singer who's had a Number One hit after having a baby?" Really? I asked. What about Beyoncé? Or Adele. Oh, yes, he said, I forgot about them. Since that time, both Janet Jackson and Cardi B could be added to that short list. But the implication was clear: motherhood while maintaining a big music career was a *problem*. Let's face it, motherhood while maintaining any big career is a problem.

◆

I'd been told that what you see with Adele is exactly what you get, but I'm always reluctant to believe any hype. Plus, she had done so few interviews and was so private about her private life, that even though I've had years of practice putting people at ease, I was hesitant about how candid she would be. But when we first met in Los Angeles in 2016, we weren't in the car five minutes on our way to Staples Center when she launched into a discussion of the post-partum depression she had suffered after the birth of her son, Angelo, in 2012. It was clear that she had wanted to talk about this, had not talked about this publicly and perhaps waited to talk about this to a woman. Most of the interviews she had done previously were perfunctory ones done with men about fashion, or tales of failed romances. This was different.

She told me that after she had her child, even though she never felt she was going to do anything to hurt her child, and she was obsessed with her child, "I felt I made the worst decision of my life." She said that the depression came in waves and different shapes and forms. She had not taken any antidepressants, but she felt that people weren't properly educated about this. She said that Simon Konecki, her then boyfriend and the father of her child, had told her to talk to other women who had children, but, she said, "I said fuck that, I ain't going to hang around with a fucking bunch of mothers. But my friends who didn't have children would get annoyed with me, while I found that women with children were a lot more patient; they knew that you couldn't just go and do whatever all the time. I could just sit there with women who had children and talk absolute mush, and none of us would judge each other." She said that one day, she told one of her friends that she just hated it, her friend burst into tears, said she hated it too, and Adele's depression just lifted—just knowing that she wasn't alone in feeling the way she did.

I asked her if she resented not having time to herself, or that her album was late, or she couldn't make music or . . . what? "I just felt I wasn't doing a good job," she said. "It had nothing to do with my feelings towards my son, but I felt very inadequate." Then, she said, she decided to give herself an afternoon a week—just one afternoon— when she could do whatever she wanted without her baby. I told her that so many women I know who have children feel guilty when they're working and not with their child, but then they feel guilty when they're with the child and not at work. "I did feel bad," she said, "but not as bad as I would have felt if I'd not given myself that one afternoon." I said I thought it was brave of her, in the midst of a consuming career, to even have a child in the first place. She replied, "I think it's the bravest thing to *not* have a child, because me and all my friends were pressurized to have kids. That's what adults do. I mean, I love my son more than anything, but on a daily basis I do have a minute or two where I'm like fuck, I wish I could do whatever the fuck I wanted whenever I wanted."

We continued our conversation in her large backstage dressing room at Staples Center, which had a play area set up for her son—who was not present. "I live a very ordinary life when I'm not doing this," she said. "My son doesn't realize that what I do isn't what everybody else's mommy does." She told me her entire life revolved around her child; everything had to be scheduled, even on tour, because he was on a routine. She said she never felt guilty when she wasn't working, and yes, sometimes she wished she was on her own, but she never was on her own because she was with her child all the time. This was four years ago, before he went to school, and when he couldn't stay awake late enough to see her shows. But despite any conflicts, she obviously adored the boy. Still, she admitted, "I'm not having that much fun in my life. I'm a mom. My fun is sitting by my swimming pool watching my son have a swimming lesson. Playing kitchen games. Reading to him. I wake up at seven a.m., sort him out, make sure a nanny is going to look after him. Then I have a few more hours of sleep, get up at ten, then we'll go out and do something. On tour, it's always something different, because it's somewhere we haven't been to before. Then he has lunch at twelve, a nap at one, and if I have a show, I go to work. Or on a non-work day, we'll do something else in the afternoon, have dinner at five and bedtime at seven. But I feel guilty because I'm doing this massive tour, and certain nights I can't put him to bed. So you're constantly feeling like you're trying to make up for shit when you're a mom. I don't mind it because of the love I feel; so . . . I don't care if I ever do anything for myself again."

But she admitted that she wasn't as carefree as she used to be, that she didn't go out as much as she used to, and that she was scared of a lot of things—even walking on the street—because she wanted to be around for her son. Then she said, "I never appreciated myself and I never was proud of myself before I had my son. People get up in airs when I say that, but I'll fucking say it again—I meant it."

✦

Let me say right here that I was married for a very long time and never, not for one second, wanted children. When I got married, I asked my husband if he wanted children—holding my breath while I waited for the answer. To me, having children always seemed like giving up anything and everything else you wanted to do. The idea of some person to whom I would have to be everything for—for at least the first fifteen years of its life—no way. I wanted freedom, and when I started a career, I wanted that career. Every few years during the first decade of our marriage, I would ask the same question hoping for the same answer. Every time, he would say no, or he hadn't thought about it, or it wasn't really something on his list, until finally he said, "I don't think it's what we're supposed to do."

When I was a child and saw the movie *Gone With the Wind*—with that birthing scene with all the screaming—it scared me off childbirth forever. (Rihanna has admitted to me that she's scared of childbirth and she thinks anyone who says they are not is lying. However, she says, she does want children.) But to give you some idea of the era in which I grew up, when I was in a college sorority, if one of my sorority sisters got engaged (which happened to nearly all of them except me), the lucky girl was given a Betty Crocker cookbook as an engagement gift. This was not a joke, nor was there any intended irony. It was just assumed that this was one thing that would be a necessity for a wife and mother. I'll never forget that book: it was a red, white and blue checked looseleaf-style binder with rings—presumably so that the new recipes you would make for your family could be added later.

When the 1960s gave us free love and feminism, the female stars of the time didn't talk about having children. By the 1970s and 1980s, when I was interviewing Patti Smith, Stevie Nicks, Debbie Harry and Cyndi Lauper—no one talked about having children. The agenda was getting a record deal, getting their music played on the radio and becoming accepted in the rock and roll boys' club. It never even occurred to me to even ask any of the women I interviewed if they wanted children. It wasn't part of the freedom or the fun of sex and drugs and rock and roll—even if sex and/or drugs were not involved, which they usually were. The highlights of the day—which meant night—were what shows were happening at what clubs and who could get on what stage to perform for as many people as possible. This was true of Patti Smith at CBGB, or later Madonna at Danceteria or Cyndi Lauper on MTV. Older, more established singers, like Tina Turner or Diana Ross, already had children, but it just wasn't part of those interview conversations; it wasn't sexy. In the 1970s, in my own circle of friends and colleagues in New York City, I think I knew of one couple who had a child. To have kids, in rock and roll, was considered a hippie thing; unwed mothers—tellingly referred to as "old ladies"—on a Grateful Dead tour bus, or cavorting with naked children at Woodstock. In the world of bigtime music stardom, for the few women who were bigtime stars, there were no visible nannies, no strollers, no mother and daughter outfits posted on Instagram, no Instagram. No one was giving up their hopes, plans and ambitions to start a family. It wasn't just that everyone was young, it was that women who wanted music careers were trying to *stay* young. To not become adults. Women had to face all sorts of misogyny, rejection, unequal pay and all the usual disadvantages just to get up on a stage or be heard. To have the added burden of a child just wasn't part of that early dream.

As the 1970s gave way to the 1980s and the 1990s, and people grew up and got into relationships and got married and had kids—especially in California—all of a sudden children started to come up in the conversation. By the time we got to the end of the 20th century, many female musicians either had a child, wanted a child, or talked about having a family. It became a thing. Very few women admitted that they didn't want children (Dolly Parton was one of the few who told me, "Thank God I never had children"), and Joni Mitchell once told me, "Women in the generation before us had the romantic notion of the white picket fence and baby makes three. Happy family life. Which has been difficult to sustain since the invention of the automobile. The man, who drove to work, had a life the women knew nothing about. Therefore, he was closer to his secretary." To put that in the context of rock and roll: the male rock star on the road was closer to the groupies and the one night stands. If these guys had children, which many of them—especially the British—did, they were stashed away with the wife on some farm back in England.

✦

In 1976, Carly Simon's daughter Sarah was just over 2 years old when Carly told me, "Now, I have some time to myself. But I love being a mother. You learn so much about yourself and your ability to love and give of yourself. The love I have for her is wonderful and it's been very expansive for me. As for work, well, I have to be more organized so I can be a mother and a wife [to James Taylor] and see my friends and shop and read and do all the things I want to do. But I have a tendency to get lazy, and you can't do that when you have a kid; I have to make an agenda for my day."

In the 1970s, Linda Ronstadt, who was the best-selling female singer of that decade, told me, "I love children, I mean they're great, but my sister has eight kids and I have an acute awareness of how much responsibility they are. I think one of the ways you can be responsible is to know what you can't take on. I have a lot of trouble having pets. No one should have a baby unless that's what they want more than anything in the world."

Linda must have changed her mind, because years later she adopted two children. But in 2012 she told me, "I'm glad I have my children, but children put so much pressure on you, and it breaks up romantic relationships. It's really hard. Children hold you hostage emotionally. And I know it's a cliché that you're only as happy as your most unhappy child, but it's true; because if you've got a child with a problem, you suffer with them. There are many things to experience as a woman, and I think having children is one of the richest ones—but it's also the hardest. And the most costly: emotionally, physically and financially."

Céline Dion went to great lengths with modern medicine to have children with her husband/manager, the now-deceased René Angélil, and she says they're the lights of her life. Bette Midler told me she couldn't have had the career she had if her husband had not really helped raise their daughter. The young, unmarried Diana Ross had a child with Motown chief Berry Gordy, then another with her husband Bob Ellis, then more with her last, now ex-husband Arne Næss Jr. But Diana never stopped working. Bonnie Raitt has never had children. So far neither have Taylor Swift or Lady Gaga—who's said she wants them because she was raised a good Catholic girl and that's just what you do. Gwen Stefani and Jennifer Lopez, both of whom have also described themselves to me as "good Catholic girls," have had multiple children. Alicia Keys has two children and manages to have a career. Madonna had a daughter by one boyfriend, a son (who, as a teenager, famously didn't want to live with her) with a now ex-husband, and then she adopted four others à la Angelina Jolie—and still, up to now, has managed to barge ahead with her career; nothing stops her. Nothing stops Beyoncé either—although she had to postpone a Coachella performance in 2017 because she was pregnant with twins; she later said that she needed an emergency C-section because there were complications with one of the twins' heartbeat. (Beyoncé wasn't the only woman to opt out of a show because of pregnancy; in 1995, Sinéad O'Connor canceled a planned Lollapalooza show when she was pregnant.) And while Beyoncé is trying to raise her three children normally, there probably is no such thing as "normal" for a child of such privilege. Still, my lasting image of her daughter Blue Ivy is not sitting courtside at the 2018 NBA All-Star game taking selfies with her mother, or shushing her parents in the front row of the 2018 Grammy Awards, but rather, walking backstage at Barclays Arena with Jay—without his security detail—on his way to his dressing room before a 2017 concert, holding his hand.

◆

"I hate that whole media spin of 'Motherhood Mellows Rocker,'" Patty Smyth told me in the late 1980s. "It has nothing to do with my work." Patty, who has an amazing voice, had been the lead singer of the rock band Scandal—who had a huge hit in 1982 ("Goodbye to You"), several albums and constant tours before they broke up and she went on her own. We talked after the birth of her daughter Ruby—the child she had with her first husband, punk musician and writer Richard Hell (she married John McEnroe in 1997). When we talked in 1985, she barely would talk about the child, because, she said, "No one talks to Sting or any of the guys about the profound difference having a child makes on their professional lives. I don't see that having children mellowed Keith Richards."

"I happen to be a woman, but I don't think of myself as a 'female vocalist,'" she added. In fact, Patty may have been the only woman ever asked to front a male, hard rock band when, after the breakup of Scandal, her friend Eddie Van Halen asked her to replace David Lee Roth in Van Halen. At the time, she was eight months pregnant, didn't want to leave New York to live in L.A., and wisely noted that Van Halen was always drunk, stoned, and fighting with each other.

In the 1990s, the great R&B singer Anita Baker was put on an involuntary hiatus from recording and touring due to legal problems, but in 1994, she told me, "Every day I was on the road I would look at this great looking guy—my husband—and think, 'I want to have babies with this man.' Once we stopped going on the road, the babies wouldn't stop coming. But we had such trauma and drama with miscarriages and surgical procedures with my two pregnancies, I don't think we're going to push our luck any further."

Admitting that nothing had come easy to her—not her music career or her children—she added, "I worked at anything I got—from my husband to my career to my family. I have to walk through walls to get it. Maybe all of it was preparing me for motherhood. I can tell my kids that nothing comes easy and I won't just be spouting garbage when I tell them that." When she went back on the road to do concerts, she said she took the children with her: "We tore up the Ritz Carlton Hotel the last time we were in New York City," she said. "We had two baby beds, strollers, anvil cases made for the bottles, the refrigeration units." When she doesn't take them with her on tour, she said having grandparents at home "softens the blow." Also, she said, instead of touring for six months at a time, she'll go for a week on, two weeks off. "But when I'm without the babies, I walk around feeling like there's a hole in me. Men can't feel this way; it wasn't inside their body, it didn't share their heartbeat and their bloodline. I always thought I didn't have what it takes to be a mother, but fortunately, when the babies got here, it came to me."

◆

A note here about what I attribute to the "*Us* magazine theory" of having children. When Janice Min was the editor of *Us* magazine in the 2000s, she had children and she constantly published photos in that magazine of baby "bumps" and actresses with their kids in a park or on a coffee run. (They're always either "grabbing lunch" or "running errands" or carrying water bottles or on a "coffee run.") And I personally think it made many young women feel that they too needed to have children so that their lives would be as complete as say,

Gwyneth Paltrow or Jennifer Garner or Angelina Jolie. And later on, Gwen Stefani and Adele. Nevermind that all of those marriages broke up, or the husbands were cheating or couldn't handle the woman's success, and those women wound up alone on those coffee runs. Nevermind that some of their careers were stopped in midstream—some because of age, but others because of the responsibilities of having to be there for the kids. Even with the financial perks of being able to hand the kid off to the nanny after the photo op—the image, the perception was that these women had it all. No one has it all.

◆

"Raising kids is hard work," Sheryl Crow told me in 2018 about the two boys she adopted in 2007 and 2010. "It's the greatest, but also the hardest. Stevie Nicks once told me, 'If you ever have kids, you'll never write a great rock song again.' But these boys have enhanced my life, and they've made me feel more urgent about saying important things in my songs."

Courtney Love told me she had always wanted to be married to Kurt Cobain and to have a child with him, but that she felt a lot of guilt about her daughter, Frances Bean Cobain. She said Frances had never been disciplined, and had to be handled with kid gloves. But after years of drama and estrangement, "Now," she said, "I'm making up for lost time."

In 1981, when Stevie Nicks was releasing her first solo album, she talked about what her life was like when she was not in Fleetwood Mac. "There are a lot of women who have devoted their lives to things I can relate to," she told me. "Jane Goodall, for example, is an incredible woman who devoted her life to these chimpanzees. When you read her books it's just heartbreaking, because she tries every day to keep these little guys from being guinea pigs. When she walks into a room she just floats; she's like an angel. I met her once in Dallas, and it's amazing to meet these women who gave up pretty much their whole lives for something they believe in. She's given up her life for research. And I've pretty much given up my life for rock and roll, and maybe to spread a little hope and joy with my songs. But I haven't been able to do a lot of things because of that."

I asked her as I had before if she felt she gave things up and if so, what? With no hesitation she said, "Well, I didn't have children, for one." Did she want children? "Yes," she said. "Yes, I did. But I didn't quit Fleetwood Mac until a year ago, and there was no way I could have taken two years off." Could she not have had a child and still maintained her place in the band? "No," she said, "I really couldn't and that's why I didn't have any. Also, there are a lot of people who depend on me—a lot of people who are involved in the band. The couple of times I actually just thought of stopping and having a baby, it was just the wrong time. There was no way I could have done it. Maybe I could adopt one day, but now it's not so important for me to have a really little baby. It's not that I couldn't do it, I would still love to do it, but by the time I'm finished with this record and I have one more solo record to do, I don't know if by then I really want to be a mommy of a really tiny baby. Maybe I'm just a little too old for that."

◆

Women in music have an abnormal life. If a woman has major hits, like Beyoncé or Adele, the record company is waiting for the next album. So there's the pressure to write songs—if she writes the songs—and be creative. That's hard to do when there's a screaming infant in the middle of the night, waiting to be breastfed, or bottle fed, or have a diaper changed, or whatever else it is that goes on. Even if the house is fully staffed and fully soundproofed, or the child is in a different wing, that child is capable of racing into mommy's bedroom at six a.m., jumping on the bed and waking mommy up. Mommy might have been in the recording studio until four a.m. Or maybe mommy had two or three hours of sleep after the adrenaline rush wore off from a great concert. Everything changes with a child in the picture. If the woman is ready to record an album, there are long days or nights in the studio, or in front of laptops with Pro Tools. Often, multiple—and I mean *multiple*—takes of one song become necessary. Do-overs if the drums are too loud or you can't hear the vocals or the vocals aren't right. When you're young and unattached, the only problem you may have in terms of how long you can stay in a studio is money. Or stamina. Or maybe there's a boyfriend waiting at home. With a child, those hours that the singer used to be able to spend in a recording studio, those days are over. Recording has to be scheduled around a child's schedule, or a child's school schedule, or vacation schedule, or one of those spring breaks that now seem to happen four times a year.

Then there's touring. If you're Adele or Beyoncé, you can travel by private plane. You can afford multi-room hotel suites, or dressing rooms with play areas set up for the child—like the one Adele had at Staples Center. But more than likely, there won't be any other children for the child to play with. (I remember during the 1970s, the very young Jade Jagger was playing with the designer *Halston*, while her father Mick was either onstage or off doing god knows what, and her mother Bianca wasn't around.) If you don't have Adele or Beyoncé funds, you shlep the kid with you on a tour bus. Or you don't tour. Or you drop the kid off with the grandparents. Then you feel guilty. But if you do tour, and you have a show at night, you can't put your child to bed and then, like Adele, you feel guilty about that. The whole situation becomes so different than when you were young and on your own and trying to Make It. Or young and on your own and having Made It. Or even older and on your own and trying to Make It. Or older and being on your own and having Made It.

✦

If ever there was a female musician who was supposed to embody the spirit of rebellion and androgyny, it was Patti Smith in the 1970s. Some found her pretentious—with all those shout-outs to Rimbaud and whatnot—but she was a champion for women in the burgeoning punk scene in New York City and ultimately, elsewhere. And not once, in the hundreds of hours we talked both on and off tape, do I recall asking her about wanting to have children. I had some vague awareness that she gave a child up for adoption at an early age, but we didn't discuss it. (Years later, after that child found Patti and became part of her life, I met her briefly, backstage at a concert.)

So, imagine my surprise—and everyone's—when, in 1979, at the height of her fame, right after a European tour that saw her perform to seventy thousand people in a stadium in Florence, Italy, and sixty thousand in Bologna, Patti left the music business to be with her boyfriend, the guitarist Fred "Sonic" Smith, one of the founding members of the legendary Detroit rock band the MC5. By the end of the 1970s, the MC5 had broken up, but Fred "Sonic" Smith still lived in Detroit, was the leader of his own Sonic's Rendezvous Band and was deeply in love with Patti—as she was with him. But there never was any thought whatsoever of him moving to New York to be with her—even though she certainly had the bigger career.

"Fred always wanted children," she told me in one of our talks after his death in 1994. "He told me exactly what he wanted; he wanted a son, and then he wanted a daughter, and I had no choice. That's what he wanted, and that's what he got [their son Jackson, and daughter Jesse]. At that time in his life, Fred wanted that, it seemed, more than anything in his life. That was his drive—even more than to do great work. And he was a great father—a loving, compassionate father."

I talked to Patti, as I always do to every mother, about how I don't understand how anyone can work with children running underfoot. And when her kids got a little older if we were on the phone—during the rare phone call when she would call from Detroit—the same things happened with her that happened on the phone with any other mother I know. We'd be in the middle of a sentence and all of a sudden I'd hear, *"Don't do that," "Stop hitting her," "Put that down," "Go outside and play," "We'll talk about that later."* Then we'd segue back into our conversation, until the next interruption. Patti told me that raising kids was "the most consuming work. But sometimes I'm just walking down our little street with them, and the kids will be in front of me—like one Halloween night they were walking in front of me with their costumes and their bags, and I just stopped and looked at these little figures in front of me, and it brought tears to my eyes. You realize you've brought them into the world, and it's quite a thing. It's not all that sappy, they drive you crazy as well, but sometimes it just hits you . . . and if once in awhile you can give yourself that moment, well, it's quite a wondrous thing."

These days, I am convinced that with all of her recognition and achievements, Patti would say that she feels the main success of her life was being a mother. And I remembered how proud she was when she told me that her son Jackson couldn't believe it when she was invited to perform at Lollapalooza, on the same bill with Metallica.

◆

Note: In the four decades that I've covered the music world, there has only been one instance and one man who talked to me about anything remotely like a child's daily schedule—and that was John Lennon when he stayed home for the first five years of his son Sean's life to take care of him. John was the hands-on father, while Yoko was downstairs in their office, handling, as John put it, "the family business." That was their deal. John described each day to me: the breakfast, the naps, the walks to the park with the nanny, the bread baking, the playtime, the teeth brushing time and bedtime. And as he went through this litany, I asked him what he felt he got from this, and he joked "well . . . the joys of motherhood."

SEX

Aretha Franklin sang, "*What you want, / Baby, I got it. . . .*"

Despite the fact that a man (Otis Redding) wrote the lyrics, or that the song was about demanding r-e-s-p-e-c-t, Aretha's delivery on that line left no question that she was referring to s-e-x. For years, female blues singers—from Bessie Smith to Big Mama Thornton to Janis Joplin—sang about sex, but they howled thinly veiled lyrics. They didn't swivel their hips the way Elvis Presley did. They didn't gyrate around like James Brown or Mick Jagger. At that time, if a woman had done that, it probably would have been considered obscene. When Tina Turner sensually stroked the microphone during live performances of "I've Been Loving You Too Long," she was simulating a sex act—even though she told me that she hadn't fully realized what she was doing; Ike Turner probably told her to do it. Jane Birkin vocally simulated orgasm on "Je t'aime," her duet with Serge Gainsbourg—and he told her to do that. And Donna Summer told me that when she emulated Jane Birkin simulating orgasm on

"Love To Love You Baby," it was initially so unnatural for her that she had to turn off the lights in the studio, lie down on the floor, light candles and pretend she was Marilyn Monroe. That was the only way she could record it the way her producer Giorgio Moroder directed her to do it.

Rock and roll was probably the first really popular music to be more explicit about sex than blues—even though raunchy blues lyrics were often more clever, more subtle, more implied. With a lot of double entendre. Blues were powerful, but never got big commercial attention. That old cliché of sex and drugs and rock and roll was the draw that made the music world such a temptation in the 1960s. But for most of two decades, it was, of course, limited to men. The big female pop stars of the 1960s and 1970s—Diana Ross and the Supremes, Lulu, Dusty Springfield, or "folk" singers like Joan Baez, Judy Collins and Joni Mitchell, or even Mama Cass and Michelle Phillips in The Mamas & the Papas—were expected to be discreet, tasteful, elegant, ladylike. They stood there, or performed little choreographed steps and twirls. Or sat there, with a guitar. When the Rolling Stones appeared on *The Ed Sullivan Show*, they had to change the lyrics of "Let's Spend the Night Together" to "*let's spend some time together*," but everyone knew what they meant. On that same TV show, Elvis Presley was shown only above the waist. "Light My Fire," a fairly innocuous José Feliciano song, was turned into a sex anthem by Jim Morrison, who got arrested when, probably stoned out of his mind, he exposed himself onstage during a live concert. Explicit sexual lyrics sung by male rock stars are far too numerous to go into here. "She Shook Me All Night Long" (AC/DC), "Pour Some Sugar on Me" (Def Leppard), "Spanked" (Van Halen), "Love in an Elevator" (Aerosmith) are just a smidgen of what the boys did.

Jane Birkin, Donna Summer, Aretha Franklin and Janis Joplin aside—women mostly held back. For awhile. Singing blatantly about sex was pretty much a man's world until the 1970s, when a few women opened their mouths and became much more specific about getting satisfaction. In the 1980s, the decidedly un-sexy Madonna sounded calculating when she sang about sex. But in the ensuing decades, female singers have been far more candid. Today, it's really nothing special for women to twerk onstage half naked. And songs about masturbation (Nicki Minaj, Christina Aguilera, Lady Gaga), S & M (Rihanna, Madonna), fellatio (Beyoncé), golden showers (Madonna), fetishes (Selena Gomez) have become staple items from female stars. (My favorite is still the much more subtle "Never Say Never," from the 1980s alternative rock band Romeo Void with its lyrical refrain: *"I might like you better / if we slept together."*)

Promiscuous sexual behavior by male rock stars was always considered one of the rock star perks. But if Madonna sat in the back seat of a limo and drove around the East Village picking up boys as was rumored in her early pre–massive fame days, that was considered shocking. When she decided to be *really* sexually shocking, she acted out masturbation on a bed during one of her concerts; for a jaded New York audience, it provoked kind of an eye-roll yawn. She also did a book with Steven Meisel titled *Sex* that included photos of her in bondage gear and totally naked, standing on a highway, pretending to hitch a ride. Undoubtedly there were people who purchased this as a coffee table collector's item, but nothing could be tackier, and less sexy than something titled *Sex*.

◆

While none of the women I interviewed admitted to me that they'd slept around, I certainly heard rumors about promiscuous behavior about many famous women—especially a few who are considered America's sweethearts. One of the women who was a little more forthright about her sex life was Lady Gaga. When I asked her what her creative director had been doing before he worked for her, she simply said, "Sleeping with me." She claimed she never was promiscuous, that she was always in monogamous relationships, or in something "very light and from afar. I don't really believe in having sex without monogamy," she said. "I don't believe in it. I don't enjoy it."

She told me that when she was younger and nobody knew who she was, if she met a nice guy in a bar, a week could go by, she could sleep with him and it really was no big deal. But now . . . if she let someone into her world, she found it hard to trust anybody. She also said that her career was such a priority for her that she went through periods of celibacy, because, as I have previously quoted her, "I feel like if I sleep with someone they're going to take my creativity from me through my vagina."

◆

According to Courtney Love, "If I'd been a man, I'd have been considered a loveable scoundrel"—instead of being called a drugged-up slut. "Guys start bands to get laid and girls start bands to get laid," she told me in 2018. "With me, it was a combination; I fell in love with the music and I wanted to have mating selections. I found that the minute I started my band, I stopped being promiscuous. I started getting picky, and I could afford to be picky."

When she was a teenager living in Portland, Oregon, Courtney said that one day, she saw some groupies at the backstage door of the Paramount Theater. "They were all in fur coats and spandex," she recalled, "and I was wearing saddle shoes and cords. They took me backstage with Cheap Trick and I thought, 'Wow, this is a wonder world.' I had a way of talking myself backstage that didn't involve anything else. I had moxie. Big fat road managers would be like, 'When are you going to give me . . . ?' and I'd say, 'I'm going to give you what your daughter gives you.' I kind of appealed to them because I looked like a kid. I was a kid. I hadn't even had a period yet. I went through some cheesy backstage shit: Sammy Hagar, Van Halen, Molly Hatchet, 38 Special. . . . But I didn't put out. I was a virgin to a very old age, considering my rock and roll history. I didn't wear spandex; I kept my preppy look and they all kind of protected me. So I got to see all these guys do all this stuff and I was really studying them. And I thought why do guys get to do all this and girls don't get to do this?"

✦

In the 1960s, *the* sexy, great looking rock couple was undoubtedly Marianne Faithfull and Mick Jagger. He was the seductive, androgynous rock star and she was the beautiful, angelic blonde. Marianne was discovered one night by the Stones' manager Andrew Loog Oldham, who thought she was so gorgeous that he could make her a star. So Mick and Keith Richards wrote "As Tears Go By" for her, it became a hit, and Marianne started touring all around England on a bus with other pop groups like Freddie and the Dreamers and Gerry and the Pacemakers. "When Andrew first found me," she told me sometime in the 1980s, "I was seventeen, they thought I was a sweet little virginal angel; a rock and roll princess. But I hated my angelic, virgin, sappy thing, I wanted to smash it, so I did. When I got together with Mick is when I stopped working—just to be with Mick. I could have formed a band—even though I didn't have the songs—but I don't think I had it in me, and I don't think Mick would have let me."

The late Ian Stewart, an original Rolling Stones band member until they decided he didn't look the part, spent years as their piano player and tour manager. "Stu" once told me that in those very early days, he would go around to Mick's place and Mick and Marianne would always be in bed, "fucking like rabbits, all the time," is the way he put it. According to Marianne, "It was a very great romance. It was almost like a fairy tale that appealed to people's imagination and sense of drama. They saw me as sort of very high class and aristocratic, which I never was, and Mick as working class, which of course, he wasn't either."

There was a famous incident in 1967 when Mick and Marianne and Keith Richards all got busted for drugs at Keith's Redlands house in Sussex, England, where, reportedly, Marianne was naked, covered only by a fur rug. There were all sorts of salacious rumors about a chocolate Mars bar being inserted into her private parts. All of this fueled people's imaginations and forever cemented Marianne Faithfull as some sort of wanton woman, and there never was any doubt that she was extraordinarily sexy.

And, after years of drug abuse and ups and downs, in 1979, she released what was considered a "comeback" album—*Broken English*, which included the song "Why D'Ya Do It?" with lyrics taken from a poem by Heathcote Williams: "*Why d'ya let her suck your cock,*" and "*Every time I see your dick I see her cunt in your bed.*" It was a raging, angry revenge song sung by a woman who was older and wiser; one whose voice was raspy from years of cigarettes, whiskey, drugs and life, and the song was, even in 1979, considered outrageous. Discussing it in 1994, Marianne said, "I don't find it that shocking. I think it's quite obvious; what does any artist work with? Sexual energy— and so what? When I first played it to the band, they were shocked, but I didn't care. I mean, it's the truth—and that's all that matters to me. If it rings true, then all that squeamishness and prudishness is irrelevant."

✦

In 1995, another singer released another controversial song. Alanis Morissette released an album called *Jagged Little Pill*, which included the song "You Oughta Know." That song introduced her to MTV and the larger pop world. "You Oughta Know" was another one of those angry, sexual female revenge songs, with the lyrics "*Is she perverted like me? / would she go down on you in a theater?*" Surprisingly, it actually got on the radio, became a hit, and the girl from a Catholic school and the pop world became a Grammy-winning "alternative" star.

In 1996, after the success of "You Oughta Know," Alanis told me, "I'm a very sexual person, and I have no problem with people seeing me that way at all. I was writing from a personal experience. I did express a fear with the man I was collaborating with—we discussed it for about a week—I wondered if it was right for me to be this unadulterated and forthright. But the other option was for me to censor it and tell non-truths or half truths. I just vowed to myself that I would never do that again. I mean, come on, it's not really something that people haven't thought about or done."

"When I was younger," she said, "I used to go out with older guys to talk to them, and younger guys to get a sexual fix. But I had sex with older men too. I wasn't that promiscuous," she added, and then laughed, "I'm kind of making up for lost time. Not necessarily promiscuity, but dating several different kinds of people. I mean when you're on the road, you meet ten new people a day."

Two years after that conversation, in 1998, Alanis told me, "I think people's reactions to 'You Oughta Know' say more about them than it does about me. That song was written as part of my anger, my sexuality, my fear, my joy—all of it is of equal value. That line '*is she perverted like me?*'—I said that sort of tongue in cheek. I don't see myself as a perverted person. But a lot of people come up to me and say, 'I have children and I would never let them listen to your records.' And I say, 'Well, you don't have to. It wasn't written for them.'"

✦

When you're young, you think about sex a lot. Most of the women I've interviewed were either young and into sex and didn't discuss it, or they were older, looking back, and only too happy to discuss it once it was no longer a major part of their lives. Sex was, much like drugs, a subject more frequently discussed by men—who undoubtedly had more access to both. Men bragged. Women were embarrassed. Men wanted to be seen as sexual conquerors; women did not want to be considered sluts.

A note about sex and marriage: It is my opinion and my experience that whenever you hear someone refer to their husband or wife as their best friend, it probably means they're no longer having sex. Unless it's in the first flush of lust and romance and they truly *believe* that this person *is* their best friend. Maybe they are, maybe it will stand the test of time. And pardon my cynicism, but no one ever tells you the truth about their sex lives. Especially when they get married. After three years, the couple stops having sex. On a regular basis. Well, maybe five years. I suppose it depends on the people. But I would bet that most married couples who've been together for years, especially those who have children, do not have sex—with each other. And if they do, it's rare. Or they have to "work" at it. Or some therapist tells them for the sake of their marriage they need to spice things up a bit in the bedroom. The minute that they *have* to "spice it up" in the bedroom—unless they were always kinky—it's on its way out. I've lived a long time, I was married for a long time, and I've had affairs—both before and during my marriage, and so did my husband. Monogamy is just not natural. The idea of having sex with *just one person* your entire life is not natural. I know I'm not the first woman to say this, and I also know there are many women who'll disagree. But I'm sorry, this is my experience, and my opinion and I'm sticking to it. Obviously, there probably isn't a man in the universe who hasn't strayed at least once from his mate; but people still assume that monogamy is more natural for women. I don't see it, I haven't seen it in the entertainment industry and certainly not among most (I said *most*) female music stars. Even in this time of "oversharing," and everyone baring everything both visually and verbally, this is just one of those things that no one talks about. When you get to that stage of familiarity, actually living in the same house with someone, even if you're a star and you're rich and you have a big house and you truly love the person—after awhile, it's just not sexy anymore.

Still, no matter how tough, how focused, how obsessed any of these women are about their careers, they still think they should have success and love and happiness and sex on top of all of that. And when it doesn't happen, many women have told me that they can get to a point where they just can't stand their stardom.

✦

Once, when Patti Smith was on the road in Europe, she sent me a letter (handwritten, on hotel stationery) from Paris, that said she was lonely in her hotel room while her male bandmates were out, she wrote, with "their whores."

In the 1970s, Linda Ronstadt told me, "If you're in the band, you get drunk, you get laid, it's fun. I don't go out and get drunk. I don't go out and get laid. I stay in and read—and I could do that better in my own house. The furniture is much better in my house than it is in the Hyatt House."

Debbie Harry told me that a guy in a band can say to their tour manager, "'Bring me back the ten best girls,' but I could never say that to my road manager. How could I say, bring me back the ten cutest boys? How would he handle that?" Debbie added, "During the peak of Blondie's success, guys wanted my underwear . . . and I had some good offers: slavery, marriage proposals, they offered to clean my house for a year—and I've met some really cute guys. But after all, most of the time I was on tour with Blondie, people wouldn't approach me because they knew I was with Chris [Blondie co-founder, guitarist and co-songwriter Chris Stein]. It's so different with guys picking up girls on the road; it depends on state to state, country to country. Girls who go after guys in bands get to experience their fantasies, but that guy whacks off in the back of the bus and then throws her out in the middle of Kansas. With women, it always has to be more about chemistry—whether it's someone you meet at a party or backstage. I haven't really partied with fans; I never had intimate sex with a male fan."

According to Belinda Carlisle, when The Go-Go's were at the height of their fame, "We weren't prudes, we were wild girls who had a lot of money and we were famous and we could do pretty much anything we wanted to do and we did it. We looked for male groupies, but we never could find them. We also were described as 'America's sweethearts'—like cute, bubbly, effervescent. I remember once smoking a cigarette and someone came up to me and seemed surprised—like

'You *smoke*??' But all that cutesy stuff was a media tag; we never wanted that image. We wanted the opposite because it was much cooler. I think the guys who came backstage to our shows might have been hoping that one of us would pick them, but I also think they were too intimidated, and so it never happened. All of us had boyfriends anyway, so we were pretty well behaved as far as that goes." There was one incident backstage at one of The Go-Go's shows, captured on videotape and circulated by an editor of a porn magazine, that showed a guy jerking off while the girls in the band watched. Belinda admitted that this was true, and said, "I'm ashamed of it. It happened and it's nothing to be proud of. Unfortunately, it got out into the world, and we couldn't stop it. But I was twenty at the time, and you make mistakes."

This was tame compared to some of the rumored orgies that allegedly took place in the 1970s with The Runaways: the band—which included Joan Jett and Cherie Currie—was managed by Los Angeles scenester/producer/provocateur and lowlife Kim Fowley. It is possible that even women on the road got so bored, or so stoned, or so encouraged to participate in wild stuff that they regretted, or forgot about, or—more likely—lied about years later.

✦

When I flat-out asked Chrissie Hynde if she ever picked up a male groupie on the road, she said, "Never." When I pressed further, and asked why not, Janis Joplin allegedly did it . . . Chrissie said, "Well, she was still going through her experimental days when she was in a band." So, I asked, does that mean you'd already done that? Chrissie replied, "I'm not saying I'd already done anything actually, Lisa, but I'd already passed my experimental streak. Plus, when you're in a band and you're a girl, it's just not the same kind of groove as a girl walking in wearing a coat with nothing on underneath or knocking on a hotel room door at three in the morning like the way it happens with guys."

There are few women in today's music scene sexier than Rihanna. She's been rumored to have been with many men that she told me she's never even met. She also said that just once, she wished she could actually live her reputation, because it sounded like so much fun. In 2015, she said, "I'm fine being by myself, because it's hard for me to trust anyone." What about all that wild, kinky sex she's always supposed to be having? The whips and chains she sings about? When we talked that year, as I've previously recounted, she said she wasn't really seeing anyone or having sex with anyone at that time because, "I don't want to wake up the next day feeling guilty. I mean I get horny, I'm human, I'm a woman, I want to have sex. But what am I going to do—just find the first random cute dude that I feel is tall enough, with big enough hands and it's going to be a great ride for the night, and then tomorrow, I wake up feeling empty and hollow? He has a great story and I'm like, what the fuck. That is the truth. I can't do it. I can't do it to myself. And that saves me. It has a little bit to do with fame and a lot to do with the woman I am. If I wanted to do that, I absolutely would; I'm going to do what makes me happy and what makes me feel good. But that kind of random sex just feels empty to me now. It's a hollow move."

"Nobody can have sex with me unless I want the sex," she added. "I hate when guys think they can make girls have sex. Girls are not having sex now unless they really want to. But people have this image of how wild and crazy and anything goes I am, and I'm not everything they think of me. I hate the assumption that sometimes, when I'm meeting someone for the first time, all of a sudden, it's all over the place that I'm *with* them. It freaks me out."

DRUGS

"I'm too old for that shit," Courtney Love told me about drugs in 2018. In the 1990s, she went through hell when children's services tried to take her baby, Frances Bean Cobain, away because of an article, written by Lynn Hirschberg and published in *Vanity Fair*, that alleged she was on heroin when she was pregnant. While Courtney told me she knew discussing it now was "beating a dead horse," and that she was reckless in the first place to tell a journalist she had taken drugs and was pregnant, she was adamant that, "As soon as I knew I was pregnant in my first trimester, I stopped taking dope." She and her husband, Kurt Cobain, moved from Los Angeles to Seattle to get away from LA's children's services, the press and drug dealers. Eventually, she said, she got off drugs altogether. "I went to rehab, then to AA," she said. "But I'm not an addict. I'm very moderate. If I feel I need an Ambien on a plane, I'll take an Ambien on a plane. But my drug of choice isn't available to me—I can't get hold of opioids and

I don't want to. I don't have dealers' numbers and I wouldn't take one if you asked me to. I can't do it, I have to say no. I want to say yes, but I can't."

Many years ago, David Bowie told me that when he tried to get off heroin in 1974, he went to Berlin—which he laughingly referred to as "the heroin capital of the world." I told Courtney that this seemed similar to the Pacific Northwest rock scene in the 1990s—where she claimed she and Kurt went to get away from LA drug dealers. She agreed, saying, "Everyone did heroin. People still do it. I think one of the keys to success is to keep a modicum of sobriety. I gave no fucks, and it's great to give no fucks, but there's a really ugly side to giving no fucks. But I really wanted to do heroin, and then I wanted to stop, and I did stop and that was the end of that. After 45, it's really sad."

✦

I never saw a female musician do a line of cocaine. That doesn't mean they never did it—of course they did. They just didn't do it in front of me. It wasn't only because I was a journalist—albeit a trusted one; male musicians did drugs in my presence all the time. In recording studios, backstage at concerts, on private planes, tour buses, vans. In hotel rooms. Especially in hotel rooms. But women hide things. Women have more vanity. Women have more guilt. Women have more shame. Men have more entitlement. Also, I was not invited to these rituals, because I didn't take drugs. Well, hardly ever. I never took heroin, never did cocaine, didn't take downs, never took a beta blocker, didn't even smoke pot after 1970. Except for a few experiences with mescaline and acid in my youth, and mushrooms in my not too distant past, or Valium to calm terror on planes, or massive doses of Advil for back pain, or wine and champagne, I was a novice, certainly a prude when it came to hard drugs. I had no idea what being high on most of this stuff felt like. And to me, the term "recreational" when referring to drugs is hilarious. Until what? It becomes professional? My favorite is when people say they "experimented" with drugs; I never know what that's supposed to mean. Everyone went into rock and roll for similar reasons: sex, attention, the love of the music, money and plenty of drugs. Drugs that made them feel free, uninhibited, have great sex, be liberated, reckless, do crazy things. Drugs that were fun. Until, as Stevie Nicks has said, they weren't.

While most women will only talk to me about drugs long after they stop taking them, I usually never believe what they tell me about the drugs they say they're not taking anyway. I think that they go on and off. An exception in candor once again is Lady Gaga. In 2010 she told me at length about the drugs she took while living in a walk-up apartment on the Lower East Side while trying to get a record deal. She talked about where she bought drugs, which ones she took, how they affected her writing—they were, she said, just a big and unfortunate part of her life. I told her about how John Cale once told me he had been fast asleep, woke up in the middle of the night and did a line of coke so he could go *back* to sleep. She had done an interview where she said she'd done MDMA, the purest form of ecstasy, and she said she loved it but didn't do it all the time. She also told me she did cocaine a few times a year—which I always assume means more than a few times a year. She was careful in talking about all this, because she didn't want her fans to be influenced by this behavior.

Since that conversation, she suffered through a bout of chronic fibromyalgia—and I have no idea what, if anything, she took for that pain. But whatever she did, it didn't stop her from being full-on Lady Gaga: from a killer halftime Super Bowl performance to an Oscar-nominated leading role in *A Star Is Born*, to a tough Las Vegas residency.

◆

In 1972, Miss Christine of the GTOs stayed at my apartment in New York City for a few days. The GTOs was an all girl group put together in Los Angeles at the end of the 1960s by Frank Zappa. It was more of a performance art outfit than an actual musical group—although they did release one album. Christine Frka was a tall, beautiful girl with long curly hair who wore vintage Victorian clothing. In another era, she would have been called a courtesan. I recall that while she was my houseguest, she went into my bathroom to take a bath and was in there for over two hours. While I didn't know at the time that she was an actual junkie, I had my suspicions. I kept knocking on the door to make sure she was okay. Actually, I was knocking on the door to make sure she was *alive*. The last thing I wanted was for her to overdose in my rent controlled apartment. Later that year, she had some sort of back surgery to straighten out her curved spine that required her to stay in bed at her parents' house in San Pedro, California—all bandaged up in a full body cast. I visited her there once and it was obvious to me that she was stoned. She told me she was taking morphine for the pain.

Then, several months later, while I was visiting Alice Cooper in his suite at the Georges Cinq Hotel in Paris, Alice told me quietly, "Miss Christine died." I was sad, but I wasn't surprised. There have been so many musicians heavily into drugs for so many years that you're just not surprised when you get *that* phone call. I have known many—many—musicians who have died of drugs. But Christine may have been the only woman I was friends with who died of that thing they call an "accidental overdose."

Today, four decades later, many—many—musicians certainly under the age of 40 still take drugs. It's more than likely that, unbeknownst to me at the time, all of the punk bands at CBGB in the 1970s were taking hard drugs—heroin included. They just didn't talk about it. At least not to me. One indie female musician in her 20s who will remain anonymous did talk to me about drugs recently, telling me that "everyone" takes ecstasy (Molly, MDMA): "It's like going to church," she said. "It teaches you how to be nice to yourself. It's a warm feeling. Women have so many body issues, and when I take it I look in the mirror and the things that

bother me don't bother me so much. It helps me be nice to myself."
She went down a list of what "everyone" takes (although this "list"
could probably be updated on a monthly basis): Ketamine, or Special K—which can be snorted, swallowed or injected and can cause
hallucinations; cough syrup (or cough syrup mixed with codeine—
"sizzurp"—which can cause seizures); and Salvia (made famous by
the antics of Miley Cyrus). This woman described Salvia to me as
"terrifying," because "when you smoke it, you're dissociative. You
don't know you're you." "Everyone" takes opioids when you can get
them, she said, "and LSD—but not the 'good' acid of yesteryear."
And while "everyone" takes Adderall (a favorite of college students
cramming for exams, or even younger students who probably have
never known academic life without that drug), it can cause anxiety
and panic attacks. And cocaine makes you paranoid. And yes, she
knew plenty of people who took heroin, although she said "that
whole thing scares the hell out of me."

So, some of the drugs have changed. But people still take all
this stuff because it works. It makes them feel "inspired." They have
better sex. It continues the myth of the cool, stoned rock and roll
star. And despite the accidental overdoses, or the suspected suicides
(often blamed on everything from autoerotic asphyxiation to antidepressants), most musicians don't *plan* to die. It's very likely that
the reason so many musicians don't do their best work after they
get sober is that they do their best work when they're young. And
when they're young, along with the burst of excitement, enthusiasm
and inspiration, comes the rush of it all, often fueled by drugs that
provide that rush. If that fun is followed by success, along with that
success comes the rigors of travel, business problems, mismanage-
ment, lawsuits, bad reviews, family responsibilities, children, a staff
and a crew on retainer. And when addiction is a factor, the down-
ward spiral can follow, along with the meltdowns and the hangers-
on—the people who are always around musicians—only too eager
to provide drugs.

✦

When I first talked to Mary J. Blige in the mid-'90s, after she had been discovered by Sean "Puffy" Combs, and when she was about to release what would be her groundbreaking album *My Life*, we did a brief phone interview, and she was extremely terse and abrupt, bordering on rude. Years later, as we got to know each other more and she blossomed—as a woman, singer and actress—I reminded her of that first conversation. She, of course, didn't remember it at all, and said simply, "I was a different person then." Mary, who was brought up in the Bronx in a rough neighborhood filled with street hustlers and gun violence, told me, "I came into this a complete savage. I went from cocaine, then traded that for alcohol. I was an alcoholic, and my spirit was dying because I didn't have any love anywhere. There was nobody around that cared about me. If I had dropped dead one day, nobody would have cared. No matter if it's family or friends, when you hate yourself, why should anybody care? I didn't like myself. The way I thought about myself was drawing negative people to me. So I was getting negative."

Mary and I have talked in person, at parties in New York and Los Angeles and at the Beverly Hills Hotel. But when we talked in 2012, just weeks after her friend Whitney Houston had died, it was clear that drugs and drink were on Mary's mind. "Let me tell you something," she said. "When I got to the point of choosing death or choosing life—I was dying. I was trying to do things on my own, it wasn't working, and I was dying, hurting myself. But the minute I spoke up and prayed, and I asked God to help me, miraculous things started taking place in my life. Life changed, and I did a 360. But I didn't think I was going to make it. Anybody can come into your life with help, but you have to make that decision, and it's not the person that saves your life, it's the decision you make right then to choose life. It's hard to choose life because you've got to follow instructions. You've got to go through all sorts of withdrawals to go through this. That decision is going to be hard, because it's not easy anymore. And there aren't going to be people around you who say yes to you all the time, and getting you high and getting you drunk all the time. There's no more of that. You've got to stop, and you've got to want to stop. The environment must change."

"If your environment does not change, you do not change. If you're trying to lose weight and your weakness is sugar, and I come around with a cake, like, 'Oh, I've got the greatest cake . . . ,' it's so disrespectful to what you're trying to do. And you might be weak. The hard part is trying to do the right thing. It's hard. That's why most singers are on drugs or recovering alcoholics."

She told me she was still reeling from Whitney's funeral, and it was difficult for her to talk about it. "She was like one of my sisters," Mary said, "and I just love and miss her. It is just so sad to watch something so great, something that God made, she was just perfect. The way she looked, the way she sang, she was just a giving, loving person. I had the opportunity to be friends with her, and sit with her in her house and have conversations with her in the middle of all that mess she was in, and just let her know how important she was. I would pray for her when she didn't know it. I would call her and tell her 'I love you and please know what you mean to the world.' It pissed me off; it really hurt my heart. We wanted her to make it—we wanted her to make it on this earth." And then she added, "I'm not perfect, Lisa. Trying to live a perfect life is work, and I still have much work to do."

✦

"I don't think anybody knew we could be sober," Bonnie Raitt told me in 2012, in one of the many phone calls we've had over the many years that we've both been doing our same jobs. "I swear to god I had not a clue that you could do this sober, nor did I want to. I thought if I became sober, I'd be a Moonie or something. You think if you play guitar sober you're not going to play funky or have any fun. Or have great sex or stay up and do crazy things. But I always waited to get high until after the show, because I wouldn't mess with my throat. That's when my day ended, and when my friends came backstage to get high. During the day it was sound check and saving your voice, and my time off was after the show until four or five in the morning. Partying was fun for those of us who did it. I wasn't moving in the echelon with the Eagles or Linda Ronstadt—those were big pop stars and I wasn't. So for me, it wasn't really a destructive scene until it personally became more self-destructive, and a nuisance, and in the way."

"Look at Judy Garland, Billie Holiday," Bonnie continued. "Most women singers have men problems, weight problems and drug problems. But by the time you've been at it for ten or fifteen years, it's going to look different on you in your mid-30s than it did in your mid-20s. I didn't have as much of a problem with it as some other people did, but by the end of my partying days—like twenty-five years ago in the late 1980s—I definitely recognized that I needed to stop. I didn't really pull myself out of it, I got a lot of help. You know how it works; the only way you can see clear to make the move yourself is to look around your close circle of friends. Then, if you see a few people who appear to be having a better time sober at everything than before—and in fact, there were three or four people who inspired me—they played great, they looked great, they were funny and relaxed and writing better songs than ever. So all my excuses went out the window."

Bonnie recalled that when she was partying, she felt terrible and looked terrible: "If your self-esteem is beat up, you know when you're not doing things the way you're supposed to. My music didn't suffer, but I think the quality of my work got better when I decided to give myself a break. Now my time off is from nine in the morning until sound check. I never was the type to get high during the day. Friends would come and stay with you and you'd be up all night, but they'd be able to go to sleep afterwards while you had to go on to the next city for the next show, and it really catches up with you. You look at those blues guys who died prematurely from all those smoky bars and years of club gigs and it's not a healthy lifestyle. I don't miss being a blithering idiot and feeling bad the next day." But, she admitted, "I do miss being out of control a little bit. Sometimes you just want to do something that's crazy and be a bit reckless."

◆

It starts out innocently enough, with a glass of wine or champagne before the show. Or a Xanax to calm the nerves. Then an Ambien to fall asleep after the show. Perhaps it escalates to a snort or two of cocaine before the show, or to get up in the morning. Then they prop you up with more drugs so you can keep that machine rolling. All is right when you're onstage feeling that high, but once the show is over and you're alone, that's when drugs can "help." In 2010, Florence Welch told me that early on in the life of her band, Florence and the Machine, "I definitely have a real self destructive streak and when I first started gigging, we used to get so drunk before we went onstage, I was a total whirling dervish. I'm surprised we survived some of our first tours, such was our quest for oblivion. But that was what I grew up with; all the art college punk bands were all wasted 24/7. That was part of it, so I thought that was what you did to perform. But over time and the rigors of touring, it became more about the show and the music than getting drunk. And now I never drink before a show. I feel very lucky to have close friends that I work with and all my band are my friends—so I have people to turn to. Touring can be very lonely. It's very tempting to just drink your way through it."

In 1994, Stevie Nicks told me, "In 1976, I was tired of all the touring. I was in my 20s and it still took me seven months to recover from a six month tour. Even with two months off. Even a tour with three days on and two days off. To come home from a two month tour, unpack your suitcases, send everything to the cleaners, have things mended that fell apart, get it all back and then repack takes weeks. And you rest for five days because you're just too tired to unpack . . . you're the only one who can do it because you're the only one who knows what you need or want. And no matter how careful you are, no matter how healthy you can try to be, if you drink or you don't drink, it all ends up taking a terrible toll. That's why all the rock and roll people I know who are 40 look 50 or 60."

Stevie, who told me she went to the Betty Ford Center to detox from cocaine, added, "I had to stop the drug that was prescribed to me when I got out of Betty Ford, because it was making me ill. I turned into a hermit. I realized it was messing up my life."

✦

The recording studio can be in a building with a curved brick wall entrance on a block in Greenwich Village. Or an unmarked building on Seventh Avenue in the middle of the Times Square area. Or it can be midtown, on the West Side of Manhattan near the Hudson River. Or nestled in between a parking lot and an alley just off Sunset Boulevard in Los Angeles. Or in the Capitol Records building on Hollywood and Vine—where Frank Sinatra recorded all those great swinging songs in the 1950s. Or a converted bus in Malibu. Or a series of modern white buildings in Malibu called Shangri-La. Or on Michigan Avenue in Chicago, or Abbey Road in London. But wherever it is, once you're inside, you're in a cosseted, soundproofed world. And even though many songs have, for the past few decades, been written and recorded with Pro Tools and laptops in musicians' bedrooms or hotel rooms, studios with multi-track mixing boards still exist. And often, musicians are in those studios all day and all of the night. Some rappers and producers hardly ever leave the studio. I was once in a recording session with one producer who wouldn't even leave the mixing board to use the bathroom; rather, he urinated in a jar he kept on the floor by his feet. Such tales notwithstanding, when musicians get into this mode, when they're working on new songs or a new album—despite the changes in the industry or dropping a surprise track online in the middle of the night—if they have the funds, the stamina and the independence, they're capable of staying there for days, nights, weeks. And it's the necessary stamina that can create the need for drugs. For some recovering addicts, the drugs of choice can be pots of coffee or cases of Red Bull or Mountain Dew. But for others, more often than not, there are hangers-on and friends only too willing to drop by with treats. To hang out. What I find hilarious is that now people have to stand outside the building to smoke a cigarette, but the overpowering smell of marijuana in so many studios is embedded in the wall to wall carpeting or the furniture in the control room. Coffee tables in front of sofas are perfect counters for lines of cocaine. Joints are passed around, bottles of Jack Daniels sit on the mixing board. Recording sessions are a world unto themselves: not only is it a place where music is made, it is the only place where total escape from real life is a perk. Escape from the mundane: no bills, no family demands, just a place to make the music. Whatever it takes.

✦

Mariah Carey's disclosure of bipolar disorder aside, she was hardly ever photographed or seen without a glass of champagne in her hand. For years, there was so much pressure on Mariah to turn out hit after hit that her public meltdowns and alleged private addictions were no surprise. Miley Cyrus' bizarre onstage behavior raised eyebrows, as did Britney Spears when she shaved her head and smashed a car window. Selena Gomez—after stints in rehab for a variety of health issues—sobbed on a TV award show that she knew she was "letting her fans down" and has recently said she's bipolar. Demi Lovato is a recovering alcoholic who stated that she once left the Met Ball to go to an AA meeting and felt more at home with the homeless people at that meeting than she did with the bejeweled and begowned celebrities at Fashion's Biggest Night. For years,

Christina Aguilera was photographed staggering out of clubs after a night of drinking. Lorde told me she has a "robust prescription" of beta blockers to overcome her shyness and stage fright. Marianne Faithfull told me that when she took 150 sleeping pills in Australia in the 1960s, the police asked her if she took them herself or did someone force them down her throat. (The implication was that her then boyfriend Mick Jagger gave them to her, whereas, Marianne told me, "In fact, Mick saved my life.")

Debbie Harry told me that Blondie originally broke up for the usual reasons that bands break up: "It's the explosive nature of rock bands. Years on the road—and who the fuck likes touring—it's physically awful. Also, tons of drugs." In the 1990s, The Go-Go's lead singer Belinda Carlisle told me, "We probably did everything there was to do, it was done in good spirit, but we definitely paid the price. Eventually, when you do drugs recreationally, it takes a toll. It very often spins out of control, and that's what broke up the band."

Talking about drugs in the hip-hop world, Erykah Badu told me in the 1990s, "I don't know anything about an opium high, but I would imagine that's what it feels like onstage, while making the record is more like a weed high. I went through smoking weed in college, and in my culture, it's a way to just escape, or to party, just have a good time. Or meditate. It was a growing experience. But I now experience the same feelings through the juices that I drink, the healing that I do. It's like my great grandparents, who are Native Americans—the peace pipe was a way of meditation. As youngsters we take advantage of it a lot of times just to numb the pain. Or to understand our vision. But I don't need to smoke anything now, because my music makes me high."

◆

In 2016 Joni Mitchell told me, "I never was much of a druggie. In general, my health was too poor to become involved with drugs. Cigarettes and coffee, that's my poison." She added, "I mean, I experimented—you had to if you were in rock and roll in the 1970s. I took a stab at it; I got in and I got out. I took acid once, and I never took it again. It was from a batch called Blue Cheer, one of Owsley's famous ones. Leonard Cohen was living on it . . . [although] how he could do that . . . One night I took one and nothing happened. I waited for creativity to strike. An hour went by and so I took another one, and I immediately went into classic DTs. The motor in the fireplace turned into lizards and the knotty pine turned into spiders. I saw violent, green jagged lines coming out of the electric sockets and outside I saw white fibers coming around from everything. I was an acid casualty. I couldn't be around electricity; I left LA, went to Canada, and lived without electricity for a long time."

Joni talked especially about cocaine, which she called "lady," saying that she and Graham Nash were a couple for a long time until "all of a sudden there was this barrier between us—especially when he'd go to play with the band [Crosby, Stills & Nash]. And people were more secretive about drugs then."

✦

Backstage accommodations, like travel, vary with the status of the act. If you're starting out, sleeping on a fan or a friend's floor, or a Motel 6, or in your van, playing in some little club, more than likely you have no dressing room at all. There may be no real backstage or there might be a spot in the hallway where you can hang out before your set. If you're the actual headliner in a club and there's a dressing room, you have a dressing room the size of a closet, with a communal bathroom down the hall. Bigger clubs have bigger dressing rooms with their own bathrooms, but do not think for one minute that these are, in any way, spacious, luxurious—or often, even clean. When it comes to theater dressing rooms, the bigger the star, the closer your dressing room is to the stage. Arenas and stadium dressing rooms are often suites, or a series of suites, with billowing white curtains and sofas and flowers. Cases of wine and champagne. Many musicians are ecstatic when they reach this level—for reasons that obviously go way beyond the size of the dressing room. The audience is bigger. The money is bigger. But then again, so is your staff and your crew and your production team and your all-around expenses. But for many, it's party time for your friends and family. It takes awhile for people to realize that there is actual work involved in putting on a show, and getting onstage. For the non-performers, the "green room" isn't a nightclub after the show—except when it is. (The origin of the green room goes back to the 1500s when, in Samuel Johnson's day, Boswell referred to some holding area backstage at London's Drury Lane that was painted green.) If you want drugs backstage, drugs will be backstage. The hangers-on just show up. Sometimes it's the same people on different tours. The dealers who traveled with Led Zeppelin in the 1970s were the same people who traveled with the Rolling Stones in the 1970s. They became friends, but they also were dealers. This kind of setup may be less obvious in today's corporate music business when a big tour is like a small traveling army. For many younger bands, they start out stoned. And now, for many aging musicians who are recovering addicts, there is a "sober" backstage. Which means a guest can't even get a glass of wine or a beer.

If you see someone hanging around a tour wearing an All Access laminate around their neck who is not a member of the band, or a significant other, or a member of the official management team or the production crew or the glam squad, or a family member, or a best friend, or a working journalist or photographer, that person might be the drug dealer. Often, a member of the glam squad or the management team or production crew is also the friend holding the drugs. It's usually easy to spot the shady ones—coming out of the bathroom with the musician, carrying a dopp kit. They might be relegated to the green room—which may or may not be the meet and greet room where the performer "meets and greets" radio station types (radio stations still matter) or record company executives. There might be another "hang room"—where actual friends are allowed to go. Depending on the act, the size of the venue and the people involved, after the show is when the party starts. If there is a party. If the star doesn't race the hell out of the venue. Even if the star does race the hell out of the venue, the afterparty happens. The music is loud, there might even be an actual DJ, the liquor flows, the room is packed and reeks of pot. Obviously, this does not happen with a sober musician; even the backstage at the Grammy Awards show has an "AA sober room." I have never seen it anything but empty.

◆

It was when I became friendly with Chrissie Hynde that I learned that most of the 1970s New York bands I loved—the New York Dolls, the Heartbreakers (Johnny Thunders' Heartbreakers, not Tom Petty's)—were on heroin. I have previously written about when, in the 1970s, Chrissie left her hometown of Akron, Ohio, and went to London and became friendly with the guys starting punk bands (The Sex Pistols, the Clash). In 1982, she told me that in her estimation, when the Heartbreakers went to London in 1977, they brought heavy drugs with them. Johnny Thunders (who died in 1991) was a sloppy but amazing guitar player and even though the Heartbreakers weren't considered punk, the English bands were impressed. They were impressed with the attitude of the New York Dolls and the Heartbreakers: "They were very New York, very street, very cool," Chrissie said. "And Johnny was a lovely guy. He wasn't one of those junkies who you think, 'what a fucking mess.'" But in London in 1976, the punk attitude actually was very anti-drug: "People drank," Chrissie said, "but Sid Vicious used to say, 'We can go over to me mum's and smoke hippie drugs.' That was the generation they left behind. The original attitude was that they were *not* into drugs. None of them had ever had any anyway. I could be wrong, but this is what I saw. The original punk attitude in London was the cleanest thing I'd ever seen in my life."

Chrissie recalled that the punk bands eventually started shooting speed, and when the Heartbreakers came to London, along with heroin they brought the junkie groupie Nancy Spungen. She was looking for someone to marry her so she could stay in London, she hooked up with Sid Vicious and the rest is history: blood on the walls and death and alleged murder in 1978 in New York's Chelsea Hotel.

Chrissie knew about drugs. Later that year, her guitar player in the Pretenders, James Honeyman-Scott, died at age 25 from cocaine, followed by the overdose death one year later of her other guitarist, 30 year-old Pete Farndon. In 1984, during one of the times she came to New York City and stayed at her boyfriend Ray Davies' apartment on West 72nd Street, we talked. Chrissie said, "There certainly were a lot of drugs around in rock and roll, but if I'd stayed in Ohio and continued working as a cocktail waitress, I'd probably be more burned out and trashed out than I am now. Because I was pretty burned out and trashed out when I was doing that." And she added, "I did some stupid things in my time; I was young and I was experimenting. Now that I have a child [her daughter Natalie, with Ray Davies], the songs I write might not be as colorful or interesting as songs about running around on an acid trip, and if the rock and roll 'edge' has been knocked off my work, so be it. That's who I am now. I feel differently at 32 than I did at 22. I feel as differently as I did between 10 and 20. My life is different; there's really nowhere to go to rock out. It's all videos now, and to me, that feels like the establishment. It's everything I wanted to get away from by being in a rock and roll band. It's like taking speed with your parents." And, she added, "When you're 23 and you get pissed—I mean drunk— you can just go crazy and it's all right. But if you're 43 and you do it, it's like your best friend's mother who used to come in pissed and everybody was really embarrassed. It doesn't go down so well after a certain age."

✦

"I have no interest in drugs," Adele told me in 2016. "When I was young, I had a relative who died of an accidental heroin overdose," she said, "and it freaked the fucking life out of me to see how upset everyone was. So I never touched a drug. I'm too scared to take drugs." Drinking, however, was a different story. "I love to be drunk," she admitted to me. "I love the feeling I have when I'm drunk. But as I got more famous, I would wake up in the morning and think what the fuck did I say last night and who did I say it to? When you have no recollection of what you said, or even who you were hanging out with, it would scare me. I didn't have blackouts, but when you go to a party, you'll talk to anyone—you don't know who you're fucking talking to. I was a massive drinker. Not anymore, but I used to be an enormous drinker, and it wasn't worth it—to tell some stupid fucking story to someone who happened to be a journalist pretending to be some hipster." While she said that since the birth of her son, she only had a glass or two of wine when out with a select circle of friends, she admitted that she wrote most of the songs on her (five time Grammy winning) album *21* drunk, saying, "A drunk tongue is an honest one."

In 2009, Donna Summer (who died of lung cancer in 2012) told me that she attempted suicide in 1976. "I was in an emotionally deprived state," she said. "I had no time for myself. I was running on empty for a couple of years and I had been secretly hospitalized on a couple of occasions." She was calling me from her home in Nashville; she told me she moved there from LA because she got tired of seeing men expose themselves on the street or in their cars—that it was no place for her to raise her children. "In 1976 I was disoriented," she continued, "and I didn't feel clear, and I felt that if it continued, at some point I would not be able to focus. Then, I was taking medication that took me two years to get off. I would say I got addicted to medical drugs, but I wasn't on the street hawking them or anything. I had a doctor who was watching over me, but at the same time, I was addicted to that. I couldn't get off them, and

I was depressed about that. It was like, 'What if the medicine isn't there one day? What am I going to do if I don't have it?' So that didn't help me; I started being depressed *on* the medicine. This is when I came to God—because it was like, either I have to take my life, or, God, you've got to help me. It was so imperative at the time, and without question, it was sink or swim for me at that moment. It's hard to describe to somebody who's never had that feeling, but if you were heavily depressed, all of a sudden I could feel like a ton was lifted from my shoulders. My neck stopped hurting, my body didn't feel weighted, I just felt like a different human. And from that point on, those things didn't happen to me. I made certain from then on to take time off and to say when I've reached my limit."

◆

Hotel rooms can have suites with kitchens and wet bars and even washer/dryers. They can have balconies or patios, or can be bungalows with private swimming pools surrounded by trees and flowers to ensure privacy. Or they can be motel rooms on the ground floor with the door opening onto the parking lot. Or a motel room up two flights of stairs—no elevator—where musicians have to shlep their guitars or their bags at four in the morning after a seventeen hour drive through a desert or mountains or the Everglades. Or it can just be something in between: a bland, decent-sized room with a queen-sized bed and a large TV and maybe a sofa in what is referred to as a "sitting area." Twenty-four hour room service. Windows that don't open. Wi-Fi so you can get Netflix on your iPad or TV, and sometimes, even a landline telephone that actually works—even though these days, they're barely functional because everyone just uses their cell phone. Or it can be a dump where there is no room service after eleven a.m. and the coffee machine provided in the room doesn't work. And if you need a wakeup call at five a.m. to make a plane and you don't have a tour manager, you're on your own. Or by the time you get to your room you're too jet lagged or exhausted from a long trip to unpack, so you can't find your toothbrush and there's no soap in the bathroom and no hair dryer. None of this is a problem for the privileged few who rent houses on tours and fly in and out to each city. But for many women on the road, life can be dramatically annoying and lonely. Even with FaceTime and instant connections via text, time changes often make communication with loved ones difficult. Or if you can't find your loved one, or if your loved one doesn't answer the texts or the phone, you get anxious and start to panic that your loved one is out somewhere with someone else.

If you're unattached and unworried and you have any sort of inner resources, you can read. Or watch movies. Or write songs. Or watch cable news—although recently, that certainly wouldn't help anyone get to sleep. But if you're like most of the women I've talked to or observed over the decades, or even me—who has been on these tours and been in many hotel rooms by myself—the hotel room can be a very sad spot. And then it starts. Valium or Xanax to calm anxiety. Ambien to fall asleep. Wine to just get into a "better mood" and stay up and write. Or, if you're in a group, especially in the early days when the band members still like each other, there's a "party room" where everyone hangs out because that's where the party is. That's the room where the drugs are. Despite the smoke-free policy of today's hotels, there is no specified drug-free policy. All you have to do is wander down the hallways of four star hotels, especially in Los Angeles or Atlanta, and the smell of pot comes wafting out—often from the very same rooms that have the booming bass well into the night. The hotel is the pit stop between the tour vehicle and the backstage and is just another precarious opportunity to get fucked up.

◆

On January 15, 2018, Cranberries lead singer Dolores O'Riordan died in the London Hilton on Park Lane. When The Cranberries were a big alternative band in the 1990s with a Number One hit ("Zombie"), they were considered the best band to come out of Ireland since U2. Dolores was known for her high voice and her yodeling. She was abused as a child, then had bouts of anorexia and back pain. Dolores, a mother of three, had been depressed, divorced, an alcoholic and always said she didn't think she'd live to be 50. In 2014, she was arrested for an air rage incident aboard an Aer Lingus flight. At the time, she claimed she was "stressed from New York hotels and the end of a twenty year marriage." She was said to be bipolar. When she died unexpectedly at age 46, those who'd been in touch with her said she'd been in a good mood, making plans for new music, hanging out in London with her boyfriend.

In 1996, when I talked to her in New York, she was 24 years old and told me that she'd already had knee replacement surgery. It was, she said, "from one of those freak moments when you jump too hard onstage—I damaged internal tissues. I have nails screwed into it, and while I'm not in pain now, sometimes it's weird—I can't be on that leg." She admitted that she didn't do the required physical therapy as much as she should have. "If you don't have a physio on tour with you to push you, you won't do it," she said. We talked about the rigors of touring. "You take your health for granted," Dolores said to me at that time. "But I'm very thin, and sometimes I can't lie on my leg; it hurts, and I can't sleep." She also told me she had a pre-occupation with death, that a lot of her friends and other artists she knew had overdosed or gone into detox, but she said that could never happen to her. "I suppose I was lucky," she said, "because I come from a different background. But when you're a celebrity, a lot of people come up and want to talk to you, and at the end of the day, it's very hard to unwind. That's why people take to escapism. Becoming famous . . . well, you try to hold on and be normal, but then there's always people arriving at your mother's house. . . . It's never ending, and everything changes. It's not that you change—but everyone changes towards you. Before, you were just regular. But after, people treat you differently. There have been times in my life when my personal life was just out of control."

While Dolores' unexplained death was ruled "not suspicious"—which technically means there was no foul play—rumors were that counterfeit fentanyl (the same drug that killed Prince and, reportedly, Tom Petty and Mac Miller) was found in her room. And then The Cranberries' 1993 debut album [*Everybody Else Is Doing It, So Why Can't We?*] went back on the charts. Like Janis Joplin, Whitney Houston, Amy Winehouse, Michael Jackson, Prince and so many others who have died from drugs—Dolores O'Riordan may be worth more dead than alive.

FAMILY

"I give my father his percentage," Janet Jackson told me in 1988 about the management set-up with her father, Joe Jackson. "He works for me."

As far back as Janet Jackson could remember, her family was in show business. When Janet was 3 or 4, she knew that her older brothers, the Jackson 5, were stars with big Motown hits. Janet grew up as the baby in a highly sheltered, Jehovah's Witness influenced family with a controlling, abusive, serial philandering father—who did god knows what with his own children—and a passive, enabling mother. Joe Jackson would not allow his children to call him "Dad" or "Daddy"—they were instructed to call him "Joseph." Her brothers were trained, rehearsed, micromanaged and beaten by their father. Joe made multiple—and often conflicting—deals for the Jackson 5; he even convinced a soft drink company that wanted a Jackson 5 soda to instead produce a "Joe Cola." And when Janet went into the family business, he managed her career too.

In 1988, following the huge success of Janet's 1986 album *Control*, she told me how her life had changed. We talked for several hours in a Los Angeles recording studio, and she said that she was always shy, except around her family. "A lot of things changed when we came of age," she said. At 18, she eloped with singer James DeBarge—probably to get away from her parents, who freaked out. The marriage was annulled a year later, and she moved back into the family home. (There have been persistent, but never confirmed whispers for years that there was a child from that marriage; it remains yet another one of the many unsubstantiated rumors surrounding the Jacksons.) As for her quickie marriage, she admitted that it didn't work out because they were both so busy with their careers: she was on a hit TV show (*Fame*), and he was in the DeBarge family singing group. Janet told me she was well aware of what everyone said about her favorite brother, Michael—the plastic surgery, the hyperbaric chamber—and knew how cruel the outside world could be. "People think that this [showbiz] world is so glamorous and there's no heartbreak and nothing bad ever happens to you," Janet said. "But they don't understand. They look at you like you're not even human. I grew up in this business, so I never worshipped fame. I saw right through it. Michael and I were always the closest growing up, and he always told me that when you hear bad things about yourself, instead of crying about it, just put the images in your music and become stronger, work harder."

"We were in a world of our own," Janet said about her childhood with her two sisters (Rebbie and La Toya) and six brothers (Jackie, Tito, Jermaine, Marlon, Michael and Randy). "We were very close. We would play with other kids once in awhile, but we wouldn't go to friends' houses. If we did have friends to play with, they would come to our house. Part of it was that our parents didn't want us to get on people's nerves, but part of it was that they didn't want us to get into bad things—like drugs. My parents were strict."

Janet described time in terms of when Michael had which hit

song, or when he got a lot of Grammys, or when she recorded *Control* with producers Jimmy Jam and Terry Lewis. She made no distinction between her family and her family's business. At that time, Michael was the biggest star in the world, and Janet, with the multi-platinum success of *Control*, was on a par with Madonna and Mariah Carey. And their father—who eventually had several different children with women other than his wife, and in later years was ubiquitous on award show red carpets with new "protégés"—had already been given the heave-ho as Michael's manager. He didn't remain Janet's manager for long either; in 1989, prior to her second smash album, *Rhythm Nation*, Janet signed with manager Roger Davies—the man who resurrected Tina Turner's career and also managed Sade, Annie Lennox and Pink.

Janet supported Michael at his child abuse trials (and she and Michael were probably financially supporting the rest of their less talented family members). She was front and center at Michael's memorial at Staples Center in 2009—hugging Michael's sobbing daughter Paris. She married—and divorced—two more times. Once to the performer René Elizondo Jr. and, more recently to the Qatari businessman Wissam Al Mana with whom—through the miracles of modern science—she had a child at age 50. She left that marriage, claiming verbal abuse, and has since resumed her career. Perhaps it comes as no surprise that women often re-create situations with the men in their lives that they experienced growing up with their fathers. But despite the estrangement, and the scandals, and general sleaziness of Joseph Jackson, after he died in 2018, she tearfully paid tribute to him onstage at the 2018 Essence Festival—saying that he taught his children everything they knew and her success in the music business was all due to his hard work.

✦

Families can be a source of strength or a problem when it comes to the female musician. For every example of someone who had a loving and nurturing childhood, there are horror stories of women with abusive parents or deadbeat relatives who wind up on the payroll. Or those who contribute stress to the performer's professional life. But nothing compares to the drama that can ensue when the parent becomes the manager. Call me callous, cynical, old fashioned—it's certainly generational; because I did not grow up at a time when people the age of millennials went on *vacations* with their parents—but I've always felt that parents have no place in the music careers of adult women. Perhaps it's because I left home at a relatively early age and never had a parent stand over my shoulder while I conducted an interview, or appeared on a TV or radio show, or sat in front of a typewriter or computer. (Still, growing up in the 1950s and 1960s I was, as was every girl who grew up at that time, expected to wind up in some conventional situation. Despite a liberal, Upper West Side New York City background, when I announced to my father that I wanted to be a lawyer like he was, he said, "Don't be a lawyer—women lawyers are too hard." And once, in the subway on the way to a funeral of some relative in Brooklyn—when Brooklyn was still the place for old relatives and funerals—I distinctly recall my father saying "Well, he died a happy man. He lived to see all his daughters married." And he was one of the more evolved men of his time.)

Rock and roll in the 1960s and 1970s was still considered rebellion—one step above a criminal. Parents were not part of the picture. You never saw Led Zeppelin's or the Rolling Stones' parents at their shows (except for regular appearances by Keith Richards' father, Bert, who enjoyed the backstage bar). You weren't really aware that these musicians even *had* parents. This probably all changed when popular music was considered a good career choice, and parents became involved the same way they did with child stars in the old Hollywood movie studio system. I still find myself totally mystified when I see a parent standing in some shmutzy bar, watching their child perform to twenty people—thinking that they too are in "showbiz." Or even when those twenty people are the friends and family of the performer or the parents. I've been witness to onstage debacles when a singer freezes—seeing a parent in the crowd. Or when the parent just happens to say the wrong thing before—or after—the show. Or calls to tell them about a bad review. Joni Mitchell once told me, "My parents always said nice things behind my back—but never to my face."

Women, especially, are more sensitive to judgmental nuance and stage fright. And the teensiest wrong comment after the show about the hair, or the makeup, or the costume, or the set list—can throw a woman into despair. Then again, I'm certain there are those women who want their parents to be there to see how well they're doing. And parents who are truly supportive and proud. They may be the same parents who encourage their kids to sing at family holiday gatherings. But then there are those who are vicariously living through their famous kids. And then there are the endless demands for tickets, backstage passes, better tickets, better backstage passes.

With the exception of orphans, or someone brought up by their grandparents, women have grown up with one or two parents, and the need for parental approval never goes away. Perhaps whatever problems a musician may have had with their parents propels the drive, the ambition, the songwriting, the need for applause and love that they never got at home. Or if they had encouragement and compliments at home (*"Isn't she adorable?"*), their self-esteem is so high that they can't ever get enough. But when business is involved, as it so often is, it is a potential problem. The examples of eye-rolls when a publicist or someone at the record label tells me that a father is involved, or a mother is part of the team, are too numerous to mention. Often, it ends in tears and/or lawsuits. And then the musician loses both their manager *and* their parent.

✦

"My family was not a Joe Jackson situation," Beyoncé Knowles told me in 2005. Nonetheless, her father Mathew Knowles quit his job to train, rehearse and manage Beyoncé's girl group when she was around 9 or 10 years old (she even referred to it as "boot camp"). He continued to do so through the success—and subsequent lawsuits—with Destiny's Child and the early stages of Beyoncé's solo career. He also managed her younger sister Solange before anyone cared whatsoever about Solange. It was a well known secret that often, when Mathew was making a deal for Beyoncé—either at the record label or an ad campaign—he would dangle the older, more successful Beyoncé by flat-out demanding that if they wanted Beyoncé, they had to take Solange too.

After Beyoncé's solo success, there were indications that she started demanding more control over her own career; after dating, and eventually marrying, Jay-Z—who certainly knew a lot about the music business—she had a different take on things. Despite Beyoncé's well known guarded demeanor, she owned up to occasional clashes with her father. "Sometimes it ends up being a drama," she told me, "the relationship you have with your parents. Especially when girls grow up and then, there's the business. It's a lot harder with my father. My mother is the balance. She always tells me if I don't want to do something, don't do it. But my father is a workaholic, and he wanted success for me. My mother would always try and tell me to go do something else—but I was obsessed."

"Personally," she added, "I'm very passive, and it's hard when it's your father and you're a little girl. Now, we butt heads and have arguments, but it's not that bad. I've heard real horror stories. People assume he was Joe Jackson and I had no childhood. But I had a healthy childhood. My mother would make sure I had slumber parties and hung out with other children. Even though we had tutors and didn't go to school, we hung out with other kids from school. It's harder now," she continued, "because I'm older and I know how it all works. People think my father just controls everything, but I actually control everything. And when we disagree, we disagree."

When I talked to Beyoncé's mother Tina Knowles that same year, she and Mathew were still married and she claimed everything was just fine. She admitted that they had briefly split up a few times, but they always got back together and they were still together. She did not address the rumors of his infidelity or that he fathered a child with another woman. (It was eventually revealed that he had two other children with two other women—both of whom brought paternity suits against him.)

When Tina talked about Beyoncé's work, she used the word "we"—as in "we did this," and "we did that" and, when Beyoncé sang all the nominated songs at the Oscar ceremony in 2005, "We got her ready for the Oscars." There was no question that Tina was, and always will be an important part of Beyoncé's team. After making the costumes and styling Destiny's Child, she fought with producers about how many songs Beyoncé could sing at the Grammys. She admitted that when it came to her kids, she was tough, but that Beyoncé was now taking more control. "She's a humble, grounded person," Tina said about Beyoncé, "and she'd rather *not* do something than not get the respect she feels she deserves." Tina added at that time that Mathew was not a controlling father, but that he did worry about Beyoncé taking on too much: "When you start looking at everything, you can just get overloaded."

Obviously, it got to a point both personally and professionally where Mathew's management style, and various lawsuits—to say nothing of his extramarital relationships—caused a break. In March 2011, Beyoncé fired him with a statement that read, *"I am grateful for everything he has taught me. I grew up watching both he and my mother manage and own their own businesses. They were hardworking entrepreneurs and I will continue to follow in their footsteps."*

◆

Families are often nuts. But when there is an extraordinary talent in the family, it changes the dynamic. Aretha Franklin's father was a pastor whose fiery sermons made him famous and rich—sort of the T. D. Jakes of the day. He also was a playboy and a philanderer. Aretha played piano at the age of 3; she sang in her father's church and traveled and performed by her father's side. She had her first child at age 12, another one at 14, and then married a man who reportedly was an abuser and a pimp. If it were not for her singular talent, Aretha Franklin would probably have ended up like any other teenage girl who had kids and a hopeless future.

Britney Spears, who has no such talent, still became a big pop star, had a very public meltdown and for years had her father as a court appointed conservator over her business affairs. Selena Gomez's mother managed Selena's career, until her mother threw in the towel over Selena's continued returns to her troubled relationship with Justin Bieber; Selena then fired her mother. Taylor Swift and her parents allegedly once marched into a record company president's office to complain that Taylor wasn't selling enough records in *Malaysia*.

Adele told me she started having depression when she was 10 and her grandfather died. "I felt abandoned," she said. While her grandparents didn't raise her, "They were a massive help to my mom," she said. "I'd go see them a lot, and I'd go for long periods of time." Adele had bitter feelings about her father—who she hadn't seen in years until she got famous and he sold stories about her to newspapers. "That was the worst thing that happened," she said. But she said she's always been close to her mother—who she described as "the most solid and constant person in my life."

Mariah Carey talked to me a lot about her mother and her parents' divorce, and blamed her lack of wedded bliss on never having seen a happy marriage when she was growing up. Miley Cyrus was managed by her mother and went wild. Jessica Simpson was managed by her father and went wild. Tori Amos' pastor father was deeply involved with her career. Whitney Houston's family issues have been widely documented both before and after she died in that bathtub in

In New York City in 1974 with a camera
shy Janet Jackson.

Patti Smith shares a secret with me
and the camera.

Yoko Ono and I are all smiles backstage at the Grammy Awards
in New York City, 1975.

Linda Ronstadt and I share a mirror backstage
in Tucson, Arizona, in 1976.

Annie Leibovitz photographs Ken Regan photographing me and
Linda Ronstadt backstage in Tucson, Arizona, 1976.
To the right, publicist Paul Wasserman.

Photo © Annie Leibovitz

Linda Ronstadt and me, not
smoking in the girls' room,
Tucson, Arizona, 1976.

Photo © Annie Leibovitz

Linda Ronstadt, me and an unidentified woman,
pre–Uber ride sharing in Tucson, Arizona, 1976.

Me and Dolly Parton deep in conversation.
She explains her hair.

Bette Midler fixes my hair.

Bette Midler and I share a laugh.

Out on the town with Chrissie Hynde.

A warm welcome from the great Patti LaBelle, in Los Angeles in the 1970s.

A rare portrait of me and Stevie Nicks.

With Tina Turner sometime in the 20th century.

Tina Turner and I share a private joke.

With Yoko Ono in the kitchen of her Dakota apartment,
sometime in the 1980s.

With Marianne Faithfull in the 1980s.

Patti Smith, Lester Bangs and me in a rare
sober moment at Max's Kansas City.

Smooth Operator Sade and I discuss hair and makeup.

Left to right: Paul Reubens,
John Waters, me, Björk—
fresh out of the swan dress—
and her mother Hildur Hauksdóttir
at the 2001 *Vanity Fair* Oscar party.

I'm thrilled to be with the incomparable
Mavis Staples, in Memphis, Tennessee,
in July 2002.

With Beyoncé, indoors in New York City,
circa 2004.

With Beyoncé, outdoors in Barcelona,
circa 2005.

Photo © Kevin Mazur

Patti Smith and I adorn the great Keith Richards.

Photo © Jonathan Becker

Jonathan Becker captured this special moment of me and Norah Jones
at a Tribeca Film Festival party in the early 21st century.

A rare smiling photo of me, with Gwen Stefani, at a party.

Gwen Stefani and me in 2016 at yet another party.

All we want to do is have some fun: Me and Sheryl Crow.

I'm with the in-crowd: Clockwise from back, left to right: Frances and Smokey Robinson, Gwen Stefani, an unidentified man, Suzanne de Passe, Berry Gordy, me and Sheryl Crow.

Me and the Divine Miss M.

Me, Romy Madley Croft of the xx and
my cassette recorders in New York City.

Alicia Keys, me and Beyoncé in a festive mood
at the 2015 Tidal Music launch.

With two favorites: Patty Smyth and John McEnroe.

The man in my life. Me and Richard Robinson.

Three New York City girls:
I'm smiling while Fran Lebowitz and
Lady Gaga are in a contemplative mood.

Me, Lady Gaga and Annie Leibovitz
in 2011 after a *Vanity Fair*
cover shoot.

Two New York City girls: Lady Gaga and me in Hollywood.

Gossiping with the legendary Joni Mitchell in 2019.

Both sides now: me and the lady of the canyon.

the Beverly Hilton in 2012. Early on, her father managed her; they had fights, money issues and a lawsuit that ended the management deal. Still, most of her family was on her payroll for most of her life. And one manager father, who shall remain nameless, said about his well-endowed daughter, "Those double Ds aren't going anywhere for less than a million dollars."

The mother of Romy Madley Croft of the xx died when Romy was 10. Then Romy's father died when she was 20 while she was on the road with her band. She told me that at that time, she just drank a lot to numb herself. But growing up, she had a good relationship with her father. "He was an alcoholic," she told me, "but he was lovely, very introspective, very creative and artistic. We certainly didn't have the normal kind of family life you see on TV. It was just me and him at the dinner table, and we'd sit there eating dinner, listening to a Velvet Underground album. His musical taste was very broad, and that's one of the things I cherish." Romy said that she never sang as a child: "Not in choir, not even 'Happy Birthday.' When I started to sing in the house, I did it very quietly so my father wouldn't hear; I was embarrassed. But he was a huge supporter of the band, and he encouraged me. It was never 'Go get a job.' He would have been so proud of the success we have now."

✦

When I met Katy Perry in 2011, I met her evangelical parents at the same time. They were right there on the Grammy red carpet. Apparently they'd managed to overcome their initial disapproval of the secular music Katy Perry had to sneak out of the house to hear. Clearly, they were reveling in their daughter's success. Over that weekend, I saw Katy's parents more than I saw her husband, Russell Brand. Her father was bald and wore a black motorcycle jacket; Katy described him to me as "unconventional." Despite the difference in their lifestyles, it was clear that Katy was close to her parents, and to her sister—who handled the VIP backstage tickets and passes for Katy's tours.

According to Gwen Stefani, "I grew up in a family with parents who met when they were in high school. All they wanted to do was have kids, and they're still in love. Our family had real Catholic morals, and family was sacred."

In addition to Beyoncé, Katy Perry, Gwen Stefani and Lady Gaga, Rihanna is close to her family too. She's close to her niece, to her mother (she bought her a house in their native Barbados), and she told me that when she first came to New York, she lived with her grandfather in Brooklyn. In 2015, talking to me about her mother, Rihanna said, "She knows me beyond. It's scary. She can warn me about things before they happen. But only recently, maybe in the last three years, did I start listening to her. After awhile you think you know better, or you think you know enough—and then there are enough failures that you just think, 'If only I had listened to my mom.'" She also told me that she's like a second mother to her younger brothers. But her relationship with her father, who is divorced from her mother and who was abusive to her mother when Rihanna was a little girl, had been problematic. "My father is very much a child," she said, "and it's very sad to say that. But I couldn't relate to him and where he's at in his mind and his stage in life. It's at a very immature place—and it's weird to say that when he's in his 60s. He's an amazing person, a wonderful father, super adventurous and very smart—but there are just things about him that I can't explain, I can't get a grip on, and I can't relate."

◆

There are plenty of examples of siblings in bands together. Brothers more so than sisters (AC/DC, The Kinks, Kings of Leon, Van Halen) but there also are Heart's Ann and Nancy Wilson, the Pointer Sisters, two of the Dixie Chicks, and currently, the twins Tegan and Sara. And then there is HAIM.

HAIM is a group of three sisters—all of whom have the last name Haim: guitarist/singer Danielle—who writes all the songs—the bassist/singer Este and guitarist/singer Alana. At the beginning of their career they performed with their musician parents as Rockinhaim at street fairs in Los Angeles. Now, as a trio, they've had hit albums and worldwide tours. They've joked with me that they've never fought about a boy, they all wear each other's clothes on tour, and they can't marry a boy who isn't Jewish—because their Israeli father won't approve. Despite HAIM having changed managers two times, their father—a former musician turned successful realtor—has become more involved in the business decisions of his daughters' group, causing the usual trepidation on the part of band's "real" management and record label.

Singer-songwriter Liz Phair, who was adopted by a wealthy family, told me that she grew up secure. She always knew her parents had her back, and that she had a safety net if "the music thing didn't work out." She also said she cared about what her parents thought, "because they impress me as people. But sometimes I feel like my mother is standing over my shoulder saying 'This is wrong, this is not how you should be carrying yourself.' And as such, I might not have been as brazen as I fantasized about being."

Patti Smith's late mother Beverly ran Patti's fan club—when people still wrote actual fan letters. Cyndi Lauper, who put her mother in her videos, talked to me about how she grew up thinking life was unfair because her grandmother worked, but her grandfather had to cash her checks because it wasn't legal at that time for women to have their own bank accounts. Cyndi said because her mother was a waitress, "she lost the opportunity to have other job skills." Cyndi—like Gwen Stefani and Lady Gaga and Jennifer Lopez—was another girl with a Catholic upbringing, and she said she used to ask God why he hated children—because the nuns were so mean.

✦

"I'm glad my mom is here to protect me," Brandy told me in 1999. "But I am 19, and sometimes I want to do what I want to do. Sometimes we clash. And then sometimes, if she's not there, I'll say 'Why weren't you here telling me what to do?' So I'm glad she and my dad are around all the time." In the late 1990s, Brandy Norwood was a teenage star on a hit TV show called *Moesha*. She also had a successful recording career, with such hits as "I Wanna Be Down" and a duet—"The Boy Is Mine"—with the singer Monica. Since those early days, Brandy's career has seen ups and downs: she was in movies, on Broadway, in reality shows with her brother Ray J (he of that archaic sex tape fame), on *Dancing with the Stars* and, more recently, she had a recurring role in Lee Daniels' now-canceled TV show *Star*. But when we met, Brandy was a big teenage star, managed by her mother Sonja Norwood—who had previously been a manager for branch offices of H&R Block.

I interviewed Brandy several times (once in a sauna at the Peninsula Hotel in New York City), and Sonja was always around. A strong, determined woman, she constantly was arguing with someone. She was considered a "nightmare" by record company executives, who would leave the building when they heard of her imminent arrival. When a female manager is described as "tough," it usually means they are doing a good job for their client—demanding more money for recording, tour support, video budgets or, nowadays, endorsement deals. Or it can mean that the manager is a pain in the ass and making unreasonable demands—such as insisting a less talented sibling also get a deal.

According to Brandy, who I saw fight with her mother often in hotel rooms and tour buses, "When women are strong, they're looked at like a bitch. If it's a guy, he's a strong male, taking a stand. But [my mother's] firm, and in this business, they don't accept females that way. I was raised to be a nice person and a good girl; and I'm nice, and I can be soft sometimes, so people can take advantage of that. But I'm strong inside and I don't like to be messed with either.

My mom doesn't care what anybody says about her. That's why she's successful."

✦

Then, there was Jewel. I met her in the 1990s, when despite the popularity of grunge and rap, the blonde, beautiful singer had such folk/pop hits as "Who Will Save Your Soul" and "Foolish Games." She was signed to Atlantic Records after a bidding war that resulted from word-of-mouth about a sold out stint at a San Diego coffeehouse. But way before that, as a very young girl, before her parents were divorced, Jewel sang and yodeled with her father in taverns and folk clubs in her native Alaska. She told me that her father had taught her how to read a room and an audience, and how to perform on a stage. As a teenager, she went to live with her mother, Lenedra Carroll, but there was no money, and she was, for awhile, homeless. She famously lived with her mother in her car. And in 1998 she told me, "I was aware that it wasn't usual. But when you're young and all your friends are on welfare, and you're on food stamps, you don't want to use the food stamps—so you shoplift. It's hard to talk about it without sounding precious, but it either makes you incredibly tenacious—or helpless and bitter."

Nedra (as Jewel's mother was called) wasn't Jewel's first manager; that was a woman named Inga Vainshtein who was let go after Jewel's debut album. The inevitable subsequent lawsuits that can accompany a big hit followed. Nedra quickly became Jewel's manager, and according to people who worked with her at the time and my own recollections, while she was not necessarily knowledgeable about the music business, she was sweet, mild mannered and lovely. But not weak. "I was raised very tenaciously and had a lot of grit," Jewel told me. "It drove me. Am I going to be beaten down, or am I going to do it? And I had a very unusual mom; she always encouraged me to do what kept me alive internally. She was much more concerned with my internal life; she knew if my internal life was taken care of the external would reflect it. She never assumed who I was—she'd ask me, and I think that had a lot to do with living in my car; it got to the point where she did it with me. She encouraged me to do what I wanted to do."

I asked Jewel if Nedra had been a stage mom, and she said, "No. She was liberating. My mom and I educated ourselves and she helped me psychologically and emotionally handle stuff. She helped me develop creatively and emotionally. Usually when fame happens, you can't keep up. But I'm so much more developed because of her support."

Then, at some point around 2003, she and the mother who helped her so much creatively and emotionally parted ways when Jewel accused her mother of stealing money from the charity they had formed together. They went to court. It was settled out of court. Jewel moved to Nashville, married a rodeo star, had a child, divorced the rodeo star, made a country album and wrote a memoir—in which she claimed her father had been abusive, and her mother—who she claimed was not the woman she thought she was—betrayed her. Reportedly, they have not spoken since.

◆

There are plenty of parents who support their children's dreams and are happy for their success. And there are also all sorts of jealousies and rejection and disappointment and things are never good enough that come along with the families of the famous—just like in real life. But then there are the scenarios when a star dies, and the family involvement lives on. The star is gone but not the royalties or the likeness or the publishing or the merchandising. And that's when family squabbles—especially when there's money, no real will, and deadbeat relatives who come out of the woodwork—can reach a crescendo. Aretha Franklin's four sons fought over who got to drive which one of her cars. After her death, Whitney Houston's family produced an embarrassing reality TV show about Whitney's troubled daughter Bobbi Kristina, who eventually died in a way eerily similar to her mother—a drug overdose in a bathtub. And more recently, that family has negotiated a Whitney Houston Tour—featuring Whitney as a hologram. The eternal meal ticket.

BUSINESS

The late, legendary concert promoter Bill Graham always used to say, *"It's not the money. It's the money."*

In 2018, Bette Midler told me, "I'm very careful about money, because I was poor. So I can never feel rich." Despite early warnings, Bette stayed with the same manager for almost a decade. "Aaron Russo [now deceased] came into my life and he thought the sun rose and set on me," she said. "He was a notorious club owner in Chicago, he was a tremendous character; even though he was fat, he was cute and he had a great sense of humor. We were a couple for about a year, and when I tried to break up with him, he got very distressed. So we stayed together for business, but then it got ugly. I thought he was an excellent manager—he made very good business decisions, but what I didn't know was that he had a side business—he had many, *many* side businesses. He was in the gold business, he dealt in all sorts of things I didn't want to know about. There was a little bit of drug action, there was con artistry, but I liked him because he made me laugh."

"People told me he ripped me off, but I never believed them," she continued. "In fact, before I signed with Atlantic Records and was thinking of signing with Aaron, Ahmet [Ertegun, co-founder and chairman of Atlantic Records] said, 'Do not sign with him, this is a bad man.' And David Geffen called me up and said, 'Do not sign with him.' And I said, 'I like him, I'm going with him.' I went with him, and I stuck with him, and he did a great job for me. I left him after *The Rose* because he hit me."

"He hit me twice. Once in front of Elton John—it was at the Palladium, the first time I'd been in London, it was 1979 or '80, and I did tremendous business. The people in the first row of the balcony had signs saying "*We Love You Bette*," and they turned the sign over and it said "*Show us your tits*," and it made me laugh so hard that I showed them my tits. And when I came offstage he hit me, in front of Elton, and Elton's jaw dropped. I didn't even know Elton that well then. It was the first time Aaron hit me. It was not the last."

London had been the first stop on a world tour to promote the 1979 movie *The Rose*—for which Bette got a leading actress Oscar nomination for playing a role loosely based on the rise and fall of Janis Joplin. Bette went all around the world with Aaron, and, "When we got to Australia," she said, "he hit me again. He hit me in the elevator, because I'd talked back to him or something, I don't remember. By that time, I'd been with him for about eight years. And when I came off the road, and *The Rose* came out, he said he wanted another deal. He didn't want the plain old manager's deal that he'd had, which was fifteen percent—he wanted fifty/fifty. And I'm not really good with numbers, but I'm not *entirely* stupid. So I called his assistant, I asked her to bring me all the files, and then I told him I was leaving him. He didn't sue me, I think he was quite shocked, but he was heartbroken."

◆

In 1974, Carly Simon told me that she wasn't all that interested in the business side of the music business. "In the very beginning of my career, I used to be more into the record company than I am now," she said. "Now I just let Arlyne handle it." Arlyne Rothberg was Carly's manager, and Carly said, "Arlyne is amazing. She's the best manager and the best friend anyone could have. She's not out to make money with me at all. She really believed in my talent, and wanted me to do whatever I could do in the most comfortable and best circumstances available. I don't think a man would be able to do that. I think a woman is very sympathetic to another woman in the same way. Men have treated her terribly because they're threatened by her; she's very strong. She used to be quite intimidating; I remember when I first met her I was scared of her. She's gotten softer recently—she had a baby, and she's married. . . . I'm very happy to have a woman manager."

After anyone has a big hit—the way Carly did with "You're So Vain" in 1972—the record company, then and now, wants the musician to make another one just like the last one. "I can't take that seriously," Carly told me at that time. "If I did, I'd be in the hit-making business and that's not what I do. I don't go in there to write a hit; I go in there and if out of ten songs on an album, there's one that I'm comfortable being a single, that's fine. But I don't think about it—even though I know people around me and especially at the label think about it."

She claimed she always had final approval over everything—except for one misfire: the use of her 1971 hit song "Anticipation" for a Heinz ketchup TV commercial. In the late 1970s she told me, "I gave them the rights to the song, it was agreed that I wouldn't sing it but I would approve the rendition done for the commercial. And Arlyne and I never got to approve it. It was an imitation of me, which I'm not fond of. I liked the idea as long as it didn't sound like me. But people wound up thinking it *was* me. I'm a little sorry that I did it, but I did it at the time that Sarah [her first child with James] was born and I never thought I'd work again. There was so much responsibility and I was so exhausted; I thought I'd better take the money when I could because I'll never make any money again. There was a lot of money involved, I'd just been through a very painful lawsuit where I'd lost about half the money I had, and I didn't have that much money because James' and my money have always remained separate."

✦

In the great 1959 movie *Expresso Bongo*, about the pre-Beatles London music business, the manager—played by Laurence Harvey—says to the musician—played by Cliff Richard—as they're about to sign a contract: "From now on, half of everything you make will go to you."

Money often becomes a problem, even for those who have made millions of dollars. In 1998, following the success of her album *Jagged Little Pill*, Alanis Morissette told me, "I was overwhelmed by the financial change in my life. I had a bit of paralysis and couldn't spend a penny. I started spending money on everyone but myself."

And reflecting back on her long career, Sheryl Crow told me in 2018, "My life became more complicated when I started making money. For a long time, I was freaked out. You start making money and you start paying everybody on your payroll and people commission your money. I'm super connected to the way I was raised, and I know the worth of a dollar, because as a kid, I always had to work during the summers. If I needed something, my parents bought it, but if I wanted something, I bought it. I remember buying an Anna Sui jacket for the first MTV Awards in 1980—it was $3,400—that's how much it meant to me, I still remember how much it cost."

In 1994, Sheryl had a Grammy winning hit with her catchy song "All I Wanna Do." But she told me that she hadn't made very much money from that song's success, because she owed the record label so much money for the tour support that kept her on the road six and seven months at a time. Her success came after years of kicking around Los Angeles as Michael Jackson's backup singer and trying to get a record deal. "You have to be ambitious when you're in Los Angeles," she told me. "Half of it is talent, and half of it is perseverance. There are all sorts of rejections, because in the music business, there are a thousand people as good as you are within a two mile radius, and you take a lot of abuse. Especially as a woman."

Back in 1995, she told me that if she ever made any real money, "I'd buy my manager a big house, because he really stuck with me and he's the most honest guy I've ever known. Bill Graham was my first manager, but he died; now Scooter Weintraub is my manager and he's an angel." (Twenty-five years later, Scooter Weintraub is still Sheryl's manager and she did buy him that house.)

✦

In 2017, Stevie Nicks told me that she always presented herself in a confident manner to record company executives. "Christine [McVie] and I bonded the very first week we met when I joined Fleetwood Mac. And we said we will never be treated like second class citizens by the men in this industry." I ventured that perhaps they wouldn't have been treated so well if they hadn't sold so many records. "Maybe not," she said. "But we did and we were."

Even so, there were problems. When they released her song "Rhiannon" as a single, "I didn't want it to be a single," she said. "The label didn't really believe in it, and I didn't want my 'Rhiannon' to be dragged through the mud." (It went on, of course, to be one of Fleetwood Mac's biggest hits.)

Beyoncé told me that when she played her debut solo album for her record label, even though she'd had many big hits with Destiny's Child, "You have to prove yourself over and over. I was so stressed out, because they told me I didn't have a single. They were right. I had four."

Years ago, Sinéad O'Connor said, "Doing a record deal is like getting married. Everyone gets burned when they *are* aware of the business—never mind when they're not."

In the late 1980s, Sade told me, "You don't have to be business-like when you're *making* a record. You don't think about money, you don't think about anything more than making a record your friends like, or that you're proud of. Then, of course, comes the promotion of it. And yes, making money helps you live comfortably—but you do not think of that when you start."

✦

Almost every successful female musician has had a man initially help guide her career. Cher had Sonny Bono, then David Geffen. Joni Mitchell also had David Geffen and Elliot Roberts. Linda Ronstadt had Peter Asher (formerly one half of the British singing duo Peter and Gordon, and James Taylor's manager). Beyoncé had her father, Mathew Knowles. Mary J. Blige had Sean "Puffy" Combs and record company executive Andre Harrell; then, for years, she leaned on her unfaithful, now ex-husband/manager Kendu Isaacs. Mariah Carey had her ex-husband and Columbia Records president Tommy Mottola, then manager Benny Medina, then a woman with whom she recently became embroiled in a lawsuit. Jennifer Lopez had Benny Medina, then guidance from Puffy, then Benny again. Tina Turner had Ike, then manager Roger Davies. Janet Jackson had her father, Joe Jackson, then Roger Davies. Lady Gaga had a New Jersey producer (who sued her), then manager Troy Carter, then Bobby Campbell—who worked for Troy—and always, the involvement of her father, Joe Germanotta. From the get-go, Adele has had Jonathan Dickins. Rihanna had two male producers who helped her get to Jay-Z and L.A. Reid who signed her to Def Jam, with Roc Nation's Jay Brown as her manager. Madonna had DJ/producer Jellybean Benitez, then label head Seymour Stein, then manager Freddy DeMann, and now, her longtime manager Guy Oseary (who probably gets a retainer rather than a percentage) who helped her start and oversee her Maverick Records label.

Dolly Parton had a mentor in Porter Wagoner and for years, a manager in Sandy Gallin. (There have been a few women here and there who have managed female performers, and a few women who have managed men—but they are *very* few and not always long-term. An exception is Jane Rose, who has managed the career of Keith Richards for thirty-five years.)

Still, even with a male protector, women have always had to work harder, were faced with more obstacles at every turn and didn't always think to ask for what they financially felt they deserved. There were, of course, exceptions. Longtime music business mogul Irving Azoff recently told me that in the music business, when it came to payment—to a male or a female—all that mattered was how many records or concert tickets you sold. "I remember in the 1970s we had a Joni Mitchell tour and a Crosby, Stills & Nash tour at the same time," he told me, "and Joni got three times as much as they did. You would get $10,000 to $15,000 for CS&N, and Joni was getting $35,000 a show. She played bigger buildings, like colleges, which had ten thousand seats—while CS&N played three thousand seat theaters. When Linda [Ronstadt] was on Capitol, and David [Geffen] signed her to Asylum Records, she had a bigger deal than the Eagles."

Also, the so-called million dollar deals everyone always hears about or are bragged about by artists' managers or publicists, come down to something like one million dollars to sign—to deliver seven albums—$150,000 to put in your pocket, $150,000 to record the first album and a ton of tour support and promotional support (which used to mean paying off radio programmers)—all of which is recoupable. That means it's a loan that the musician or the band has to pay back to the label before earning a dime of profit. Today, even though the entire business model has changed with downloading and streaming and commercials and direct to consumer merchandise, "The artist is still getting fucked," says Azoff. "Male and female. They're making their money from touring, branding, merchandising, publishing, and a little bit on their recorded music." So why do they still make albums instead of just concentrating on touring or their makeup or lingerie or sneaker lines? Apparently, they still care about making new music because that's what they do, that's who they are. Or, the more cynical view is that they care that the fans think that they care enough to make new music. And except for the current vinyl LP fad, for those who prefer analog or the generation that never saw them before and likes nostalgia, physical albums—CDs—have been phased out in favor of streaming—although radio still matters in country music and places where you're in a car much of the day.

And, as hard as it is to believe, people still care about the Billboard charts and Nielsen SoundScan—both of which keep track of how many albums are sold each week. Hence: "bundling"—a relatively new scam that helps the musician sell more albums and rise higher on the Billboard charts. If you purchase a concert ticket, it can be bundled with some merchandise—a t-shirt, or some nonsense like a laminated pass that might get you into a mass meet and greet with the star at a concert—and an album. Or, you can opt in to download the album along with the concert ticket, and that album is then considered a "sale." If Taylor Swift sells four slightly different versions of the same album—one with a deluxe package of lyrics or another with a bonus track—some sucker will buy all of them and that's counted as four sales. Or, if you stream the same track from an album ten times, that's also considered a sale of that album and helps it get higher on the charts. This has caused extraordinary competition and chaos in the business as well as unbelievably creative ways to sell music, concert tickets, and merchandise. And, of course, it soothes the musician's ego by making certain she gets higher on the charts.

✦

Despite the fact that every so often, women dominate those charts, women in the music business today still go through many of the same things that their older counterparts did. Lest we forget that "wardrobe malfunction"—when Justin Timberlake mistakenly ripped off part of Janet Jackson's bodice and exposed her nipple on the 2004 Super Bowl telecast. The result was that for years Janet was virtually blackballed from performing or appearing on Grammy shows. Justin Timberlake, however, was invited to headline what turned out to be a truly awful set at the 2018 Super Bowl halftime show. And we all know about how Neil Portnow, the then head of the Grammys in 2017—when there was only one woman nominated for Album of the Year (Lorde), and she was not even asked to perform on the telecast—actually said, "Women need to step up." (Which women was he talking about having to step up? The multi-Grammy winners—Beyoncé? Adele? Rihanna?) Women in the industry were so outraged by this that their public outcry did force Portnow to finally step down.

A lot of the ongoing misogyny is most obvious in the world of hip-hop. Despite the fact that rap recently became the largest selling music category all over the world, and that back in 1998–99, Lauryn Hill sold fifteen million albums and won five Grammys for *The Miseducation of Lauryn Hill*, women in the rap game have problems. There are hundreds of rappers currently recording today; only about 10 percent of them are women. For years, women were seen as bikini-clad playthings in male rap videos. Then, after Lil' Kim and Foxy Brown started performing in various stages of undress, using their sexuality the way Madonna had years before, Nicki Minaj, Cardi B and a slew of others followed. Sex sells. Label executives want their female stars to be sexualized: they still think that all women should want to *be* her, and the men should want to *fuck* her.

So, even when the stars are so famous that they can get dressed in free gowns from Balenciaga or Balmain or Givenchy, we've arrived at a time when the ensembles are getting skimpier; half-naked is the norm. (It's funny to remember that there was once a time in the 1970s when Linda Ronstadt raised eyebrows performing onstage wearing an adorable Boy Scout uniform with little shorts.) These days, it's hard to find someone other than Billie Eilish or Adele who is fully clothed in concert. All that cleavage baring and butt flaunting has reached a level that eschews any mystery whatsoever and leaves absolutely nothing to the imagination.

And then too, there are those male executives who don't want to sign a woman; they think she'll be too "expensive." The budgets won't cover the hair, the makeup, the styling. They want a diva, but they're not sure they want to front the money to pay for one.

◆

In 2016, Adele told me, "Money makes everyone act so bizarrely." While Adele didn't need the money she was making as she reluctantly trekked her way across the U.S. on tour, she said she felt an obligation to perform live for all her fans who had bought millions of her physical albums—especially *21* and *25*. "I don't come from money," she said. "It's not an important part of my life. But people are intimidated by it; it's like I'm *wearing* my fucking money. Obviously I have nice things and I live in a nice house, but money was not the goal. I just wanted to get out of where I was living when I was 'growing up.'"

"When I started out, I never had any real examples of people who had a rough time in the music business. It's not like I had a friend who was thrown around like a piece of meat. I've never been treated like that, although obviously, I've seen other artists treated like that. But when I walk into a room, and there are twelve fucking men in fucking suits who think they know more about my career than I do, I like making them really nervous."

"I hate it when artists blame their managers," Adele added. "Each time an album flops, they blame their manager. Your record just ain't fuckin' good enough. My manager and I butt heads all the time, we raise our voices, but if he says, I don't think you should do something, I'm like fine, I won't do it. There also are things that I haven't wanted to do that he said would be good for my career, and I've done them. But we probably say "No," more than any other artist. I'm a control freak, but there's no way that anyone can be involved in every single thing. I trust him completely with my career."

◆

A note here about what a manager actually does: My husband Richard Robinson once likened managing a musician to "running backwards holding up a mirror." A manager can do anything and everything from getting a record deal to negotiating the terms of that deal. Shlepping the guitars to the van after a club gig when the band is on the way up, to negotiating the arena or stadium tours when the band is big. Finding a record producer, a band, a choreographer. Working with—or fighting with—the record company. Overseeing the terms of all the concert fees, corporate gigs, merchandising, royalties on album sales or these days, streaming percentages. Getting endorsement deals. Getting the act on TV. "Creative" decisions about clothes, glam, styling, music. Getting the calls in the middle of the night that the equipment truck broke down in Detroit. Or that the guitars were stolen from the equipment truck. Helping staff the household if there's money for a household staff. Finding a house if there's money for a house. Helping to furnish the house. Making the best private plane deals or finding the best gluten-free chefs. Approving interviews and magazine photo shoots. Approving final video edits. Dealing with travel and hotel room needs. Dealing with—and often initiating—litigation. Setting up the act's social media accounts. Often pretending that the manager *is* the act on social media (although that job usually falls to the publicist). Finding doctors and dealing with the star's health issues. Preventing drug problems. Enabling drug problems. Managing drug problems. Finding rehabs or sober "coaches." Enrolling children in school. Watching the children. Paying the employees. Buying the groceries. One manager I know used to cut the food for his client right at the table. There have been managers who have become famous themselves—

Brian Epstein with the Beatles, Peter Grant with Led Zeppelin, Irving Azoff with the Eagles, Paul Rosenberg with Eminem, to name a few; most famous managers have been men, including Scooter Braun, who has been managing Justin Bieber since Scooter discovered the teenage Justin on YouTube. Scooter also manages Ariana Grande and Demi Lovato and has managed Kanye West—who has fired and hired him back on a regular basis.

There is no end to both the larger than life deals when an act is a success, to the minutiae and the chores—whether the act is big or small. The job is a combination of a parent (especially when it *is* a parent), babysitter, businessman/woman, lawyer, psychiatrist, teacher and saint. The real job is to provide support, encouragement and success to help the musician realize her hopes, dreams and ambitions. And to give advice. But if the advice is not what the star wants to hear . . . when the management is no longer the Greek chorus, if the star needs that chorus, the partnership can fall apart. It is, frankly, very often a thankless task. And when the act has a success, they did it all by themselves. And when they fail, they usually say it's the manager's fault.

◆

Lorde is a successful young woman who had no hesitation walking into a record label meeting and telling the executives what she wanted to do. "I never felt like it was frightening or a big deal," she told me in 2017. "I was so sure of what my work needed, and that only I could protect it. What else would I do? I was a teenager and I knew what wouldn't fly with other young people. But a lot of it had to do with being 16 and having no qualms about walking into a room and shooting down a bunch of million dollar ideas." And, she added, "I've been told that they could work out the numbers of how recognizable I am in certain markets—which is not a good thing to know. I've told people I don't want to know the numbers; I don't want to walk around with a number in my head."

In 1994, Salt-N-Pepa's Cheryl James told me, "As females, you have to be more demanding and more assertive. But that's not just in the music business, it's in any business. It's sad but it's true; you just have to let people know you're intelligent, that you can do the job, and not question you because you're a woman. If you're wimpy and you take a lot of crap from people, they're going to give it to you."

"The reason Salt-N-Pepa have been around so long," she continued, "is that we have never limited or confined ourselves to any rules of what we can or cannot do. A lot of rappers feel that they have to just be a certain thing and only that thing, but we don't accept that. We do what we want to do. Our expectations of what we think we can do are very high."

Joan Jett has been in a partnership with Kenny Laguna since the breakup of The Runaways in 1979. Laguna, a musician, songwriter and producer, is more than just Joan's manager. He and his wife Meryl, and their daughter, Carianne Brinkman—who runs their Blackheart record label—and Joan's band, the Blackhearts, are Joan's family. Everyone says this about the people they work with, or their "team"—but in Joan's case it's really true. "It's like a gang," she told me in 1982, "but without the violence. Kenny did not tell me how to dress or how to talk; we wrote songs and they spoke for themselves. Even though he's not onstage, he is a big part of the band; he'll play things on the record or he'll help with the arrangements. But it's definitely not a Svengali situation, I'm not his puppet. It's just good to know that there's someone around to make sure you don't run off or get into trouble somewhere."

While Joan has basically been slogging away on the road for over forty years, despite her recent (and long overdue) induction into the Rock & Roll Hall of Fame, she had the usual problems with radio: "I was told, 'We can't play you on the radio,'" she told me in the 1980s. " 'We're playing a woman already. We're playing Pat Benatar.'"

Pat Benatar may have had radio airplay in the 1980s, but things weren't all that easy for her either. Like Alanis Morissette, she felt she was a "victim of other people's ideas." In 1986, she told me, "There was a time when I felt like just chucking it all because I was trying to be my own person and I got caught up in what everyone else wanted me to be. Now I'm in control of everything, because otherwise what happened before will happen again. Maybe because I'm little, people think I'm easy to push around, and I'm not. You didn't know you'd have to be the big business mogul, the corporate woman, and maybe you don't have to be. But I don't want to wake up in ten years and have someone say, 'Sorry, the money's all gone.' I work too hard," she said. "I've got to care. I know where the money goes—I worked in a bank."

In 1984, Cyndi Lauper told me, "At first, they wanted me to be Pat Benatar. Then, when I was being myself, they said you're just like Debbie Harry. I didn't do the business thing, I just did the work. But I went through a lot of stuff. My albums weren't promoted right and I was touring and I kind of lived under the tyranny of what I was allowed to do, or what I was told to do, or what I was told I shouldn't do. I'm not a rules kind of girl. I had to go back to doing what I knew was right for me. I was tired of fighting for years and years. You can't take somebody who comes from left field and try to make them be mainstream."

In 2010, Donna Summer told me that in the beginning of her career, she was incredibly ripped off because her deal was with the German producer Giorgio Moroder, who then licensed her to Casablanca Records in the U.S., and the German mark to the dollar was not in her favor. "Later, when I got successful," she said, "I tried to rectify it as much as I could. But part of the problem was that [Casablanca label head] Neil Bogart wanted to keep selling records and I wanted to grow as an artist. There definitely were conflicts. Neil wanted to give 'Bad Girls' to Cher, but I wrote the song, and if anybody was going to sing it, it was going to be me. Neil thought it was too rock and roll," Donna continued, "and it sat in a closet for two years. Then I went back to Germany and played it for Giorgio and for Neil and then, he liked it. The same song. Then I wrote 'She Works Hard for the Money' because of all the women who work hard and aren't paid properly. They basically run companies for their bosses and their bosses take all the credit. Neil and I definitely had our conflicts, but we resolved them and in the end," she said, "he was a mensch."

◆

Radio airplay for women was a problem in the 1980s, and in country music especially, being a woman definitely still has its disadvantages. Kacey Musgraves won the Grammy Album of the Year in 2019 as well as the Country Music Association's 2018 Album of the Year Award. But despite all of her accolades, awards, and record sales, she still is considered somewhat of an "outlaw" in Nashville because she sang about smoking pot and gay marriage. Kacey was signed by Luke Lewis (he also signed Ryan Adams, Willie Nelson and Lucinda Williams), who was a champion for all kinds of music. "He signed me," Kacey said, "and told me, do whatever the hell you want to do. Then he left the label, and I was devastated. But I was already doing what I was doing and what I wanted to do, so no one could come in and change it. Not that I would have let them anyway."

But, Kacey said, "Every measure of success in country music is based on whether you're getting support from country radio. Critical acclaim, Grammys, even the quality of the music—none of it matters. What matters is how much radio play you're getting. And when it comes to that mindset, women do not get the same support when it comes to radio play or festival billing. There are indications that it's changing, but I haven't seen any hard proof yet."

In 1997, Erykah Badu talked about the state of soul music and told me, "The music and the music business have two totally different agendas. The art has never left, we just don't get to hear it as much because of the radio programmers' ideas of what soul music is. For awhile, every single song on the radio sounded exactly alike: the same beat, the same kick, the same snare drum, same bassline, same samples and you just didn't know one from the other. For most of the 1990s, people were led like cattle by the music programmers." However, Erykah said she was very "blessed" with her record company, who let her co-produce her debut album in 1997. "The president of my record label knew exactly what I wanted to do, he appreciated me and he allowed me to be me. He didn't try to dress me in any kind of way, or put any kind of music on me; I didn't have those kinds of problems at all."

✦

The record business has always been thought of as one of the sleaziest and more corrupt sides of show business. In the music business, there are so many ways to steal or hide profits from record sales or now, downloaded singles, publishing royalties, or even concert grosses. A long time ago, Ahmet Ertegun told me, "Etta James really didn't care about the money—she *wanted* the Cadillac instead."

(Also, let's look at the word "artist," and how deceptive that word can be in this industry. Around the mid to late 1990s, musicians started being referred to as "artists" instead of singers or guitarists or bands. Call me cynical, but I feel that by using that term for every single singer, rapper or guitarist, they get unearned gravitas and an exaggerated sense of grandeur. And more importantly, it also flatters them—which makes it that much easier to rip them off.)

You'd need to take a course in the music business (and there are now plenty of them) to understand royalty rates and how people get ripped off, or the tenets of entertainment law, or percentages from streaming vs. physical CDs, or international synch rights. I start seeing triple when people describe any of that to me. One thing to know is that the writer of the song makes more money than the performer who sings it. So Aretha Franklin made less from "Respect" than Otis Redding, who wrote it. Dolly Parton, who refused to split publishing royalties with Elvis Presley on the song she wrote—"I Will Always

Love You"—made six million dollars when Whitney Houston made it a hit—much, much more than Whitney made for singing it. Carole King made way more money on "You've Got a Friend" than James Taylor did, even though his version was the smash hit. Then there's the money that does not go to the artist when their song is played on the radio or now, on YouTube—because it's all considered promotion that helps the artist's global "brand." Despite the analytics and research and focus groups, no one knows which song is going to be a hit, they never have. Had they been able to figure out the formula, everyone would have one. Granted, every few years there certainly are some formulaic songwriters who churn out a bunch of same sounding hits—for awhile. For years, everyone in the music business wanted to sign "the next Beatles." I remember in 1975, my husband Richard said, "The next Beatles is going to be a machine." And of course, the music business fought the digital revolution as long as it possibly could. Obviously, it was generational, but they sued their *customers*, and it took them years to figure out a way to actually *make* money from this "machine."

Ahmet Ertegun always said you walk along and if you're lucky, you bump into a genius. He probably was referring to Ray Charles or Aretha Franklin, but knowing him, he also could have meant Led Zeppelin. Clive Davis has been praised for years for having gone to the Monterey Pop Festival to sign Janis Joplin; but quite frankly, you would have had to be an idiot to not know about Janis Joplin by 1967. Yes, Clive signed Whitney Houston—after her mother Cissy brought her to him—but he did not sign Bob Dylan or Bruce Springsteen (John Hammond did). Yet, somehow, that's gotten all shmushed into his bio. As for Clive's "magic ears" that pick singles, some musicians who've worked with him have told me he never picked their singles. As with many things, the myth is often greater than the reality.

Hence, the music business is replete with terrible business encounters, numerous lawsuits and rejections—and while George Michael sued his record label, and for years David Bowie had to pay half of what he made to a former manager, and Prince wanted out of his label deal, and both Billy Joel and Bruce Springsteen couldn't record for years because of management disputes—more often than not, the bad stories are women's stories. Destiny's Child was dropped from Elektra Records before they signed with Columbia. Lady Gaga was dropped from her first record label. After Kesha became embroiled in the aforementioned lawsuits with her producer Dr. Luke (her claims were eventually dropped but his are still pending), she still was prevented from recording new music for anyone else because she was signed to that guy's production deal.

The Australian rapper Iggy Azalea told me, "When I started out, I had no business people, and one person said, 'Let me handle everything for you, and I'll get this guy and this guy,' and then they're all in cahoots. Other people were in control of everything. They tell you, 'Well, we're paying your rent,' but you don't have any money. I signed a fuckload of shit I wish I had never signed and I still have to pay for it. It sucks, because if you get successful, you still have to pay people off who were around when you were seventeen. In no way were they helpful to me or did anything significant in what I achieved, but unfortunately, I was trigger happy and now they get to reap the benefits of my hard work."

◆

Anita Baker was told by her very first label that she "couldn't sing." In the 1990s, Anita told me, "They said I didn't have what it took to make it in the music business. At that time, as naïve as I was, I thought that what it took to make it in the music business was talent, and so they thought I didn't have talent. I've since come to realize that talent isn't all there is to making it in the music business. But I stopped singing. I put my record player and my radio in my mother's house. In my mind, I buried it. I moved back to Detroit, waited tables for six to eight months, then answered an ad for a receptionist. I moved from being a receptionist to being in charge of a workers' benefit program, and I learned word processing. I was earning five figures a year, which for someone who was not a college graduate was a lot. I had a week's vacation, I had my own apartment, and I was very proud. But I had to let my music dreams go."

Two years later, she got a call from someone who told her, "We don't want to just record you, we want to make you a star." She said, "That was the clincher. He got me. So I packed up, and in 1982 I went to LA against the advice of my family, and in 1983 my album *Songstress* was released. That album charted in 1984, and we were looking to record another album," she said. "But the company did not allow us to record another album, which meant I'd have to stay on the road—which I didn't want to do because I was playing small clubs and small clubs will kill you. I came off the road, got my 'salary' of two hundred dollars a week, which was what that company paid me at that time, and waited to do the next album. I had never had a manager before; so I went and got management, and my manager told me you can't sit around for a year waiting to make a record, you've got to keep hammering. It took a *year* for him to get a dialogue going with the executive branch at the label, and they basically said, 'Do what we want or you can drop dead.' So my manager said, 'We're not going to drop dead, we're going to walk.'"

Attorneys were consulted, notification of breach of contract was sent, but one year later, Anita won the freedom to pursue other employers. She signed with the major label Elektra, but immediately after signing, she was sued by her original label. "I was giving depositions in the daytime and recording at night," she told me. "I dealt with it. I got guts that I didn't even know I had."

✦

In 1997, Chaka Khan, who reportedly had a lot of problems with record labels about the "vision" for her career, told me, "I have to take my hat off to a lot of these guys who start their own labels. Because they start their own labels and make deals with big companies and get their stuff out there and have full artistic control. They don't have people telling them what they can't sing, or what they can't do. And there's a lot of racism in this business. Because of the color of my skin, they expect me to be a certain type of artist; I'm actually much more versatile than they think."

When Rihanna went to Def Jam to sign with L.A. Reid and Jay-Z, she had already had an unsuccessful audition with J Records, and in 2016 she told me, "It was good that I went to J Records first, because I needed to feel rejection. I needed to feel the real industry. But I remember later on, there was a big discussion with the Def Jam marketing department about what kind of artist was I? Was I urban [the industry's term for black music and hip-hop] or pop? This was the first time I ever heard those words. I never knew there was a difference. Coming from Barbados, I never even knew there were genres of music. I just knew there was music you liked, and that was it. Eventually I kind of got it: would I be gearing more towards my culture and gearing to the urban audience, or would I be gearing to the kids who listen to Z100?" Eventually, of course, Rihanna was successful with both.

The day Rihanna auditioned for Jay-Z and the other Def Jam executives, they made her and her lawyer stay in the building for about twelve hours because they didn't want to take the chance that she would leave and sign with another label. "We signed the deal at three a.m. in the morning," she said, "and it was a great deal, an impressive deal."

According to Forbes, Rihanna is the world's richest female musician—more because of her clothing, lingerie, and beauty lines and a deal with retail giant LVMH than for her albums, which she releases at her own glacial pace. But this was not always the case; there was a time when she had a very low six figure amount in her bank account despite having had hit records. But now, Rihanna owns her own master recordings. For years, musicians couldn't own their own catalogs; record labels owned the masters probably in perpetuity, and it took people years and years to fight to get the rights to their own music. (A recent example of a battle over masters is when Scooter Braun purchased the rights to all of Taylor Swift's masters for $300 million. Her solution: the same as what many musicians now do— they just re-record their early "master" songs so they own those themselves.)

Rihanna told me, "I worked very hard and I know when to cooperate and when I've earned the right to call the shots. Getting my masters is a very big deal and it was the right opportunity for me. I think it's important for young women to see that a woman who's in a position of power can control her own product—even in an industry that's so dominated by male executives."

✦

What industry is *not* a male-dominated industry?

In the music business, the men who run things are mostly in their 50s and 60s (some are in their 70s and 80s), and they worked their way up from radio promotion or marketing departments of various labels. There are a few examples of early and important female executives: Suzanne de Passe at Motown Records in the 1960s, Sylvia Robinson—co-owner of Sugar Hill Records—in the 1970s and Monica Lynch at Tommy Boy Records in the 1980s. Today, there are only five truly major female executives, four of whom *really* run important companies, and three of whom I've talked to off the record. One came up through the 1960s concert business at her manager father's knee. She told me that she saw the blowjobs backstage behind the stacks of Marshall amplifiers at the concerts in the 1970s. Janis Joplin snuck into her room once at a Holiday Inn to smoke a joint. She regularly held $15,000—the night's "settlement"—in her purple and green suede fringed purse when she went to Ratner's with her father after a Fillmore East show, because, she told me, "no one would think a kid had that kind of money in her bag."

Another woman started as an intern at a management company,

then became an assistant to the head of a record label, to the head of promotion and marketing at that label, to the president of a label, to the chairman, where she now oversees budgets, corporate, promotion, marketing—everything except the "creative." Another one ran nightclubs, then went into business with a world famous artist and mogul; she now runs his billion dollar company. The degree to which they project confidence and efficiency is impressive. Two of them went to at least one year of law school, they all can read a spreadsheet and QuickBooks and they use expressions like "marketplace value." They've all personally been through abuse, competition, jealousy, but mostly, hard work. They also all had the encouragement, support and protection of their male mentors. And while they all expressed it slightly differently, they all said to me, "I don't care about my title; just give me the power and let me do my job." Two of them think of their artists as "their kids." One of them told me, "When I was at a major label, I was 34 years old, this Jewish girl from New York City, and a 57 year-old man in Nashville had to report to me. Let me tell you, he was not happy about it. And then what was worse, a year later I had to fire him. That did not go down well. But I think in this day and age, if a man has to report to a woman, it's not that big a deal. A lot of this is generational." Another one said, "I have a great advantage in signing a woman. Women come in and see me and they see a different kind of leader—someone who is sensitive to their needs. I give the maternal vibe, but I also give the 'I'm going to kill for you' too."

And yet, one of these women told me it took her awhile to ask for what she felt she deserved financially because she didn't want "to make waves." And another one said that even though she runs meetings in conference rooms, there are still men who will talk over her, or when she doesn't smile they think she's a bitch, and there is always—always—the adjective "tough," and not in a complimentary way. These are women who make millions of dollars a year—yet a few of them have wrestled with the work/life balance. When a woman executive has a child but wants to be the first one in the office in the morning and go to every concert or event at night, it's the same juggling act as in every business. With the music business so skewed toward nightlife, if you're a woman and a mother, there is a lot of guilt involved. Now if someone could just figure out a way for a *man* to give birth . . . I mean, they're not that far off. Surely it could be a possible medical procedure in the not too distant future.

✦

In the 1970s, Linda Ronstadt told me that the minute she met Peter Asher, "I knew I could trust him. And I've never been wrong. I've had some horrible experiences, but they've only served to sharpen my instincts. In fact, as my manager, Peter does manipulate me, but for good reason, and there's nothing wrong with being manipulated if you're aware of it and willing to cooperate. I'm lazy. If Peter didn't kick my ass, I wouldn't work."

Linda added, "People have asked me if being a woman and having a lot of male employees—in my band and crew—makes it hard. Of course it's been difficult, but it's never been impossible. I know a lot of girls who say, 'Well, I'm a chick and they won't hire me to play guitar' and they use it as an excuse. I find that musicians are musicians, and they just love to play. I get real tired of that 'She plays real great for a girl' kind of thing. I get tired of anyone who even thinks that—because you either play well or you don't."

For most of my own career, I just thought I was underpaid because I was a music journalist, not because I was a woman. I just forged ahead. I assumed that all music journalists were underpaid. But then Jon Landau, who had been a music journalist, went on to manage Bruce Springsteen. And Cameron Crowe, who'd been a music journalist, made—and is still making—big Hollywood movies. When I convinced Sony president Walter Yetnikoff to sign the Clash and Elvis Costello in the 1970s, I never even thought to ask for a finder's fee. In retrospect, I now realize the difference in the way men and women felt they were "allowed" to act or pursue opportunities. Like drugs, women hardly ever talked to me about money—unless it was about how they didn't care about it (Adele), or it wasn't appropriate to discuss (Beyoncé), or the many horror stories of how they got ripped off. But they didn't really talk about the actual figures. The only musicians who talked in depth and at great length about money were Jimmy Page and Mick Jagger—both of whom complained often and loudly about the taxes they had to pay in England.

Courtney Love told me in 2017, "When you're young, you don't listen. Stevie Nicks warned me," Courtney said. "She told me she lost fortunes—and when she said fortunes, she didn't mean little namby-pamby fortunes. She meant part of her empire. And the band kept her on tour even when she didn't want to be. But I didn't listen to her advice." Courtney talked about a seriously bad personal and managerial situation she got into after Kurt Cobain died. She had been dating the actor Edward Norton but broke up with him to be with someone who—as she claimed—"seduced me, and kept me pretty stoned on Oxycontin and Vicodin. I wanted to numb myself, mainly from him. It was a ridiculous mistake. But I couldn't get rid of him. I left my manager Peter Mensch [who also managed the Red Hot Chili Peppers and Metallica] for him. It's every rock and roll cliché—you're a great meal ticket. I couldn't get rid of him. I used to hit him, I kicked him, I cheated on him like crazy, and he would not go away."

Eventually, she got rid of him, but she was still involved in an ongoing legal battle over money with the two living former Nirvana members, Dave Grohl and Krist Novoselic. "There was litigation—bizarre litigation," Courtney said. "Chaos. They justified it by saying, 'She's on drugs, she doesn't deserve it, we'll just take it.' I *was* on drugs, but I was pretty lucid. Dave Grohl and I had beef about this for about twenty years, but now we're friends and we buried the hatchet and I'm in an LLC with him and will be for the rest of my days."

✦

Generally, things are better for women in the music business now. Not always wonderful—unless you're having huge hits—but better. The 20 year-old singer/songwriter King Princess, who grew up around her father Oliver Straus' recording studio in Brooklyn, told me, "What I noticed about women in the studio was the lack of women producing themselves. This was ten years ago, but they'd come in, record a whole album, then come back with the edits that the label made, and they'd re-record the whole album again. My dad and I would talk about the politics of the thing; he'd comment on what was wrong about their deals and what the labels were saying—but it was startling to watch music get mutilated. And there was only one instance of a woman producing her own music."

"I watched a documentary on Joan Jett," King Princess continued, "and it seems that no matter what genre you're in, if you're a woman, after years and years of the same shit, the label only knows how to deal with you in one way: they want to see marketable and packageable. It's changing—that's the good part. Women are getting more resourceful and finding alternate ways of getting into the business."

STAGE FRIGHT & BAD REVIEWS

"This is the first year I felt truly unbridled confidence," Lorde told me in 2017. "I'm a very shy person. I'm a writer, and writers are some of the most introverted kooks out there. But this is not an introverted job, and I have to bridge the gap and do what needs to be done for the work—which is to perform in front of twenty thousand people at something like Coachella. I really have to bargain with myself, and talk myself down to get on that stage. It's not an easy thing. I have horrific stage fright. Every time I do it I think, this is the last time . . . you have to draw yourself out in such a way that you think you can never do it again."

Adele told me that she used to get so nervous that projectile vomiting was involved before—as was crying after—a show. Now she says she just gets nervous. "I'm not very confident chatting away to the audience," said the woman who is known for having such a great connection to her audience. "I feel like they're probably having a shit time. That perhaps I should talk less."

Years ago Sinéad O'Connor told me she was "terrified" onstage, so, "I look at the floor. I can't look at the audience. You throw yourself onstage and to the public so that you can overcome shyness." Romy Madley Croft told me that at first, she was so nervous and shy that the xx performed onstage in near darkness. In 1985 Sade told me, "I'm getting better, but I'm afraid of performing. I don't think I'll ever *not* be nervous." And King Princess said she used to be nervous to perform onstage, but is more comfortable now, "because I'm usually stoned."

Annie Lennox told me, "It's very daunting to go onstage. It's like walking a tightrope; you could go either way. You could fall off or go straight on that rope. There have been times I felt I had to leave; I've gone onstage so full of paranoia and nerves I almost hallucinated."

After years of writing songs in New York City's Brill Building, then recording an album in a Los Angeles studio with producer Lou Adler, Carole King was apparently so petrified of performing in public that James Taylor had to practically push her onstage to sing a duet with him.

Back in the 1970s, Linda Ronstadt told me, "One time, the anticipation of going on the road was so bad, I wasn't even admitting to myself how scared I was. I threw up on the way to the airport. I was so scared, I was a wreck. And the first week of rehearsals, I couldn't eat anything at all; I was taking stomach relaxers and Maalox. I thought I was getting an ulcer. But I signed all those contracts, and you think well, you either go home and have a nervous breakdown, or you just show up and do it. I got drunk a lot on that tour—which I don't like and I don't like people who get drunk. You don't sing as well, but I got a couple of shows under my belt not being afraid, and then I didn't have to drink to get loose. I'm always scared—even when I go into the recording studio. You never really get more confidence in what you're doing, but I get more ability to have confidence in being able to handle my fear. I know I'm going to be afraid, but I know it's not going to send me out of the room in tears."

One of the most well known cases of stage fright was Carly Simon's, who in 1974 told me, "I started out as an opening act and I didn't feel scared, because I didn't think they were coming to see me. As I became more and more successful, I got more and more scared, and I wouldn't perform live." At the time, she was uncomfortable talking about it. She discussed potential solutions she had considered—like performing in total darkness with people just wandering in. But people paying to see her was the problem. "If I feel the spotlight is on me, I'm terrified, I prefer to be performing in a club with drinks clinking or something, I'm not afraid of doing a bad show; it's like a fear of flying—of being in a closed in space. I'm afraid of being trapped."

✦

I have asked all of the women I've talked to who have stage fright, or get nervous, or have fears and doubts—why choose this particular job? They've all said similar things: they'd be happy just making records, but then you have to be able to perform live to promote the music you make that you want people to hear. Or they eventually learn to live with it. Or they take beta blockers or have a few drinks or smoke a joint. Also, with practice, it gets better. It gets so much better that I have heard horror stories of potential mishaps that could totally derail someone's career, and yet, the audience doesn't have a clue.

These women only seem to have it together. Obviously, the more anyone does it, the better she gets. Beyoncé always insisted she was shy, so she had to create her "Sasha Fierce" stage persona to be able to do what she does onstage. Nowhere was this more evident than when she performed all the songs at the 2005 Oscars. In 2005, she told me, "When I did the second song, the Andrew Lloyd Webber song from *Phantom of the Opera*, my shoe wasn't on. It wasn't snapped. So when I went down the stairs, not only was my shoe not on, my ear monitor was not on. The sound was bouncing, and I'm thinking, 'Oh my god, my shoe's not on and my monitor isn't on and this is going to be embarrassing. I'm going to fall down the stairs.' I'm all offbeat, looking at the conductor, trying to keep time. . . . And then, when I get down the stairs, my shoe comes off. It's stuck in the tulle in the bottom of the dress. So I'm singing on one tiptoe, trying to balance it. It was a mess."

However, Beyoncé's professionalism—from years and years of training, practicing, rehearsing, performing—was such that the millions watching on television had no idea this was happening. This was not the case when Adele sang at the Grammys in 2016 and something went awry with the piano mics. They fell on the piano strings, and it threw Adele off. It sounded like a guitar and as if the entire song—"All I Ask" from her smash album *25*—was off key. She knew it was happening, anyone who knew the song and was listening could tell, and afterward, Adele was devastated and in tears. When I talked to her about it in 2016, she agreed with me that should that ever happen again, she should just stop and start over. And at the 2017 Grammys, during her tribute to George Michael (who had died on Christmas Day, 2016) when her pitch was slightly off, she stopped and started again.

Jennifer Lopez is another performer who is so seasoned that once, at Staples Center during a performance of "On The Floor," her hit with Pitbull, "I came out from underneath the stage at the end of the song," she told me in 2011, "and boom, in the middle of my song, the entire sound system goes out. This has never happened in the history of Staples Center, they don't even know how it happened, it was such a freak accident. Meanwhile, I'm singing, my mic is on, the music is blaring, and I hear nothing. I think my ear monitors went out, so I popped one out, I hear nothing. I pop the other one out—nothing. I'm like, what the fuck is going on, I'm not hearing myself. But I keep going and the dancers can hear me, so they keep dancing. Pitbull's still on the stage, the guys are playing percussion, I'm still singing and dancing, and we all got into a circle in the middle of the stage . . . there was so much adrenaline. Eventually the sound came back on. My manager told me anyone else would have left the stage." There was another incident when J.Lo fell in the middle of a number but jumped right back up and made it appear as though that fall was deliberate, part of the routine.

✦

The internal fears and doubts never really go away. Many of these women worry that they're faking it. They worry that really, down deep, they're a fraud, an imposter, have nothing special, just got lucky, they're doing the same old thing, people will lose interest, the next big thing is right behind them. Men have doubts and panic attacks and anger and depression too. Men worry about their looks, losing their hair, staying in shape, not having a hit, not making money, not getting an erection. With the exception of the latter, they're not immune to the same problems women have. But let's face it, women have greater burdens of being the caretakers, the more involved parent . . . they worry more about their age and their looks—for no one is judged on their looks the way women are. And nothing can send a woman spinning into despair the way a bad review can—to the point where she might actually not want to leave the house.

No matter how big the star, and no matter how much they claim they never read them, they read them. And years later, they can quote one line out of one bad review—even if there were dozens of good ones.

✦

In 1977, Jann Wenner had moved *Rolling Stone* magazine from San Francisco to New York City. Despite the fact that he hired the former *Detroit Free Press* columnist Loraine Alterman (who later married the actor Peter Boyle and is currently a Broadway producer) to run the New York office, that magazine was a boys' club. All the main album reviewers and feature writers were men. There was that *Hunter Thompson thing*. Jann was reportedly not nice to his female staffers who—with the exception of Loraine and photographer Annie Leibovitz—were not memorable. Despite the fact that Annie made her initial reputation at that magazine, she certainly went on to have a prominent career post–*Rolling Stone*. Jann and I never got along; I thought he was a bully. But there was a time when *Rolling Stone* mattered. One bad review could seriously stain a musician's reputation. That was not only limited to women—men were eviscerated too. One blistering John Mendelsohn review of Led Zeppelin, in which he wrote that "Robert Plant sings notes that only a dog could hear" was so mean, that the band could not stop talking about it for years. *I* still remember it. Years later, of course, that same magazine listed Zeppelin as one of the best bands ever in the history of the universe. But when it came to women, most of the reviews were often sexist and downright cruel. (There was the aforementioned chart of all the men Joni Mitchell had reportedly slept with during the Laurel Canyon scene. No such chart was ever published about Mick Jagger.)

"I went to a singing teacher," Bette Midler told me in 2018, "because Jon Landau gave me a bad review for my second album in *Rolling Stone*. It basically ruined my life. I ruined my voice because of Jon Landau. He said I sounded 'callow.' I started to panic—and everyone is susceptible to this. I'm not the only one—Eric Clapton broke up Cream because Landau said he was a 'by-the-book' guitar player."

In 2018 Sheryl Crow talked to me about the rumors about her in the *National Enquirer*: "They said I was a heroin addict and I was having Michael Jackson's baby. The Michael Jackson thing was, I think, an inside job; they were trying to align him with a woman. As for the heroin rumors—well, I guess I was so much more fabulous than I thought." But the thing that really got to her, and so much so that she remembered it decades later, was a particular bad story. "I was on a plane to Nova Scotia," Sheryl said, "at the end of a touring cycle, and I had sworn off reading anything about myself because I'd seen a picture of me in *Glamour* magazine, I'd had my hair cut, and I looked like a soccer mom. But I was sitting on this plane and there was a copy of *Rolling Stone* next to me, with a piece on me written by David Fricke. It was so ugly and so personal—it was just a weird thing. I was just stunned. And for three to four days I carried this sick feeling around with me, and I never read anything about me again. I don't even watch myself on TV."

It wasn't just *Rolling Stone* that could be unkind. I wrote such a sarcastic piece about The Runaways in *Creem* in the 1970s that years later, I apologized to Joan Jett. That all girl band was made fun of, turned into sex objects to the point where Joan has said, "We got tagged with all that sex shit, when all we wanted to do was rock. We were aware of what the press was saying, but we didn't care—we were just happy to be in a rock and roll band."

In 1995 Mariah Carey told me, "I guess I had a misconception. I thought the job of a reviewer was to inform the buying public of a record in an unbiased manner. It gets to the point where if someone gives me a good review, of course it makes me feel good, but then I immediately go to that place where I think well, what is this other guy gonna say? The bad stuff stays with you so much longer. And even if you try to make yourself feel better by thinking well this other person said this good stuff, the bad still penetrates you. There's a guy who seems to be very bitter, and every time I put out an album, he reviews it, and basically he says this is the worst thing ever made and don't buy it. Now I admit that I was glad when I got a bad review of my very first show, because it helped me get to the next level. But why do they have this guy reviewing *every single one* of my albums when he so obviously hates me?"

In 1997 Patti Smith—who was an instant and constant music press darling for years—released her *Dream of Life* album, produced by her husband Fred "Sonic" Smith. It was the first and only time they had collaborated on a music project and Patti had high hopes. "I did have expectations that the album would be better received, and when Detroit pretty much ignored it, I thought with pride, well, I can count on New York. And it was brutally panned in the *New York Times* and the *Village Voice*. I didn't really care for myself, but I wanted to show Fred that the city would be behind us."

"I know we had people who liked it," she continued, "but with the way the music business machinery is, we couldn't get much radio airplay. I can say truthfully I don't care that much about these things for myself, but these things can be hurtful, and I felt bad for Fred."

◆

Stevie Nicks told me in 1976, "The good things go unnoticed. The bad things are the ones everyone knows. The worst interview you ever do on TV, the one you hope no one sees, is the one your parents have on video cassette when you go home." She added, "I got a horrible review once from John Rockwell in the *New York Times*, and I never forgot it. I was so nervous for our show at Madison Square Garden. I flew my parents out for it—and I was so terribly nervous I didn't eat, I drank too much, I was out there onstage, and it was a disaster, I just knew it. Then the bad review comes out and everybody knew about it, because it was in the *paper*, and that paper goes all the way to Phoenix, Arizona, to my parents." (Today, of course, between Twitter and online media, the bad reviews are instantaneous and go much farther than Phoenix, Arizona.)

"Don't they realize when they write something like that that you get so bummed you have to go to Mexico and hide," Stevie said. "There are just bad nights. But the next time I came to New York, I didn't leave my hotel room for eight days. I slept, I did yoga, I exercised, I prayed. I never went shopping. I came to the city with combat boots on saying no one will ever write anything like that about me again. And he did take it back: saying 'This writer could have been wrong'—by the way, about the show he came to for about ten minutes. He did *not* say, 'I'm sorry I ruined your life for three years.'"

MUSIC & INFLUENCES

"My mom loved Anita Baker," Beyoncé told me in 2005, "and Donny Hathaway, and Rachel Ferraro—who was a jazz singer. So I grew up with all that. And my dad had this Motown series, which was just the most fascinating thing—especially The Supremes—I was obsessed." When I asked Beyoncé if she had listened to any of the rap music that was so popular when she was growing up, she said, "To be honest, I had to sneak it, because of the profanity. I liked it to a certain extent, but I was just in love with soul music. That was my life. When my friends would come over, we'd listen to rap, but I never loved it as much as I loved Anita Baker or Luther Vandross."

I remember when Beyoncé once told me she could rap, but it wasn't until I saw her video with Jay-Z for "Apeshit" that I realized just how well she can rap. And while she's no Aretha—no one is—she can "go to church" and sing soul music with the best of them (witness "Love On Top") when she chooses to—which, I think, she doesn't do enough. But I've been in rooms with Beyoncé when an old O'Jays or Michael Jackson or Stevie Wonder or Temptations song came on the sound system—at a party, or backstage, or even at a photo shoot—and she knows every word of every song. Jay-Z once told me, "She's listened to music her whole life; she's a student of the game." Beyoncé once told me, "As a kid I'd go to stores that had karaoke machines and I'd sing pop songs—like Whitney's and Mariah's—but I'd rewrite the lyrics."

✦

What is it that makes someone want to sing, or play a musical instrument, or get on a stage and entertain people? When a child "performs" in their house in front of their mirror or for their parents, it's considered either showing off or isn't she cute? When that child grows older, she sees other people do it—on TV, or she listens to the music her parents play, or her friends tell her about bands they like, or she goes to a concert to see one of those people who loomed so large in her fantasies and she thinks, *I want to do that, I can do that.* And that's when the dream and the drive kicks in and it becomes a quest. It isn't any different than a bookworm obsessed with reading who thinks, *I want to write, I can write,* or a person who looks at a painting and thinks, *I can do that, I can draw, I can make art.* And if the talent is actually there, especially when it's music, it touches your mind and your heart and takes over your soul. For most of the successful women who make music, they took their initial inspiration and never gave up.

In the 1970s, when rock and roll became a serious business, for little girls who grew up wanting to be rock stars, there were no women to emulate—with the exception of Janis Joplin and maybe Grace Slick. (And in fact, there really weren't that many women who influenced Janis Joplin—except, perhaps, the rocking country singer Wanda Jackson or the blues belter Big Mama Thornton, who did the original version of "Hound Dog" before Elvis Presley.) If you wanted to play electric rock guitar, you looked to Keith Richards or Eric Clapton or Bob Dylan for inspiration. I remember being on tour with the Rolling Stones in 1975 in Los Angeles and a girl came by the house where Keith Richards was staying. She claimed she was a great guitar player and all she wanted to do was play for Keith or jam just one time with the Stones. She was laughed out of the house. Chrissie Hynde wanted a guitar when she was a teenager and her parents reluctantly bought her one. Joan Jett wanted a guitar and she got one, taught herself how to play, and then was ridiculed for her 1970s all girl band The Runaways. With the exception of Bonnie Raitt who played blues guitar, and the "folk" music of Joan Baez, Judy Collins and Joni Mitchell (who never considered herself a folk singer and once compared her music as being more like Schubert), musical inspirations were—for the most part—men.

In 2015, Rihanna told me that as a young girl growing up in Barbados, "Reggae music was the first music I loved. Barrington Levy, Beres Hammond, Booji Harrington. Then I got into Mariah Carey, Celine Dion and Whitney Houston. I was obsessed. From the age of 5 or 6 on, I would just watch these people on TV and dream about it. I loved that Mariah song 'Vision of Love.' And my mom used to tell me stories about Mariah—that she was both black and white, between two cultures, and that just made me even more interested in her."

In 2010 Lady Gaga told me that when she auditioned for her vocal coach Don Lawrence, she sang Mariah Carey's "Hero," and that she loved pop music. "Don told me I should really listen to Carole King. I listened to *Tapestry* and when I went to see her live, I cried all through 'You've Got a Friend.' When I met her, I cried in her arms, and she said, 'My dear Gaga, you're so sweet, why are you crying?' And I told her that when I would come home from school I would feel so sad and miserable, because of all the mean things that had been said about me, and I didn't feel like I fit in anywhere. But then I would listen to *Tapestry*, and feel better. That's why if I can make any of my fans feel the way Carole King made me feel, nothing is more important."

Gaga told me she also loved the music of Joni Mitchell and Patti Smith. I noted that these two women made very different types of music. She said, "But it was the spirit of strong, opinionated females that I was gravitating towards." And then, in 2015, when she sang the Julie Andrews medley at the Oscars, she told me afterward that Julie Andrews had always been an inspiration. When she sang standards with Tony Bennett—both in concerts and on two albums—she nailed songs like "The Lady Is a Tramp" and "What's New?" Following her Oscar-nominated role in *A Star Is Born*, she claimed that she had always adored Judy Garland and Barbra Streisand—both of whom had starred in previous versions of that movie. (She did not mention Janet Gaynor, who played the lead in the film's original version.) Musically, Gaga is all over the map. I have no doubt that eventually she can, and will, play Dolly Levi in *Hello, Dolly!* on Broadway—and then we will hear about how she was inspired by Carol Channing and Pearl Bailey and Bette Midler. She's a student of show business; she always told me she was a "theater girl"—she played the part of Adelaide in a high school production of *Guys and Dolls*. Someone should consider casting her in the next revival of that great musical on Broadway.

◆

I first heard Mavis Staples' self-titled, debut solo album in 1969, when my husband Richard played it on his late night radio show on WNEW-FM in New York City. You could hear the gospel, blues and R&B influences even in songs she covered written by Burt Bacharach. Years later, when I got to know her, Mavis told me she grew up aware of Lena Horne and Billie Holiday but with her family group, The Staple Singers, their music was firmly rooted in gospel. They initially performed wearing choir robes. She said that when the group started getting calls requesting that they perform at rock shows at the

Fillmore West or at blues festivals, "I said 'Pops, why are these blues people calling us? We don't sing no blues. And he said 'Mavis, if you listen to our music, you will hear every kind of music in our songs. You'll hear the blues and R&B and gospel—that's our background. And all those different people just took to us."

Mavis Staples' influence endures. In addition to all sorts of accolades, lifetime achievement honors, various Hall of Fame inductions and the much-deserved Kennedy Center honors, Mavis has been a collaborator and muse to musicians as diverse as her good friend Bob Dylan (she reportedly turned down his marriage proposal), Bonnie Raitt, Arcade Fire, Prince, Wilco's Jeff Tweedy, Ray Charles, Norah Jones—and she's been sampled by rappers including Pusha T, Ice Cube, Ludacris and Salt-N-Pepa.

"I always wanted to go back to basics with music," Joan Jett told me in 1983. "No heavy meanings, just fun: dancing, partying, meeting people, falling in love—things that people can apply to their lives. I get fan letters from girls who say that I'm a model for them because I don't back down." I asked her why people had initially thought she was such an oddity, or that she was threatening. "I don't know," she said. "I'm a risky type. I just keep going, I challenge. If somebody says you can't, I say, 'yes, I can.' I've been going since I was 15—I never gave up."

When Joan played guitar in The Runaways in the mid-1970s, the band was ridiculed because girls didn't play rock and roll guitar. While calling them sluts was sexist and unfair, what was troubling was that they were put together by the creepy, manipulative producer Kim Fowley. The lead singer, Cherie Currie, wore a corset onstage— nothing any more outrageous than what Beyoncé or Nicki Minaj would wear today or Madonna still wears today—but at the time, it seemed exploitative and cheesy.

"But," Joan said, "I was a fan of bands, I still am. I went to see the Rolling Stones at Madison Square Garden. I loved Cheap Trick, the Ramones, Iggy, Rush . . . we all sort of started at the same time." She did not mention any women, but, to be fair, there were hardly any women playing guitars in rock and roll bands when The Runaways started, and, Joan said, "There never was an all girls band that was as hard as The Runaways."

Since the demise of The Runaways, lots of girls have played guitar onstage: Chrissie Hynde, Courtney Love, St. Vincent, Alison Mosshart of the Kills, the riot grrrl groups, Cat Power, the three sisters in HAIM, Brittany Howard, Romy Madley Croft of the xx, King Princess—many, many others. And while Taylor Swift may have incongruously played Joan Jett's "Bad Reputation" over the sound system at the beginning of her 2018 concerts, when it comes to Joan's influence in terms of attitude: take a look at Miley Cyrus. Forget Miley's past twerking, the drug hijinks and the tabloid exposés of her love life; she brilliantly combines a Joan Jett–like grit with an incredible voice that evokes the country roots of her godmother, Dolly Parton.

"My mother played a lot of Billie Holiday and Ella Fitzgerald and John Coltrane," Alicia Keys told me. "And growing up, I was listening to a lot of Mary J. Blige, Salt-N-Pepa, Biggie and Tupac. Then I started listening to Aretha Franklin, Donny Hathaway and one of my absolute favorites—Patrice Rushen. I read about Nina Simone, and that was a big inspiration for me. The thing that was so incredible about her to me was that she played classical music, and that's what I had studied—and I'd never been introduced to another black woman who played classical music. I remember reading how she was at the Apollo Theater and she played piano and didn't look at the audience, and I could just imagine myself in that theater one day, on that stage, playing with my back to the audience—Miles Davis style. That's what I wanted to do."

◆

"From the first time I heard Judy Garland sing," Sheryl Crow told me in 2018, "this was all I ever wanted to do." Sheryl had the distinction of being the one girl who was widely accepted in that rock and roll boys' club. She opened shows for the Rolling Stones, Eric

Clapton and Bob Dylan and, she told me, "I felt uniquely accepted by the people who had inspired me and who also had written the book on the music I was trying to make. But at the same time, I felt shunned by my peer group. I felt I was considered uncool and unedgy by what was going on at the time—which was Hole, Beck, and the whole grunge scene. Those were my peers and I wasn't included in that—I wasn't even noticed by them. Then Alanis [Morissette] came out and I maintained a sort of under the radar status, because I was never embraced or invited into that 'alternative' thing."

"Instead," she continued, "I was invited into what was more historically important, by the people who were the reason I was doing what I was doing. There were so many people I loved and admired who really championed me. Bob Dylan watched me open for him at Roseland in New York and his crowd was quite brutal to me—but he invited me into his dressing room the next night and offered me his friendship, and a passageway for utilizing him over the years. I have called him over the years and said I have writer's block—and I've had him talk me off the ledge." (I have written previously about when Dylan got the Grammy for his amazing album *Time Out of Mind* in 1998, I was backstage with him, his publicist and the photographer Kevin Mazur, and Bob wouldn't take a photo holding the award until someone found Sheryl and got her to come backstage and "present" the Grammy statuette to him; he wanted a woman in the picture.)

Sheryl recalled that she was only 7 years old at the time of the original Woodstock Festival in 1969, but her older sister had all the records of all those artists and she grew up loving Joe Cocker, Jimi Hendrix, Janis Joplin, "That whole genre of blues-based early rock and roll," she told me. "The Stones . . . the Faces. Later, when I grew up at a time when corporate rock was popular—like Journey and Foreigner—I was the kid who was a fan of Eric Clapton and I walked around with Cream and Derek and the Dominos albums. But," she emphasized, "nobody was more influential to me than Bob

Dylan." (Sheryl would later open shows for Clapton; he also was one of her high profile romances that included the actor Owen Wilson and a broken engagement to Lance Armstrong. But her appeal to the bands that invited her to open for them or to jam with them was her own unique blues-based, guitar-based music.)

Then she added, "Aside from Dylan and the Stones, one of the biggest influences of my life was Stevie Nicks. I remember when I was a kid, getting my hair cut like hers, wanting to be like her. She was the first woman I could look at and say she's writing rock and roll and she's cool. When I was coming up, there were women doing more mainstream stuff—Heart, Pat Benatar—and I knew all those songs because I had played in cover bands before I left Missouri for Los Angeles. But I didn't relate to that as much as I did to what Stevie was doing."

◆

When Janet Jackson got her Black Girls Rock! award in 2018, she paid homage to Nina Simone, Gladys Knight, Patti LaBelle, Queen Latifah, Lena Horne, Dorothy Dandridge, MC Lyte, Aretha Franklin, Mary J. Blige, Missy Elliott and Salt-N-Pepa.

In the 1980s, Missy Elliott told me that Salt-N-Pepa were her inspirations because "They were some of the first women to stick with it in rap, and it's amazing how long they've remained and took it to another level."

When hip-hop began in the late 1970s, it was a boys' club just like rock and roll had been. It was a boys' club for quite awhile, and not only did women have only male rappers to listen to, they also had to keep hearing themselves referred to as "bitches" and "hos." But then, a few women started to get attention.

Queen Latifah, whose "Ladies First" was not only a hit, it was a female hip-hop manifesto—with an accompanying video that featured images of Sojourner Truth, Harriet Tubman, Angela Davis and Winnie Mandela. Latifah—who later would influence Lauryn Hill, MC

Lyte, Da Brat, Missy Elliot, Salt-N-Pepa and many others—became a one woman entertainment empire with successful careers in music, movies and television.

And then there was Mary J. Blige, who is still considered the "Queen of hip-hop and soul." When I first asked Mary who her early inspirations were, she replied without hesitation, "I'm going to start with Aretha, and then, Gladys Knight, Mavis Staples, the Staple Singers. My mother would play music in the house and walk around singing—Anita Baker, Teena Marie, Chaka Khan, Shirley Brown and the Clark Sisters—just every female. And of course, a lot of Otis Redding, Sam Cooke, the O'Jays and Bobby Womack. Outside of the house, by the time I was a teenager in the Bronx, it was just hip-hop. Hip-hop parties all the time."

Recently, Mary and I had a chat about all the young women singers and rappers coming up today. She talked about H.E.R., Ella Mai, Summer Walker, Megan Thee Stallion and Normani. Then there's Lizzo, whose influences range from Tina Turner to the drama of Freddie Mercury and the classical flute she studied at the University of Houston. Other current stars, such as Nicki Minaj and Cardi B, were clearly influenced by the earlier, and far more explicitly sexual, Lil' Kim and Foxy Brown. (And then Nicki and Cardi get pitted against each other. Whether it's Taylor and Katy or Nicki and Cardi—social media has escalated this sort of competition. In fairness, male rappers are always having "beefs" with each other too; some have even resulted in violence and death. Still. When it comes to women, everyone seems to love a good "catfight.")

◆

Anita Baker worshipped Sarah Vaughan, but was too nervous, she told me, to go backstage to meet her. Florence Welch told me she always wanted to sound like a man, "like Jeff Buckley or Tom Waits." Linda Ronstadt's musical inspirations ran the gamut: from rock and roll to country to standards and the Mexican music of her heritage.

Janelle Monáe told me she loved James Brown, Outkast and Prince, but mostly, she was inspired by Lauryn Hill.

St. Vincent told me she sat in her room in Austin, Texas, listening to John Coltrane's *A Love Supreme* album over and over. Cyndi Lauper told me about how, when she was 9 years old, she was doing her Al Jolson impersonation in the schoolyard. But, she added, "All my life I wanted to go to Canada, because I would listen to Joni Mitchell sing about Canada. It sounded so beautiful, I wanted to see it. Then I went during black fly season, got bitten up and had huge welts all over me." Katy Perry snuck out of her house to listen to Gwen Stefani and Shirley Manson, and both Gwen Stefani and Shirley Manson told me that they loved Debbie Harry.

Erykah Badu said her favorite male artist was Stevie Wonder and she carried a picture of Marvin Gaye around with her for years. But, she told me, "When I met Chaka Khan and she said I was her favorite new artist, it made me feel like it doesn't even matter what anyone says about me again; this is who I looked up to and admired growing up. I want to make people feel the way she made me feel. That gives me the motivation to keep going on."

Courtney Love told me that in the 1980s, after receiving a letter from her estranged real father who told her he was a professor in Ireland and that he had regular lunches with the likes of Bono and Bob Geldof, Courtney traveled to Dublin, thinking she'd go to a fancy university and meet rock stars. It turned out that her father wasn't a professor, and he didn't know any of those guys. But she went to a pub, met Julian Cope of the band Teardrop Explodes, who gave her his keys and let her stay in his apartment while he went on tour. The drummer from Echo and the Bunnymen was there too, and she said he taught her a lot. "In the U.S. I had been through a lot of cheesy rock stuff, but I started listening to the music that was happening in England, and it was so much cooler. I had a 1958 Melody Maker guitar and I learned the Bunnymen songs, I listened to Television's *Marquee Moon*, and I went back to Portland with all this knowledge."

She wanted to start an all girl band that would just play Beatles cover songs in a hostess bar in Japan (still a great idea), but instead, fate took her to San Francisco, then to Los Angeles where, at the age of 19, she met all sorts of movie stars, spent five hundred dollars a month from a trust fund on drugs, stripped in strip clubs, was briefly the singer in Faith No More until they kicked her out. Then she formed her own band—Hole.

✦

Music was central in my own family when I was growing up. Classical music on WQXR was on the radio every weekend, Gilbert and Sullivan operettas were on what used to be called a hi-fi system. Under duress, I took piano lessons, and in addition to the classical music and the sacred Hebrew music my mother studied and later, wrote, we listened to what was considered "avant garde"—Igor Stravinsky and Aaron Copland and Hector Berlioz. I was also exposed to the "left wing" folk music of Pete Seeger, Woody Guthrie, and Alan Lomax's *Sounds of the South*. Growing up, I was influenced by Thelonious Monk, John Coltrane, Miles Davis, Gerry Mulligan, Stan Getz—these were all sounds that informed me there was another world—a sophisticated, sexy world—out there. I memorized every single note of Lambert, Hendricks & Ross' "Twisted" (which Joni Mitchell covered years later), as well as Dizzy Gillespie's "Salt Peanuts," played by the Charlie Parker Quintet. John Coltrane's "My Favorite Things" was a favorite—I can still hum all the instrumental parts; it was years before I ever even knew it was a song from *The Sound of Music*. But it was the voices of the women—Annie Ross, Anita O'Day, Chris Connor, Mabel Mercer, Sarah Vaughan, Dakota Staton, Ella Fitzgerald, Lorez Alexandria, Della Reese (decades before she was known for playing an angel on TV), Morgana King (decades before she played Mama Corleone in *The Godfather*)—those were the voices that got to me the most.

As a kid, I also went to rock and roll shows, and when Elvis Presley came out with that album—the one with the black and white photo and the pink and green cover that the Clash copied years later—I was hooked. The mix of all that music got me out of the house—both metaphorically and literally. By the late 1960s, I became obsessed with rock and roll: mainly the Rolling Stones. I was never really a Beatles fan—I thought they sounded too "white," and while this has become a boring debate that has gone on among male rock critics for over fifty years (the same kinds of guys who are Boston Celtics fans or who argue about who's better—Michael Jordan or Lebron James), at that time, you really had to draw a line in the sand. The Stones were sexier. End of discussion.

At the same time, I also liked Joan Baez and Richie Havens and Joni Mitchell, and Bob Dylan's three great albums (*Bringing It All Back Home, Blonde on Blonde* and *Highway 61 Revisited*). I loved Laura Nyro, and I went to the Cafe Wha in the Village to see Frank Zappa and The Mothers of Invention and The Fugs because they were weird, and I always liked weird. I saw Jimi Hendrix once, at a club called Salvation in Greenwich Village's Sheridan Square. I think it was 1969, and I remember I wore a Greek fisherman's tank top as a mini dress. With nothing on underneath except two band aids covering my nipples and bikini underpants. I seem to remember that there were, at most, ten people in the club that night watching this wild guitar player onstage. A few months later, I found out that one of those ten people was Richard Robinson. And, as I've previously recounted, before I ever met him, I was deeply influenced by the music he played as a disc jockey on late night "free form" New York radio station WNEW-FM. The music he played, in fact—Ike & Tina Turner, Mavis Staples, Isaac Hayes, The Stooges, Howard Tate and all sorts of R&B—was considered so "unfamiliar" that he was fired and rehired several times; the final time for playing what he was told was the "unpatriotic" Jimi Hendrix version of "The Star Spangled Banner."

For many people, the music of their youth is the music they love and remember—just witness the audiences singing every word at an Eagles or Billy Joel concert. But for me, it's always been the music that's *good* that mattered, and still does. It hits you in your ears, then your heart, and then it takes hold of your soul. Because of all of the different music I was exposed to early on, and my eclectic taste—from jazz to hip-hop, soul music to hard rock, and initially the music Richard turned me on to—I have remained a fan and even today, when I do interviews with musicians, we share a common language. We were influenced by the same music, heard the same music or, in the case of younger musicians, they want to know my war stories about the musicians who influenced them.

Early on in my career, there were very few women doing what I was doing. I was never a critic; I wrote features, did interviews, edited fan magazines and wrote chatty columns. Female colleagues were few. Penny Valentine wrote a column for *Disc and Music Echo* in London—the paper that hired me to take over a column previously written by my husband. The Australian journalist Lillian Roxon wrote a wildly entertaining Rock Encyclopedia, as well as regular columns for the *Sydney Morning Herald* and the New York *Daily News*. Lillian became a mentor and my very close friend; she died in 1973. Gloria Stavers was a sophisticated woman who modeled in the 1940s, dated Jim Morrison and Lenny Bruce in the 1960s, and eventually wound up editing the teen publication *16* magazine in the 1970s. Gloria became a good friend too; she died in 1983.

But compared to men, there were very few women writing about music: there were the respected critics Ellen Willis, Ellen Sander and Janet Maslin. The columnist for the *Cleveland Plain Dealer* was the now-deceased Jane Scott. At the *Chicago Tribune*, there was Lynn Van Matre, now deceased. Jaan Uhelszki was at *Creem* in Detroit and Caroline Coon was in London. Later on, there was Ann Powers and Edna Gundersen, and from England, Julie Burchill and Sylvie Simmons. But in New York City, and the circles in which I traveled when I started out, there were so few women writing about rock and roll compared to what was going on at *Rolling Stone*, *Crawdaddy*, the *Village Voice*, the *New York Times* and everywhere else. Like everything else, rock music journalism, just like rock music, was a boys' club.

◆

Every musician has told me that often, their very best songs just get plucked out of the air. "It just came to me and I wrote it in two minutes," Beyoncé once told me about "Bootylicious," which she wrote on a long plane ride after listening to a playlist that included Stevie Nicks' "Edge of Seventeen" (which is sampled on "Bootylicious"). Sheryl Crow and Joan Jett and many others have told me that they dreamt the *best song ever*, only to wake up and not be able to remember it. Lady Gaga told me she got the idea for "Born This Way" out of the blue while in a movie theater in Australia watching *The Hurt Locker*. She said she left the theater and wrote the song in two minutes. In the olden days, when others had eureka song ideas, they might have called their answering machines and sung into them. Today, everyone just records songs on their phones. (Although St. Vincent told me she dropped her phone into a pool once and lost everything. I keep trying to tell these girls to back everything up on flash drives, but this seems to be too much of an old school concept to grasp. I'm so paranoid that I've backed up 5,000 plus hours of interviews on disks and various hard drives—including three external hard drives kept in three separate locations. I do not trust the Cloud.)

Everyone has a different songwriting process. Some people write all the time. Some don't start writing songs until they have to deliver an album—although those record company schedules are less important now that anyone can release music as a surprise, online, in the middle of the night. But some of the old rules remain: some women still lock themselves away to write—with or without a co-writer or a team. I was once in the recording studio with Gwen Stefani and two songwriters who were writing songs with her, and they were all so excited with what they'd come up with that there was dancing and champagne drinking all night long. Then, the two songs I heard that I thought were great never made it onto her solo album—because the record label didn't like them. In the hip-hop world, there are often ten different people or more credited with writing a song—which can also include the original writers of the songs that are sampled on the track, or the producer who came up with the beat, or the arranger, or someone who contributed a lyric, or an assistant who orders the food. Just look at the credits on a hip-hop song—if you can even find credits now that physical albums are scarce artifacts from the previous century.

Still, despite the technological changes, the "creative" remains the same. Someone actually has to be inspired enough to write something new, something that will appeal to their fans, their followers, their team, and most importantly, themselves. Then hopefully, people will like it, buy it, and the musician can sell concert tickets where they make their real money. Some people love the process, some people dread it. Some people find it easy, others are tortured. When Adele played new songs she had been working on for her album *25* for producer Rick Rubin, he listened, then told her he "didn't believe her." So she went back to the drawing board and spent almost another year writing the songs that wound up on that eventual gazillion selling, Grammy winning success.

✦

Adele is another one of those artists who was—and still is—a fan. In 2016, she freely admitted to me that she grew up loving Britney Spears and the Spice Girls. "In London there was a big record store like HMV called Our Price," she told me, "and it was right opposite the Britain tube station. And every time I'd come up from the Britain tube station, I'd go and buy CDs at Our Price. I wanted to be cool, and they'd have the record of the week, so I'd listen to that. It wouldn't be the Spice Girls, it would be something different and

I always wanted to know about all kinds of music. There was a jazz section, and I found an Ella Fitzgerald album in a bargain bin. The CDs in the jazz section were always cheaper than the Top 20, which blew my mind, and I'd buy them, and I loved them."

"My mom also had great taste in music," she said. "She loved Jeff Buckley and Bob Dylan, she loved 10,000 Maniacs and the B52s; she had really cool taste. You know how you get obsessive over people when you're young—so it was Jeff Buckley on all the time." I asked her that with taste like that, how did her mother feel about Adele's love for the Spice Girls? "She loved them too," she said. "I mean that was girl power. She absolutely loved it. I love girl singers. I absolutely worship Beyoncé, and Bette Midler, and Stevie Nicks. I wasn't born when Fleetwood Mac's *Rumours* came out, but my mother had it, and good music just comes through, good records last."

While Adele obviously had not been alive during the first Fleetwood Mac incarnation, when they reunited and came to London to perform at the O2 Arena in London in 2015, it was her birthday, she got a box and invited her friends and they all went. "Then I get there in my box," Adele said, "and I get summoned, so I'm being taken backstage—but they're *Fleetwood Mac* and I felt, why would they know me?" I pointed out that she'd had a very big success with her previous multiple Grammy winning album *21*, and *of course* they would know who she was. She went backstage, got taken into Stevie's dressing room and, she said, "I can't find the words to say how much I love her. She's standing there looking like an actual angel, she's glowing. It's like I could see dust particles floating around me; time slowed down, it was an out-of-body experience. She's like, 'How's the baby?' So I was like, she knows me, she knows I have a baby. Then she asked me how my record was coming along, and said she was dying to hear my new record. I just collapsed. I was sobbing my heart out."

"She was amazing, but I couldn't stop crying. And I fucking hate it when people get overwhelmed meeting me and they start crying, and I bet she hates it—she's been doing it for forty years. But she invited me into her personal dressing room and all I'm doing is snotting all over her and she's laughing. Then later, in the show, after I had been snotting all over her, she dedicated 'Landslide' to me. I was speechless."

✦

I've talked to Stevie Nicks a lot over the years, and in 2017, I asked her who had influenced her. She said Aretha Franklin. And Grace Slick—because she was a singer in a band. And Tom Petty, The Beach Boys, Janis Joplin, Crosby, Stills & Nash, her grandfather—who taught her how to sing harmonies like the Everly Brothers. And, she said, Carole King. But she said, "In the 1970s, when I got a new Joni Mitchell album, I would lie on the floor, smoke some pot, and listen to that album for ten days. I called her my 'phraseology person,' because that's where I learned all my phrasing from. Her coming out with a record, for me, was ten days of pure bliss. By myself, lying on the floor, reading every word of the lyrics. If anyone walked in the room it was like, 'Get out, I'm busy. I'm listening to Joni Mitchell's *Court and Spark*, go away.'"

"All the guys realized she was not only a great singer," Stevie said, "but she also was a great songwriter and a great musician. It was like, 'Oh my god, this girl is better than us.'"

AGE

Let's go back to three summers ago, to that backstage VIP hospitality suite at a sold out classic rock concert in an 80,000 seat stadium—the one where a major music booking agent told me that no woman who ever had a baby had a Number One hit again. Onstage, the band lineup that day consisted of men in their 60s and 70s. They all performed—without a visible shred of embarrassment or concern—with white hair or bald heads, their bellies hanging over belts and in some cases, the unattractive visuals of tight t-shirts. I asked that same agent if there was any woman in her 60s or 70s—other than, perhaps, Barbra Streisand—who could sell out a stadium alone. No, he said. No one. Female stadium headliners—Beyoncé, Adele, Lady Gaga—all were in their 30s. Stevie Nicks could only sell out those venues with Fleetwood Mac, not alone. "But," said another man sitting with us, "none of the women from the 1970s were as good as the guys."

✦

In the 1990s, talking about her career, Chaka Khan, who was in her 40s at the time, told me, "The whole term of the geriatric, older person has been redefined. You have to make it work in the most healthy way for you; everyone has different ways of doing it. I just try to get enough sleep. And I find that I really need to take time away from everybody else—just for myself, totally for myself."

In 2018, when Mariah Carey was 48, she announced that she was bipolar. Lady Gaga, who's 34, had lupus when she was younger, and more recently, she's had chronic fibromyalgia. At age 41, Melissa Etheridge had breast cancer. And at the age of 73, Marianne Faithfull had decades of health problems, including hepatitis and several forms of cancer.

In the 1980s, Cyndi Lauper told me she had endometriosis, that it was a stress thing and it happens when you travel a lot and a lot of athletes get it. "I had two major operations that really didn't have to be major operations, but I didn't know enough about it. I had three operations, actually, but the one on my throat was endometriosis related, and today, if someone went to the doctor, they would be treated for something else. It was hard for me at first because I traveled and traveled and worked and worked until I just dropped. Then I got up again and worked and worked until I dropped again. Now it's different. I work out, I take care of myself a little better."

In 2012, when Linda Ronstadt told me that she hadn't been able to sing for three years due to Lyme disease, she said that if she could sing, nothing would stop her. This was the woman who was considered the single best vocalist to come out of the 1970s California scene. In 2013 she was finally diagnosed with a form of Parkinson's disease—too late to correct the vocal and muscular problems—and at age 67, she officially retired.

In 1985, the 46 year-old Tina Turner told me, "People always say 'What? She's still doing it?' And then they say 'How old is she?'" But it wasn't until Tina had retired, was 79 years old and published her second memoir that she revealed she'd had a stroke and kidney failure. And now, even while she's living quietly in Switzerland with her husband Erwin Bach of seven years (and her partner for twenty-seven years before they married), who gave her one of his kidneys, here comes the inevitable Broadway show about the older female star: *Tina!* All this started with *Beautiful,* the Carole King musical, followed by the somewhat successful Donna Summer musical—six years after her death—then the flop *Head Over Heels* with the music of The Go-Go's, *The Cher Show,* and now there's the musical based on Alanis Morissette's album *Jagged Little Pill.*

◆

Health problems are not limited to women, the elderly or the famous. But for women in the music world, aging and illness are added liabilities. We've all got enough stuff we have to fight: business, men, lack of opportunity, unequal pay. For the female musician, getting a record deal, or onto a stage, or tour support, radio airplay or a song on Spotify has often been a challenge. When Lady Gaga won a Golden Globe for her song "Shallow" from *A Star Is Born,* she said as a woman in music, it was hard to be taken seriously as a musician and songwriter. Add illness to that, and it means more weakness and less money. If the people in charge—usually men, but whoever is in charge—think that a woman has a life-threatening illness, or even something that would prevent her from generating income, the offers dry up. It's highly unlikely that the face of L'Oreal is going to be a breast cancer survivor or someone who's had a stroke. Unless, of course, some cosmetic or clothing company decides to cash in on this and photograph a whole group of sick women together in some politically correct "campaign" for something. Other than attempts at glorifying "body positivity," I haven't seen it yet.

One manager, whose name I won't mention, told me about his 50 year-old client, "Her album is so good; if she was 30, it would be a hit." Female stars—especially singers and musicians, and especially those who dance as part of their act—have a limited time on the stage. For the female star, a year quickly turns into five, then a decade, and the decades turn into a lifetime. Much more so than men. The 77 year-old Mick Jagger may look silly with dyed hair, prancing around a stage, but all you ever hear about him is what great shape he's in, how he has such a fabulous blues voice and is such an amazing, crowd-pleasing entertainer. No one says anything of the sort about any woman near that age—except maybe Bette Midler and Stevie Nicks. But when people say they both still look good, there is always that word in there: *still*. Given everything we're up against, women are in a fragile position. Aging women in music have three choices: try as long as you can to just deal with it, rely on surgical "enhancement" and dress inappropriately, or get out of the way. Or, for a few, with age comes that wisdom you've always heard about . . . that supposedly comes with age.

✦

"I feel like I finally get it," Sheryl Crow told me in 2018. At 56 years old, living on a farm in Nashville with her two adopted sons, she said, "Clearly I'm not a young mom, but while you may be having a fabulous career—shit happens to you. I've had several public relationships fall apart and I did go through breast cancer. But as much as I hate watching myself get older, there is something super liberating about not giving a shit anymore."

"I'm super happy," she continued, "I wish I was lonely so I could manifest a relationship. But I've got to be honest—I've had great love affairs and great relationships, and if a guy walked in right now and knocked me off my feet, great. But I'm really content. I think there's a mellowing out that happens when you get older. And for me, watching what's happening with music now, it's inspired me more to write. Because I know that at my age, I'll never get played on radio anyway, so I can say whatever I want to say. I feel liberated onstage— and that's largely due to the fact that I have things surrounding me that I love and I want. And I'm not going after anything. There's something about going after something and setting yourself up for these huge goals—you get on a trajectory where you miss all the good stuff. And I've spent a lot of my life doing that."

"The female thing makes it more complicated," Sheryl admitted. "Because women give birth to a whole other body and your job is to take care of everybody first and put yourself last. That's what we do. And if you're someone like me, who's always defined myself by being productive—and not just productive, but good, like Dylan or Joni—it's a real mind bender. But I don't feel that way anymore." I asked her how having gone through breast cancer (Stage One in 2006, a double lumpectomy and radiation) gave her a different take on life. "Well," she said, "it was six days out from breaking up with Lance [Armstrong] and losing my dream of a wedding. I was like, 'You think you control everything and you don't control anything.' It was awful, it was emotional whiplash, it was harrowing and it was awesome. It was the best thing that ever happened to me. For one thing, I would have continued to go back into that relationship over and over, and that relationship already was toxic. But it broke the story I had been telling myself about who I am. I had to learn how to say 'No.' I had to learn who was bringing me energy and who was sucking my energy. I had to cut people out of my life. I decided to adopt a child while I was going through radiation, and in a weird way it helped tie everything together and is the reason that my life is the way it is now."

In terms of her career, and the current music business, Sheryl said that she resents having to publicize herself on an iPhone instead of just releasing music. "It's so counter to the way I was brought up," she said, "which is play your ass off to one hundred people in a club, then play for one thousand people, then they buy your record and you build a following and they like your music. But I was 30 when 'All I Wanna Do' came out, and by the standards of what was going on at the time, I was already elderly compared to Britney Spears and other 18 year-old girls."

✦

When I talked to Diana Ross in 1996, she was 52 years old, had been out of The Supremes longer than she'd ever been in that group, and while her solo career wasn't exactly flourishing, she was still in the game. "As I get older, I realize that music comes from deep in your soul," she told me, "and a lot of it comes from pain. And I wonder sometimes how young girls can write if they haven't had any deep experiences. I've had over a thirty year career, and five kids, and I had to learn a long time ago when to say 'No.' Career-wise, because of my children, I've missed a lot; I probably could have done more movies."

"But," she said, "music has been my life and my career. I work hard. I realized when I was leaving Motown, and at the end of my first marriage, that I couldn't sit around and wait for someone to take care of me. I had to take care of myself, and it made me stronger. I think all of us go through important decisions: like I'm scared to go this way, or I'm scared to go that way, but I've got to pick one. Each doorway could possibly be painful but you've got to take chances. That's what I did when I left The Supremes, because dissatisfaction makes you want to try something else. It was a very painful time, but you've got three girls in a group who weren't sisters, forced to be with each other all the time. And Motown was like our protector. You'd work, you'd travel, you'd pack your suitcases, you'd get on the bus and it wasn't fun anymore. You start getting on each other's nerves. Someone takes someone's lipstick. . . . Just because you're in a singing group doesn't mean you're supposed to spend the rest of your lives together. Some groups can do it—the Rolling Stones seem to be able to, but they have other lives too. If you grow up, you change. You want different things in your life. And as many years as I've been in this business, I feel like I'm grounded."

Diana said she would have liked to have had the hits that Whitney and Mariah had, but she never wanted to retire. "The music is my life.

Even when I walk or I'm on an elevator, I'm singing or humming to myself, and someone will say 'thanks for the concert,' and I'm not even aware that I'm humming or singing. I hope I never stop singing, but I think I'll know when it's time for me to stop performing. I'll get the message. Because of my love for jazz, I could probably make records until the record companies say 'OK, Diana Ross, it's time for you to stop singing.' And then I'll probably go on singing somewhere else. I've always had a record deal, it's just getting them to not think of you as a 'veteran' artist. But it's like anything else; if you can make money for them, the music business is there for you. When we started, artists were geared for longevity. Now they throw someone out there and if it makes money, great. If not, on to the next one. But when I run into kids who say that I inspired them, that means the most to me."

(*Note:* In 2002, Diana Ross briefly entered a rehab facility for alcohol problems. She released an album of new music in 2006. Since that time, she performs, has received various Icon and Lifetime Achievement awards and a Presidential Medal of Freedom, and has done a residency at the Wynn in Las Vegas. She has not retired.)

◆

Joan Jett, who still tours, told me in 1983 when she was just 25 years old, "Hopefully I'm going to know when it's time for me to no longer go out onstage. There could come a point where maybe, because of the athleticism of our stage show, I'm not able to satisfy the audience the way I think it should be done. Who knows, maybe I'll just retire from the stage; it's hard to even think about stopping playing music." I mentioned that Muddy Waters and Howlin' Wolf and all the blues guys played until they died, and undoubtedly so will Keith Richards, and she said, "Who's to say you should stop at 50 if you feel there's a lot of life left in you? Even though we live in an ageist society, it's all in your head about age anyway. It's like a challenge to me. Whenever people say you can't, I say yes I can. You have to open that door, then realize that there's a lot of people behind you. So you just have to run faster through that door."

In 1994, when she was 52, Tammy Wynette told me she had recently had a "little bout" with pneumonia, and that she'd had a lot of health problems in her life. In 1986 she went to the Betty Ford clinic for an addiction to painkillers, and, she said, "I've had stomach problems, scar tissue, multiple operations—and when I went into the hospital this past year I was in excruciating pain. I was poisoned from bile duct, my blood pressure dropped to like thirty over ten and I was on life support for two days. When my blood pressure dropped, I got numb and I was frightened."

"But," she said, "I take antibiotics every day and I feel great now. *The National Enquirer* said I was a walking skeleton, but I am *not*." Was she a regular reader of the tabloids? "I read them every week to see if I'm in them," she said. "I don't believe them, but most of the time, they have parts of the story right." She said doctors had been telling her for years to take time off, but, she said, "That's *hard*. It's hard when you want to go ahead and work. I want to be back in the mainstream."

Tammy Wynette, who was called the "First Lady of Country Music," had more than twenty Number One singles on the Billboard country music charts, was married five times, and wrote songs that dealt mostly with love, loneliness and divorce. ("Stand By Your Man" is considered one of the most influential songs of all time.) In 1998, at the age of 55, after more than a three decade career of nonstop recording and performing, Tammy Wynette died, supposedly from a blood clot in her lung. Several years later, her daughters filed a wrongful death lawsuit against her doctors and her then-husband. After her body was exhumed, it was discovered that she died of cardiac arrhythmia. Fifteen hundred people attended her memorial service at Nashville's Ryman Auditorium.

◆

Some women never lived long enough to worry about how they would look or sound when they reached 30, 40, 50 or beyond. Janis Joplin died at 27 and will forever be remembered in photos wearing that feather boa in her hair, and on film for her mind-blowing performance at the Monterey Pop Festival in 1967. Amy Winehouse, who also died at the age of 27, lives on, pictured in her Ronettes-inspired hairdo and signature winged cat-eyeliner. Whitney Houston didn't exactly have a graceful exit—dead of a cocaine overdose in a bathtub in the Beverly Hilton Hotel, and an embarrassing reality show prior to that—but who knows how much worse it might have been had she just continued as a sad drug addict who had permanently lost the upper registers of her voice. All of these women's voices live on in their recordings. No one knows where they would have gone vocally or what other avenues they could have explored had they lived. And there are many—like the Scottish singer Maggie Bell and British singers Julie Driscoll and P. P. Arnold and others—who had amazing voices but who aged out of the music scene. Even for some of our greatest talents, aging is rough.

✦

Even though she was under appreciated at the height of Blondie, Debbie Harry has had an enduring influence. She and her music partner Chris Stein brought rap into the pop mainstream, they thought that Blondie was an art project—a kind of cynical take on a pop group. But because she was so adorable, some people did not like her. People are jealous not only of talent (Joni Mitchell, others), but when it comes to women, they are also jealous of their looks (Joni Mitchell, Debbie Harry, others). She was always generous when talking to me about how she was flattered when younger women musicians such as Gwen Stefani and Shirley Manson said they had been influenced by her. "I'm very warmed by that," she said, "it's still amazing to me that we had that kind of impact. With all these girls coming up and using Blondie as a reference, it's given us a longevity and a lifeline."

At the height of her fame in the 1980s, Pat Benatar told me, "When I started, it probably drove Linda Ronstadt and Stevie Nicks crazy. Then I got asked all the time about Madonna and Cyndi Lauper, and in a couple of years someone else will drive them crazy. But it's a relief for me to have people looking at Madonna's underwear instead of mine. It's like having twenty pounds lifted off my shoulders. I'm glad she's here; I can move on."

In 1998, Shirley Manson told me, "Part of the excitement about rock and roll, always, has been the sexual chemistry. With women, we are expected to look a certain way or we are not considered sexy. The music business will eventually spit me out, because it's a limited life span." I mentioned that there are many women who altered the idea of conventional beauty: Janis Joplin, Patti Smith, PJ Harvey, to name a few. (And today, certainly Lizzo has broken the mold.) "But unfortunately," Shirley said at that time, "they come across once in a lifetime. Their talent is such that it demolishes the discriminatory rules. There aren't that many women that have that much talent and confidence." (Years later, in 2017, Shirley—a seemingly strong, aggressive woman when fronting the rock band Garbage—wrote an essay for the *New York Times* and admitted that she had spent years cutting herself.)

✦

The Joni Mitchell who sang "Both Sides Now" in her 20s had a very different voice than the Joni Mitchell who sang it in her 50s and 60s. Her older vocals had more depth—a richer, slower and world-wearier sound. Gwen Stefani's "Underneath It All"—a cutesy hit she'd had with No Doubt when she was in her 20s—sounded much sexier after the crushing blow she faced with a cheating husband and failed marriage; she slowed the song down and it took on a whole different meaning. When Bette Midler sings her slow version of "Do You Wanna Dance" these days, there are decades of living in her voice. It's the same way when Stevie Nicks sings "Landslide" now as opposed to the way she sang it in 1977. And it certainly was true of Marianne Faithfull.

When Marianne was Mick Jagger's angelic blonde, beautiful girl-friend in the 1960s, she had a hit with a sweet song, "As Tears Go By." When she sang it in her 50s and beyond, it was sultry, smarter, sexier; a voice full of whiskey, cigarettes, drugs, illness, heartbreak and experience. In the 1990s, Marianne, who was then in her 50s, told me, "I'm absolutely at the right age now to be perfectly happy being a worldly and sophisticated woman who's been through a lot. I wasn't very happy to feel that way in my 30s. I had to change the feelings that I had for years that I could just have a normal life and be like everybody else. I had to let go of that. In order to have any kind of normal life, I would have had to stop being so exotic."

Reflecting back on her youthful beauty, she said, "I really did take my looks for granted. What I'm looking for now is to feel good, more than to look good. But obviously, when I feel good I look good—it goes together. I'm not crazy about being in film, because I'm not as beautiful as I was. I know I'm not, and I feel that I'm not coming through properly. I wish I'd made more films when I was younger. But I couldn't, because I didn't have the discipline. I did a lot of very dreadful things to myself, but what can we do? I always knew that if I got through it all, I was very lucky."

◆

In 2010, the 41 year-old Jennifer Lopez tried to look on the bright side. She told me that *People* magazine had done a story that year on actresses over 40: "Me, Halle Berry, Jennifer Aniston, Sandra Bullock," she said, "and everybody started noticing. I think there was a time in Hollywood when women got into their 30s, people thought, they're not worth anything; we need someone younger, hotter, better. But I think it's a different time now. They realize that this generation of women has more experience, more wisdom and much more to offer. We also can still be amazing looking as well."

Recently, when she had what seemed to be a month long celebration of turning 50, she made sure to post fantastic bikini shots of herself on Instagram and said that people just don't get to write a woman off when they reach a certain point in their life.

In the talk Jennifer and I had ten years ago, I said I doubted there was a woman in Hollywood who hadn't been forced to have plastic surgery to try to look younger so they could get a job. Even Janet Jackson, in 1985, when she was 23, before she'd ever had any plastic surgery, told me that she saw nothing wrong with it. Obviously, she was defending her brother Michael at the time, but she also said that everyone in Hollywood and show business did some cosmetic enhancement, and if they could afford it and if it made them feel better, why not? Men in Hollywood and music are victims of aging too: I think for whatever reason George Clooney seems to have lost his looks, Robert Redford looks like he had something done to his face, Tom Cruise just looks weird, period, and Michael Jackson aside, don't get me started on David Lee Roth or any number of male rock stars. If I had to bet, I would say with some conviction that the only male rock star who probably has had absolutely no plastic surgery is Keith Richards.

◆

In 1993, the 47 year-old Patti Smith talked about how she didn't expect to reach a younger audience, that it wasn't her job. She told me that there was a lot of work being done by younger people addressing each other, addressing youth, and she respected that. "Even if it's stuff I don't relate to," she said, "I still understand where that energy comes from. I had my time when things were directed toward me, and I think each generation translates things over and over again, re-translating for themselves. The music that's being produced now is theirs."

In 1997, she told me that she didn't feel any nostalgia for the 1970s: "If I feel any nostalgia it's just that the '70s were a time when all my friends were alive. That's the only thing I feel nostalgia for. I don't feel nostalgia for the music or my place in it. But I do actually appreciate it more now than when I was doing it. I outgrew my own work really quickly and I never listened to it in the '80s. Hearing it again, I feel affection for it because the one thing that comes through to me is that we had a lot of guts, we had a lot of bravado, and we had a lot of heart."

Katy Perry once told me that she worked as hard as she did because she knew that fame was fleeting; but she was 26 at the time, and while she may have understood the concept, she really did not understand how fast fame can flee. While she got $25 million to be a judge on the underwhelming reboot of *American Idol*, she also worked for over a year on an album that flopped, and she claimed that the failure of that album left her "heartbroken."

The old adage that age is just a number becomes a cruel joke when you age. Like athletes, very few stars can beat that clock. The 19 year-old Britney Spears singing "Oops! . . . I Did It Again" on the MTV Awards, shaking her ass in a sheer, sparkly jumpsuit, with a snake around her neck is a very different Britney than the 35 year-old Britney with the newly augmented breasts, lip-synching her way through the same song in 2017 in Las Vegas. There was a time when U2 and the Spice Girls were the biggest acts in the music world. Pat Benatar had hits in the 1980s (her "Hit Me With Your Best Shot" can now be heard as a TV commercial for Applebee's). The Go-Go's wrote their own songs, traveled the world and made a fortune in the '90s. The Bangles were hot. Until they were not. And here we are again, with women at the top of the charts: Beyoncé! Rihanna! Adele! Cardi B! Until they're replaced. Madonna copied street style and wanted to rule the world and sort of did. Until she didn't. Now, she just seems to be aging gracelessly with what appeared to be démodé butt implants, attention-getting, inappropriate clothing, and is as narcissistic as ever.

Women are always aware of the younger, prettier, equally talented ones right behind them. And even if it takes years for them to realize that they're no longer the draw they once were, the realization and despair when it finally hits is not good. They might have money, they might have loved ones, they might have children, they might have an entourage. But once they had that hit, it felt so good, they wanted another one. And there is no way that an older anyone can look at a picture of their younger selves and not be less than pleased. And when their stardom is diminished, so goes their spirit.

◆

In 1994, Patti LaBelle told me that she never lied about her age and she was very proud of being 50, because, "It's a milestone for me. None of my sisters ever made it [her sisters died of breast cancer at earlier ages]. But even if they had made it to this age, I'd still be proud to be 50; I would boast about it and tell the world that I'm 50 years young and feeling like 20. As I got older, things started happening for me—I went on the Oprah show, and even though I don't have the hits that Madonna and Toni Braxton have, I know my records are just as good." (Or, I added, better.)

In 1995, Bette Midler told me, "The day after I turned 49, I started saying I'm almost 50, so I've been saying it for six months now. I feel pretty good about turning 50; I want to have a big party, something fabulous."

Twenty three years later, in 2018, Bette was 72 years old and had just finished a year's sellout stint on Broadway starring in *Hello, Dolly!* She talked about what she had learned over the years. "You get caught up in the fantasy of showbiz and it takes you years and years to finally realize you've been had," she said. "Growing up, you had one record: Joni Mitchell said that she had one record, and I had one record. And you listened to that record over and over again until you managed to get to a store—it might have been fifty miles away—and you got another record. We didn't have all this . . . stuff. We weren't entertaining ourselves to death."

"I knew I had a talent, I knew I could be funny as a solo artist, but for some reason, I understood very early on in life that what I was doing was so obscure; three people understood what I was doing. I was smart, but I wasn't beautiful, and I knew that you were not going to be young forever, the bloom of youth was going to fade. And you had to be careful about money, about who you hung with, or you would fall to wrack and ruin. Because there were so many traps."

Bette told me that she never said it publicly before, but she was the highest paid woman in Hollywood in the movies in the 1980s, "And I'm saying it now. But for me, it was never the fame, it was the work. Fifty years later and I'm still fascinated by the work."

Then there is the 32 year-old Adele, who may be the sole artist of her generation who really doesn't have to worry about moving into old age. For a start, she simply stands on a stage and sings and chats to the audience in a funny, bawdy way that no one has since Bette Midler. She doesn't dance around or wear Ice Capades ensembles or stripper clothing or have a row of backup dancers. Her live shows don't rely on massive production, costume changes, flying through the air or fireworks. She has an incredible voice, and as long as she takes care of that voice, she can sing and record music for as long as she wants. In 2016 she told me that she would like to perform on Broadway, and specifically to play the part of Mama Rose in *Gypsy*. I asked her, when? "Oh," she said, "when I'm 50."

She also said, "Every day as I get older, I appreciate women more and more. When you're between the ages of 15 and 20, you don't appreciate other girls so much, you see women as competition—as opposed to lifesavers and people that hold your hand or have experienced pretty much every single thing that you've experienced as a woman. I underestimated that. So the more women I have in my life, the better."

As she nears 40, Beyoncé seems to have figured out her place in the musical landscape. The woman who performed a blistering two hour set at Coachella in 2018 has come a long way from the teenage pop star in Destiny's Child. It wasn't just her embracing black culture, or the HBCU-influenced marching bands, or the uplifting, ambitious, intense, angry and emotional performances. This was a woman who had pushed herself, was relentless, still ambitious, envisioned a massive production, and managed to combine everything she had learned in her twenty two year career. In her Netflix documentary, she's seen at rehearsals directing the dancers and the crew. She was wearing no makeup and looked twenty years younger but seemed twenty years wiser; more experienced and more confident than the girl I'd known fifteen years ago when she released her first solo album. She's become the woman that I'm not sure even she imagined she would become.

◆

No one seems to have the time to lie on the floor and listen to an album for ten days the way Stevie Nicks said she did when a new Joni Mitchell album came out. People listen to music as it goes streaming by, in the air. Even if they select a song, or an album, or a playlist, it's often on in the background while they're also watching something else. Or "following" someone else's Instagram—if they're not busy updating their own—or catching up on Twitter. Or going down that online rabbit hole from one gossip site to another, one video on YouTube to another. Or checking their news alerts. Or following the suggestions given to you when you purchase something online—a book, or an album or a song—and an announcement appears: "If you liked this, you'll like *that*." Or on Netflix when they claim "Since you watched this, you'll like *that*." All of these suggestions are annoying to those of us who either are old enough to have always been able to make up our own minds or select our own entertainment, or those who are younger and prefer to make their own choices. Then there are those stars taking part in actual activities—skiing or jumping off cliffs or diving off a yacht into the water—who then post it on their Instagram to prove that it actually happened or to promote something. At some point, all this posting and following and alerts and whatnot becomes *work*. Apparently, people have not yet gotten sick of themselves. Or sick of following others. Where are the leaders? People will eventually move on to something else, or there'll be a backlash, or there'll be something new. There always is. Does anyone remember Myspace? Facebook is now the provenance of the older generation, while the younger generation seems to be discovering flip phones along with vinyl LPs—all of which are considered "vintage," and supposedly "coming back."

With everyone's life so cluttered with real and virtual reality, it remains to be seen if any female stars will have staying power or long careers anymore. I would bet on Adele and Lady Gaga, and I think Beyoncé is not going away. But we are no longer in an age where every few years another star replaces another star; we're down to months . . . or weeks. Many singers are famous online before even releasing a song. And no matter how much they provide music directly to their fans, or control their own narrative, and remove the middleman, it all sort of merges together into one big hot mess. In the 1970s, when everyone in Fleetwood Mac was sleeping with everyone else in the band, no one really knew about it unless you dissected the song lyrics—and those albums sold millions. People now are interested in Ariana Grande as much for her romantic breakups as her music. More people follow Beyoncé on Instagram than buy her albums. Music will always matter. Women will always matter. It's how you'll hear it and who will be doing it that changes faster now, more than ever.

✦

In 1997, the 49 year-old Stevie Nicks told me that when Fleetwood Mac are onstage for two and a half hours, "We go back to the past a lot. All the things that made us write those songs are still there. All the tensions that were there when we wrote those songs are still there. But we're older and wiser and not so willing to let little, stupid things blow this thing out of the sky. If one person is angry about something, we sit down and talk about it, whereas before, we would just walk out." (Of course, at the time we talked, the reunited Fleetwood Mac had not yet been on a long tour together for years; they were still in rehearsal and could go home to their own houses every night.) "It's quite another thing when you're not able to go home," Stevie said. "You have to do the show, get on the plane, fly to another city, have breakfast in the same place, and go to sound check together. You'd better like these people."

Apparently in 2018, she decided she no longer liked her former boyfriend, co-songwriter and bandmate Lindsey Buckingham enough to get on a stage with him. There had been numerous fights, breakups and personnel changes in Fleetwood Mac over the last four decades, but this time, Stevie said it was either him, or her. Obviously it was easier to get other guitar players (Mike Campbell from Tom Petty's former Heartbreakers and Neil Finn from Split Enz and Crowded House) than get another Stevie Nicks; there isn't one. When I asked someone involved in their tour what happened, I was told: "Money. Scheduling. Mean."

But in 2016, before this estrangement, she and I talked about the problems with bands and old boyfriends and touring and the vocal problems Linda Ronstadt and Bette Midler and Adele had all had, and Stevie said, "That's the dreaded thing that every singer goes through; that something could go wrong with your vocal cords. Even if you have enough days off and you're careful, still, sometimes the perfect storm happens. It can be nodes or a hemorrhage, those are the words I never want to hear." We talked about Adele, and Stevie said, "It's very satisfying to see someone who has actual talent become so successful. Also, she is so damn polite, and has such beautiful manners and is so funny. I think she's a very old soul who writes a lot about being older. I tried to tell her to enjoy her 20s—but when I was 25, I wrote 'Landslide' [with the lyrics '. . . *time makes you bolder, even children get older / and I'm getting older too*']. As songwriters we tend to write about getting old for some reason, and about looking back on your youth. Even if you're 27, you're looking back on what you call your youth."

"What Adele does appeals to all different age groups," Stevie said. "She probably has fans in their 60s like me, then she has little baby fans and everybody in between. I have a group of younger girls I've taken under my wing—Adele, HAIM, Vanessa Carlton. I feel it's important to take an interest in them, because I won't be around forever. And I want to spoon feed them as much information as I can while I'm still here."

◆

In 2012, Joni Mitchell talked to me at length about having Morgellons disease, a nerve disease that she described as "feeling like strings are coming out of my arms." A lot of people always thought Joni was nuts, but of course, she was brilliant. At the age of 24, she wrote *"So many things I could have done / but clouds got in the way."* She used to always feel misunderstood and under appreciated. She collaborated with Charles Mingus, she thought she should be played on black radio stations, she compared herself to classical composers—and then she also had to deal with competition within the youthful LA music scene. *And* she had ongoing health problems. She told me, "I haven't been well my entire life. Up and down, up and down."

Reflecting on her youth and the Laurel Canyon scene, she told me, "The women of song did not get along. [Joan] Baez was completely hostile to me and sabotaged me whenever possible. If we were on the same bill, she pushed me to the front of the show and cut back my songs. I was the new kid on the block, and Baez was threatened by me and very unfriendly."

In 2012, she told me that she'd basically retired, and said, "But my career goes on without me, which is fantastic. There are seventeen annual international festivals of my music." I also told her that there were courses in schools devoted just to her songs. In 2015, Joni was named the face of Yves Saint Laurent at a time when it appeared that it was going to be yet another one of those years of the older woman.

Then she had a debilitating stroke. No one talked about what really happened to her. She was in a facility for several years, and the rumors were she couldn't walk or talk. It was hard for me to imagine Joni—who was always so outspoken and unfiltered with the few people she trusted and talked to—silent. But she started to appear again, at a party here, or a tribute to her there, and at a party for her 75th birthday in 2018. Then, at the 2019 Vanity Fair Oscar party, she was sitting in a wheelchair, being photographed by Mark Seliger in a studio built on site for taking portraits at the party. I was so happy to see her. We hugged. We laughed about the "women of song did not get along" line—which she remembered. She was wearing an ensemble by her favorite designer, Issey Miyake, and we gossipped for a bit. I looked into her eyes and asked her, "How are you Joni?" She looked at me, deadpan, and said, "I've been better."

◆

Addendum: Several months later, at Lincoln Center, there was a premiere of Martin Scorsese's *Rolling Thunder Revue* film about Bob Dylan's 1975 traveling tour of the Northeast—with performers that included Dylan, Joan Baez, Patti Smith, Allen Ginsberg and others. But the scene when Joni plays her new song ("Coyote") about the tour, with alternate tunings and complex lyrics, caused the Lincoln Center audience to spontaneously burst into thunderous and prolonged applause. No one else in the film got this reaction. I was so excited I called Joni the next day to tell her. Her longtime assistant Marcy said she was doing some rehab in the pool, but she would tell her—and that Joni was starting to walk again, with a cane. Forty years ago Joni may have been dismissed in favor of Bob Dylan when a guitar was passed around a room in California, but here, at the New

York City premiere, she was the hands-down highlight of this movie. You could see the combination of admiration and bewilderment on Dylan's face as he tried to absorb her guitar tunings. And I remembered what Stevie Nicks had said about Joni: that the guys at that time thought, "She's better than us."

Epilogue

The world in which I began writing this book three years ago has changed in many ways. First, my husband of forty nine years became ill while I was writing this, then died in November 2018 while I was still writing it; I finished it the following year. Girls still don't run the world, but #MeToo changed the way women are treated and the way men have to act. Women are speaking up and speaking louder. In some instances, the effects have been positive. Not enough, but some.

I was lucky that my husband, Richard Robinson, gave me both the opportunity and the encouragement to start my career writing about music. He was an evolved, lovely, smart and savvy man who not only did not stand in my way—ever—but rather, opened the door that I was able to barge through into a long career. And one of the last things he did for me was to digitize more than five thousand hours of my taped interviews, for which I will be eternally grateful; it enabled me to write this book. Listening to many of the interviews I did with all of these women—then and now—over many years, I am struck by the fact that famous, rich, talented and often beautiful women still have anxiety, depression, addictions, romantic problems, conflicts about motherhood, business and financial disasters, health issues and wildly swinging ups and downs in their careers. Money and fame don't eliminate problems—except for money problems or the wanting to be famous problems. But the love of the music, the need to perform, the belief that they can *do* this—all of that has been stronger than the obstacles put in their way. No matter how tough it's been, these women all took risks, faced rejection, and made something happen. All while being—to paraphrase a Joni Mitchell song title—frail and cast iron.

The great ones, the ones who matter, will last. And each month there are new voices, new women coming up. The way we get our music has changed. The voices and the faces will continue to change. But balancing a life with fame and success in music goes on. The strength and fortitude of these women is inspirational. Just not giving up can make a real change. Things are better for these women now. Not enough. But better.

Acknowledgments

Richard Robinson: No him, no me.

Fran Lebowitz: Ditto—no her, no me.

At WME: my agent Suzanne Gluck; Andrea Blatt and Sabrina Taitz. At Henry Holt: Amy Einhorn, Barbara Jones, Ruby Rose Lee, Maggie Richards, Carolyn O'Keefe, Caitlin O'Shaughnessy and former editors Gillian Blake and Libby Burton. At *Vanity Fair*: Radhika Jones, Claire Howorth, Geoff Collins, Sara Marks, Cate Sturgess and former editors Punch Hutton, Louisa Strauss and Aimee Bell.

And John Skipper, Craig Hatkoff, Paul Rosenberg, Irving Azoff, Lindsey Cohen, Peter Feingold, Karen Mulligan, Laura Cali, Ruth Levy, Annie Leibovitz, Bob Gruen, Kevin Mazur, Mark Seliger, Jonathan Becker, Kate Simon, Justin Bishop, Patrick McMullan, Patrick Demarchelier, and other photographers who generously gave me the photos in this book.

Index

10,000 Maniacs, 207
38 Special, 114

AC/DC, 112, 152
Adams, Ryan, 172
Adele, 15, 22, 24, 32, 33, 40, 41, 42–43, 46,
    48, 55, 91–92, 97–100, 108, 138, 150,
    163, 167–68, 181, 183, 186, 206–8, 209,
    223, 225, 226–27
Adler, Lou, 184
Aerosmith, 112
Affleck, Ben, 63, 79
Aguilera, Christina, 33, 113, 132–33
Alabama Shakes, 12. *See also* Howard,
    Brittany
Alexandria, Lorez, 202
Al Mana, Wissam, 145
Alterman, Loraine, 187–88
Ambrose, June, 37
Amos, Tori, 60–61, 76–77, 150
Andrews, Julie, 195
Angélil, René, 9, 103
Angelou, Maya, 72
Aniston, Jennifer, 219
Anthony, Marc, 79, 80
Apollo Theater, 15, 197

Apple, Fiona, 9–10, 60, 71–72
Arcade Fire, 196
Arista Records, 71
Armstrong, Lance, 199, 213
Arnold, P. P., 217
Asher, Peter, 163, 180
Atlantic Records, 68, 155, 159
Aucoin, Kevyn, 34, 38
Avedon, Richard, 34
Azalea, Iggy, 41, 55, 63, 175
Azoff, Irving, 164, 169

B52s, 207
Bach, Erwin, 211
Bacharach, Burt, 195
Bad Company, 25
Badu, Erykah, 30, 133, 172–73, 201
Baez, Joan, 20, 112, 194, 203, 227, 228
Bailey, Pearl, 195
Baker, Anita, 104–5, 175–76, 192, 200
Balenciaga, 166
Ballard, Glen, 14
Balmain, 166
Bandy, Way, 34, 38
Bangles, the, 221
Baptiste, Marc, 31

Bardot, Brigitte, 35
Bayley, Roberta, 21
Beach Boys, The, 208
Beatles, the, 21, 169, 203
Beck, 69, 198
Bell, Maggie, 25, 217
Benatar, Pat, 55, 57, 73, 94, 170–71, 199,
    218, 221
Benitez, Jellybean, 163
Bennett, Tony, 195
Berlioz, Hector, 202
Berry, Halle, 219
Betty Crocker, 100
Beverly Hills Hotel, 30, 127
Beyincé, Angie, 6
Beyoncé, 6–8, 27–28, 29, 32, 39, 46–47, 51,
    60, 62, 69, 82, 87, 97, 103–4, 108, 113,
    147–48, 152, 162, 163, 181, 185–86,
    192–93, 205, 207, 209, 223, 225
Bieber, Justin, 150, 169
Biggie, 197
Birkin, Jane, 111, 112
Björk, 10, 30, 55–56
Blackhearts, the, 170
Blige, Mary J., 16, 31, 63, 127–28, 163,
    197, 199, 200
Blondie, 6, 24, 119, 133, 217. See also Harry,
    Debbie
Bogart, Humphrey, 53
Bogart, Neil, 171–72
Bolan, Marc, 34
Bono, 26, 34
Bono, Sonny, 163
Bowie, David, 10, 26, 29, 34, 43, 69, 123,
    174
Boyd, Eva, 74–75
Boyle, Peter, 187
Brackman, Jacob, 88
Brand, Russell, 87, 95–96, 151
Brandy, 9, 154
Braun, Scooter, 169, 178
Brinkman, Carianne, 170
Brown, Bobbi Kristina, 157
Brown, Chris, 61, 75
Brown, Foxy, 166, 200
Brown, James, 19, 111, 201
Brown, Jay, 163
Brown, Shirley, 200
Bruce, Lenny, 204
Buckingham, Lindsey, 62, 85, 226
Buckley, Jeff, 200, 207
Buffalo Springfield, the, 84
Buggles, 24

Bullock, Sandra, 219
Burberry, 40
Burchill, Julie, 204
Bush, George, 66

Cale, John, 124
Camilletti, Rob, 81
Campbell, Bobby, 163
Campbell, Mike, 226
Campbell, Naomi, 37
Cara, Alessia, 28, 40
Cardi B, 32, 46, 97, 166, 200
Carey, Mariah, 13, 16, 26, 45–46, 61, 87,
    90–91, 132, 150, 163, 189, 189–90, 194,
    210, 214
Carino, Christian, 58
Carlisle, Belinda, 119–20, 133
Carlton, Vanessa, 227
Carlyle Hotel, 68, 69
Carroll, Lenedra "Nedra," 155–56
Carter, Blue Ivy, 104
Carter, Shawn. See Jay-Z
Carter, Troy, 163
Cass, Mama, 20, 25, 112
Cat Power, 197
CBGB, 17, 32, 101, 125
CBS Records, 45
Channing, Carol, 195
Charles, Ray, 49, 196
Cheap Trick, 114, 196
Cher, 6, 31, 81, 163, 171, 211
Childers, Leee Black, 21
Clapton, Eric, 72–73, 188, 198, 199
Clark Sisters, the, 200
Clarkson, Kelly, 28
Clarkson, Lana, 74
Clash, the, 136, 180, 203
Clinton, Bill, 71
Clinton, Hillary, 82
Clooney, George, 220
Cobain, Frances Bean, 106, 122
Cobain, Kurt, 59, 106, 122–23, 181
Cocker, Joe, 198
Cohen, Leonard, 134
Collins, Judy, 20, 26, 84–85, 112, 194
Coltrane, John, 20, 197, 201, 202
Columbia Records, 7, 61, 90, 163, 175
Combs, Sean "Puffy," 16, 63, 79, 127,
    163
Connor, Chris, 202
Cooke, Sam, 200
Coolidge, Rita, 72–73
Coon, Caroline, 204

Cooper, Alice, 34, 125
Cooper, Bradley, 58
Cope, Julian, 201
Copland, Aaron, 202
Cornell, Chris, 69
Costello, Elvis, 180
Cranberries, 140, 142
Crawford, Cindy, 37
Cream, 188, 198
Creamer, Richard, 21
Creem, 21, 36, 38, 189, 204
Croft, Romy Madley, 13, 28, 91, 151, 184, 197
Crosby, David, 5, 83–84
Crosby, Stills & Nash, 84, 134, 164, 208
Crow, Sheryl, 5, 77–78, 106, 161–62, 188–89, 197–98, 205, 212–13
Crowe, Cameron, 180
Cruise, Tom, 220
Crystals, The, 74, 75
Currie, Cherie, 120, 196
Cyrus, Miley, 15, 126, 132, 150, 197

Da Brat, 200
Dandridge, Dorothy, 199
Daniels, Lee, 154
Darlette, Miss, 6–7
Davies, Ray, 89–90, 137
Davies, Roger, 145, 163
Davis, Angela, 199
Davis, Clive, 71, 75, 174
Davis, Miles, 202
DeBarge, James, 144
Def Jam Records, 29, 163, 177
Def Leppard, 112
Del Rey, Lana, 74
DeMann, Freddy, 163
de Passe, Suzanne, 178
Derek and the Dominos, 72, 198
Des Barres, Pamela, 67
Destiny's Child, 7–8, 15, 37, 148, 175, 224
Diana Ross and the Supremes, 29, 112. *See also* Supremes
Dickins, Jonathan, 163
DiLeo, Frank, 77
Diltz, Henry, 21
Dion, Céline, 9, 13, 103, 194
Dixie Chicks, the, 152
Driscoll, Julie, 217
Duran Duran, 37
Dylan, Bob, 18, 29, 37, 69, 70, 71, 174, 196, 198, 203, 207, 228, 229

Eagles, the, 129, 164, 169
Echo and the Bunnymen, 59, 201
Eilish, Billie, 41, 167
Elizondo, René, Jr., 145
Elliott, Missy, 37, 69, 199, 200
Ellis, Bob, 103
Eminem, 169
Epstein, Brian, 169
Ertegun, Ahmet, 68, 159, 173, 174
Etheridge, Melissa, 210
Evangelista, Linda, 37
Everly Brothers, 208

Faces, the, 198
Faithfull, Marianne, 15, 115–16, 133, 210, 219
Faith No More, 202
Farndon, Pete, 137
Feliciano, José, 112
Ferraro, Rachel, 192
Ferry, Bryan, 34, 41
Field, Patricia, 22
Fincher, David, 37
Finn, Neil, 226
Fitzgerald, Ella, 197, 202, 207
FKA twigs, 49, 55
Fleetwood Mac, 20, 62, 73, 85, 106–7, 162, 207, 209, 225–26
Florence and the Machine, 18, 130
Flowers, Gennifer, 82
Fowley, Kim, 67, 120, 196
Foxy Brown, 166, 200
Franklin, Aretha, 111, 112, 149–50, 156, 173, 192, 197, 199, 200, 208
Freddie and the Dreamers, 115
Fricke, David, 189
Frka, Christine, 124–25
Fugs, The, 203

Gabrielle, 15
Gainsbourg, Serge, 111
Gallin, Sandy, 164
Garbage, 218
Garland, Judy, 129, 195, 197
Garner, Jennifer, 106
Gaye, Marvin, 201
Gaynor, Janet, 195
Geffen, David, 70, 159, 163, 164
Geldof, Bob, 201
Germanotta, Joe, 163
Gerry and the Pacemakers, 115
Getz, Stan, 202
Gillespie, Dizzy, 202

Ginsberg, Allen, 228
Giraldo, Neil, 94
Givenchy, 166
Glitter, Gary, 34
Goffin, Gerry, 74
Go-Go's, The, 119–20, 133, 211, 221
Goldsmith, Lynn, 21
Gomez, Selena, 113, 132, 150
Goodall, Jane, 106
Gordon, Jim, 72
Gordy, Berry, 9, 103
Graham, Bill, 158, 162
Grande, Ariana, 35, 47, 169, 225
Grant, Peter, 25, 169
Grateful Dead, 101
Grohl, Dave, 181
Gruen, Bob, 21, 36
GTOs, the, 124
Guinness, Daphne, 30
Gundersen, Edna, 204
Guns N' Roses, 37
Guthrie, Woody, 202

Hagar, Sammy, 114
HAIM, 152–53, 197, 227
Halston, 108
Hammond, Beres, 194
Hammond, John, 174
Hansen, Patti, 10
Harrell, Andre, 16, 163
Harrington, Booji, 194
Harris, Calvin, 73, 81
Harris, Emmylou, 69
Harry, Debbie, 6, 22, 24, 25, 29, 36, 73,
    101, 119, 133, 171, 201, 217
Harvey, Leslie, 25
Harvey, PJ, 12, 48, 56, 218
Hathaway, Donny, 192, 197
Havens, Richie, 203
Hayes, Isaac, 203
Heart, 152, 199
Heartbreakers, the, 136–37
Hell, Richard, 104
Hendrix, Jimi, 69, 198, 203
H.E.R., 200
Hill, Lauryn, 15, 37, 166, 199, 201
Hirschberg, Lynn, 122
Hit Parader, 21, 25, 36, 38
Hole, 5, 59, 198. *See also* Love,
    Courtney
Holiday, Billie, 129, 195, 197
Honeyman-Scott, James, 137
Horne, Lena, 195, 199

Houston, Whitney, 13, 37, 127–28, 142,
    150–51, 156–57, 174, 194, 214, 217
Howard, Brittany, 12, 24, 25, 197
Howlin' Wolf, 215
Hudson, Jennifer, 29
Hynde, Chrissie, 8, 21, 25, 40, 73, 89–90,
    120, 136–37, 194, 197

Ice Cube, 196
Ike & Tina Turner, 203
Interview, 38
Iovine, Jimmy, 87
Isaacs, Kendu, 163

Jackson, Jackie, 144
Jackson, Janet, 6, 97, 143–45, 163, 166,
    199, 220
Jackson, Jermaine, 144
Jackson, Joseph, 6, 143–45, 148, 163
Jackson, La Toya, 144
Jackson, Marlon, 144
Jackson, Michael, 5, 23, 29, 37, 77, 142,
    144–45, 162, 193, 220
Jackson, Randy, 144
Jackson, Rebbie, 144
Jackson, Tito, 144
Jackson, Wanda, 193
Jackson 5, the, 6, 143
Jagger, Bianca, 34, 108
Jagger, Jade, 108
Jagger, Mick, 15–16, 26, 34, 53, 67–68,
    111, 115, 133, 181, 188, 212, 219
Jam, Jimmy, 145
James, Cheryl, 169–70
James, Etta, 173
James, LeBron, 71, 203
Jay-Z, 6, 29, 47, 62, 69, 82, 148, 163, 177,
    192, 193
Jett, Joan, 8, 21, 40, 120, 170, 182, 189,
    194, 196–97, 205, 215
Jewel, 6, 26–27, 69, 81, 155–56
Joel, Billy, 175
John, Elton, 159
Jolie, Angelina, 103, 106
Jolson, Al, 201
Jones, Norah, 48–49, 196
Jones, Sue, 49
Joplin, Janis, 11, 20, 21, 23, 24, 25, 26, 28,
    33–34, 40, 111, 112, 120, 142, 159, 174,
    178, 193, 208, 217, 218
Jordan, Michael, 203
J Records, 177
Judd, Cris, 79

Kanal, Tony, 88
Kardashian, Rob, 81
Kelly, Ruston, 93–94
Kennedy, John F., 66
Kennedy, Robert, 84
Kent, Andy, 21, 36
Kerr, Jim, 90
Kesha, 62, 175
Keys, Alicia, 33, 103, 197
Khan, Chaka, 176–77, 200, 201, 210
Kills, the, 197
King, Carole, 61, 74, 75, 174, 184, 194–95, 208, 211
King, Morgana, 202
King Princess, 13, 182, 184, 197
Kings of Leon, 152
Kings of Rhythm, 11
Kinks, The, 89, 152
Kinney, Taylor, 58
Kiss, 67
Knight, Gladys, 199, 200
Knowles, Beyoncé. See Beyoncé
Knowles, Mathew, 62, 147–49, 163
Knowles, Solange, 6, 35, 148
Knowles, Tina, 6, 62, 149
Konecki, Simon, 91–92, 98

LaBelle, Patti, 199, 222
Lady Gaga, 16, 26, 28, 30, 31, 33, 35, 40, 43, 55, 58, 61, 68, 76, 81–82, 103, 113–14, 124, 152, 153, 163, 175, 194–95, 205, 209, 210, 211, 225
Laguna, Kenny, 170
Laguna, Meryl, 170
Lambert, Hendricks & Ross, 202
Lambert, Miranda, 50
Landau, Jon, 180, 188
La Roche, Pierre, 34
Latifah, Queen, 199
Lauper, Cyndi, 5, 22, 30, 37, 57–58, 101, 153, 171, 201, 210, 218
Laurel Canyon, 83
Lawrence, Don, 194
Le Bon, Simon, 47
Led Zeppelin, 21, 25, 36, 66, 67, 135, 169, 188
Leibovitz, Annie, 21, 35, 69, 188
Lennon, John, 70, 94–95, 110
Lennon, Sean, 110
Lennox, Annie, 77, 145, 184
Levine, Larry, 74
Levy, Barrington, 194
Lewis, Luke, 172

Lewis, Terry, 145
Lil' Kim, 166, 200
Little Eva, 74–75
Little Richard, 17, 20
Lizzo, 24, 200, 218
Lollapalooza, 104, 110
Lomax, Alan, 202
Lopez, Jennifer, 12, 27, 31, 51, 63, 79–80, 103, 153, 163, 186–87, 219–20
Lorde, 15, 48, 133, 166, 169, 183
Lovato, Demi, 132, 169
Love, Courtney, 5, 58–59, 74, 106, 114, 122–23, 181, 197, 198, 201–2
Ludacris, 196
Luke, Dr., 175
Lulu, 112
Lynch, Monica, 178
Lyte, MC, 199, 200

Mackie, Bob, 11
Madison Square Garden, 190, 196
Madonna, 13, 22–23, 26, 29, 31, 35, 37, 44, 56, 61, 69, 71, 101, 103, 113, 163, 166, 218, 221
Mai, Ella, 200
Malone, Post, 28
Mamas & the Papas, The, 19, 112
Mandela, Winnie, 199
Manic Panic, 22
Manson, Shirley, 15, 201, 217, 218
Mapplethorpe, Robert, 17
Mardin, Arif, 49
Maripol, 22
Marshall, Jim, 21
Maslin, Janet, 204
Max's Kansas City, 6, 17
Maxwell, 69
Mazur, Kevin, 198
MC5, the, 70, 109
McEnroe, John, 10, 104
McQueen, Alexander, 30
McVie, Christine, 162
Medina, Benny, 163
Megan Thee Stallion, 200
Meisel, Steven, 34, 35, 38, 72, 113
Mendelsohn, John, 188
Mensch, Peter, 181
Mercer, Mabel, 202
Mercury, Freddie, 200
Met Ball, 29, 40, 132
Michael, George, 37, 174
Midler, Bette, 3–5, 33, 43, 51, 62, 103, 158–59, 188, 207, 212, 218, 222–23, 226

Miller, Mac, 142
Min, Janice, 105
Minaj, Nicki, 28, 113, 166, 200
Mingus, Charles, 227
Mitchell, Joni, 5, 20, 21, 25, 44–45, 52,
    69–70, 83–84, 102, 112, 133–34,
    147, 163, 164, 188, 194, 195, 201, 203,
    208, 217, 218, 222, 224,
    227–28, 230
Miyake, Issey, 228
Molly Hatchet, 114
Monáe, Janelle, 5, 35, 201
Monica, 154
Monk, Thelonious, 202
Morissette, Alanis, 12, 15, 43, 116–17, 161,
    198, 211
Moroder, Giorgio, 5, 112, 171–72
Morrison, Jim, 18, 112, 204
Mosshart, Alison, 197
Mothers of Invention, The, 203
Motown, 9, 103, 143, 178, 192, 214
Mottola, Tommy, 45, 61, 90, 163
MTV, 15, 19, 21–23, 24, 32, 37, 39, 46, 49,
    57, 101, 221
Mulligan, Gerry, 202
Musgraves, Kacey, 73, 93–94, 172

Næss, Arne, Jr., 103
Nars, François, 38
Nash, Graham, 84, 134
Nelson, Willie, 49
Newton-John, Olivia, 11
New York Dolls, 36, 136
New York Times, 9, 45, 190, 205, 218
Nicks, Stevie, 9, 20, 21, 25, 26, 28, 40, 62,
    73, 85, 101, 106–7, 130–31, 162, 181,
    190–91, 199, 205, 207, 208, 209, 212,
    218, 224, 225–27, 229
Nirvana, 37, 181
Noa, Ojani, 79
No Doubt, 15, 29, 49–50, 73, 88, 218.
    See also Stefani, Gwen
Normani, 200
Norton, Edward, 181
Norwood, Brandy. *See* Brandy
Norwood, Sonja, 154
Novoselic, Krist, 181
Nyro, Laura, 203

Obama, Barack, 71
O'Connor, Sinéad, 104, 162–63, 184
O'Day, Anita, 202
O'Jays, 193, 200

O'Keefe, Michael, 81
Oldham, Andrew Loog, 115
Ono, Yoko, 68, 70, 94–95, 110
Ora, Rita, 73, 81
Oribe, 38
O'Riordan, Dolores, 140–42
Oseary, Guy, 163
Outkast, 49, 201

Page, Jimmy, 26, 66, 181
Palmer, Robert, 37
Paltrow, Gwyneth, 51
Parker, Charlie, 202
Parton, Dolly, 28, 37, 49, 102, 164, 173, 197
Patitz, Tatjana, 37
Pattinson, Robert, 49
Pei, Guo, 29
Perry, Katy, 14–15, 28, 32–33, 40, 50, 87,
    95–96, 103, 151–52, 201, 221
Peter and Gordon, 163
Petty, Tom, 73, 142, 208
Phair, Liz, 52, 153
Phillips, Michelle, 19–20, 112
Pink, 28, 145
Pitbull, 186
Plant, Robert, 188
Pointer Sisters, the, 152
Pop, Iggy, 70, 196
Portnow, Neil, 166
Powers, Ann, 204
Presley, Elvis, 111, 112, 173, 193, 203
Preston, Neal, 21, 36
Pretenders, The, 89, 137
Prince, 23, 37, 142, 175, 196, 201
Pusha T, 196
Putland, Mike, 21

Q-Tip, 49
Quatro, Suzi, 21

Raitt, Bonnie, 26, 81, 103, 128–30, 194,
    196
Ramones, the, 36, 196
Ray J, 154
Redding, Otis, 111, 173, 200
Redford, Robert, 220
Reed, Lou, 26
Reese, Della, 202
Reid, L.A., 163, 177
Remm, Pete, 49
Reynolds, Burt, 82
Rhodes, Nick, 41
Richard, Cliff, 161

Richards, Bert, 146
Richards, Keith, 10, 16, 18, 26, 29, 49, 67,
    115, 146, 164, 194, 215, 220
Righteous Brothers, 74
Rihanna, 13, 21, 28, 29, 32, 53–55, 61,
    75–76, 95, 100, 113, 120–21, 152, 163,
    177–78, 194
Rimbaud, Arthur, 93, 108
Roberts, Elliot, 163
Robinson, Richard, 168, 174, 195, 203, 204,
    230
Robinson, Sylvia, 178
Rock, Mick, 21
Rock Scene, 21, 25, 36, 38
Rockwell, John, 190
Rolling Stone, 21, 35, 69, 187–88, 189, 205
Rolling Stones, the, 17, 19, 21, 34, 36, 52,
    66, 112, 115, 135, 194, 196, 197, 198,
    203, 214
Romeo Void, 113
Ronettes, The, 19, 26, 74
Ronstadt, Linda, 16, 21, 35–36, 52, 83,
    102–3, 119, 163, 164, 166, 180, 184,
    200, 210, 218, 226
Rose, Jane, 164
Rosenberg, Paul, 169
Ross, Annie, 202
Ross, Diana, 9, 11, 25, 28, 29, 101, 103,
    112, 214–15
Rossdale, Gavin, 50, 63, 87, 88
Roth, David Lee, 67, 68, 104, 220
Rothberg, Arlyne, 160
Rowland, Kelly, 7
Rowling, J. K., 71
Roxon, Lillian, 204
Rubin, Rick, 206
Runaways, The, 8, 67, 120, 170, 189, 194,
    196–97
Rush, 196
Rushen, Patrice, 197
Russell, D'Angelo, 63
Russell, Ethan, 21
Russo, Aaron, 62, 158–59

Sade, 12–13, 47, 145, 163, 184
Saint Laurent, Yves, 228
Salt-N-Pepa, 169–70, 196, 197, 199, 200
Sander, Ellen, 204
Scandal, 104
Scorsese, Martin, 228
Scott, Jane, 204
Seeger, Pete, 202
Seidmann, Bob, 25

Selassie, Haile, 21, 40
Seliger, Mark, 228
Sex Pistols, The, 136
Shakur, Tupac, 197
Shankar, Ravi, 49
Sheeran, Ed, 28
Shelton, Blake, 50
Shrimpton, Jean, 25
Simmons, Gene, 67
Simmons, Sylvie, 204
Simon, Carly, 88, 102, 160–61, 185
Simone, Nina, 197, 199
Simple Minds, 90
Simpson, Jessica, 150
Sinatra, Frank, 131
Sinclair, John, 70
Sire Records, 71
Slick, Grace, 20, 21, 25, 193, 208
Smith, Bessie, 20, 111
Smith, Beverly, 153
Smith, Fred "Sonic," 92–93, 109, 190
Smith, Jackson, 109
Smith, Jesse, 109
Smith, Patti, 16–18, 21, 25, 29, 32, 36, 40,
    41, 44, 71, 73, 92–93, 101, 108–10, 119,
    153, 195, 218, 220–21, 228
Smith, Sam, 41
Smyth, Patty, 104
Solange, 35
Sonic's Rendezvous Band, 109
Souther, JD, 83
Spears, Britney, 23, 132, 150, 206, 221
Spector, Phil, 61, 74–75
Spector, Ronnie, 61
Spice Girls, 15, 206, 207, 221
Springfield, Dusty, 19, 112
Springsteen, Bruce, 73, 174, 175, 180
Sprouse, Stephen, 22
Spungen, Nancy, 137
Staples, Mavis, 49, 195–96, 200, 203
Staples Center, 14, 33, 42, 97, 99, 108, 145,
    186
Staple Singers, The, 195, 200
Starr, Paul, 69
Staton, Dakota, 202
Stavers, Gloria, 204
Stefani, Gwen, 15, 29–30, 31, 37, 49–50,
    63, 69, 73, 87–88, 103, 152, 153, 201,
    205, 217, 218
Stein, Chris, 6, 119, 217
Stein, Seymour, 71, 163
Stewart, Ian, 115
Stigwood, Robert, 73

Stills, Stephen, 84–85
Stone the Crows, 25
Stooges, The, 70, 203
Straus, Oliver, 182
Stravinksy, Igor, 202
Streisand, Barbra, 195, 209
St. Vincent, 9, 197, 201, 205
Sugarcubes, The, 55. *See also* Björk
Sugar Hill Records, 178
Sui, Anna, 161
Summer, Donna, 5, 61, 111–12, 138–39,
    171–72, 211
Supremes, The, 9, 29, 112, 192, 214
Swift, Taylor, 44–45, 46, 62, 103, 150, 178,
    197

Talking Heads, 36
Tate, Howard, 203
Taylor, James, 88, 102, 161, 163, 174, 184
Taylor, Sarah, 102, 161
Teardrop Explodes, 201
Teena Marie, 200
Tegan and Sara, 152
Television, 201
Temptations, 193
Thomas, Clarence, 77
Thompson, Hunter, 188
Thornton, Big Mama, 20, 111, 193
Thunders, Johnny, 136
Timberlake, Justin, 166
Tommy Boy Records, 178
Truth, Sojourner, 199
Tubman, Harriet, 199
Turlington, Christy, 37
Turner, Ike, 11, 61, 64–65, 111, 163
Turner, Tina, 10–12, 28, 61, 64–65, 74, 75,
    101, 111, 145, 163, 200, 210–11
Tweedy, Jeff, 196
Twiggy, 25

U2, 221
Uhelszki, Jaan, 204
Us, 105

Vainshtein, Inga, 155
Valentine, Penny, 204
Vandross, Luther, 192

Van Halen, 66, 67, 104, 112, 114, 152
Van Halen, Eddie, 104
Vanity Fair, 31, 32, 34, 44, 69, 122
Van Matre, Lynn, 204
Vaughan, Sarah, 200, 202
Versace, 27
Versace, Donatella, 30
Vicious, Sid, 136–37
Vogue, 32, 34
Vreeland, Diana, 34

Wagoner, Porter, 164
Waits, Tom, 200
Walker, Summer, 200
Walsh, Joe, 62, 85
Waters, Muddy, 215
Webber, Andrew Lloyd, 185
Weintraub, Scooter, 162
Welch, Florence, 18, 130, 200
Wenner, Jann, 69, 187–88
West, Kanye, 169
White Panthers, 70
Who, The, 21, 36, 66
Wilco, 196
Williams, Heathcote, 116
Williams, Hype, 37
Williams, Lucinda, 87
Williams, Serena, 45
Willis, Ellen, 204
Wilson, Ann and Nancy, 152
Wilson, Owen, 199
Winehouse, Amy, 26, 74, 142, 217
Winfrey, Oprah, 71, 222
Wolman, Baron, 21
Womack, Bobby, 200
Wonder, Stevie, 69, 193, 201
Wood, Ronnie, 67
Woodstock, 101
Wynette, Tammy, 82–83, 216

xx, the, 13, 28, 91, 151, 184, 197

Yetnikoff, Walter, 180
Young, Neil, 69, 70
Young, Nick, 63

Zappa, Frank, 124, 203

ABOUT THE AUTHOR

For the past twenty years Lisa Robinson has been a contributing editor at *Vanity Fair*, where she produced music issues and pro-filed many major musicians. Prior to that, she was a columnist for the *New York Times* syndicate and the *New York Post*, the American editor of England's *New Music Express*, and the editor of several rock magazines. Additionally, she has hosted various cable TV and radio shows, and published a memoir, *There Goes Gravity*, in 2014. She was born in New York City, where she still resides.